The Dynamics of Inequality and Poverty

The Dynamics of Inequality and Poverty

Comparing Income Distributions

John Creedy

Truby Williams Professor of Economics, University of Melbourne, Australia

Edward Elgar
Cheltenham, UK • Northampton, MA, USA

Published by
Edward Elgar Publishing Limited
8 Lansdown Place
Cheltenham
Glos GL50 2HU
UK

Edward Elgar Publishing, Inc.
6 Market Street
Northampton
Massachusetts 01060
USA

A catalogue record for this book
is available from the British Library

Library of Congress Cataloguing-in-Publication Data
Creedy, John, 1949–
    The dynamics of inequality and poverty : comparing income distributions / John Creedy.
    Includes bibliographical references.
    1. Gini coefficient. 2. Lorenz curve. 3. Income distribution- -Mathematical models. 4. Poverty—Mathematical models. I. Title.
    HB523.C733 1998
    339.2'01'5118—dc21   97-39371
                                                                CIP

ISBN 1 85898 801 2

Printed and bound in Great Britain by Biddles Ltd, Guildford and King's Lynn

Contents

II Cross-sectional Comparisons

CONTENTSix

12.1.1 The Redistributive Effect 212
12.1.2 Disproportionality of Tax Payments 213
12.1.3 The Effect of Re-ranking 214
12.1.4 A Decomposition 215
12.2 Some Numerical Comparisons 217
12.2.1 Income Profiles 217
12.2.2 Annual Incomes Over the Life Cycle 218
12.2.3 The Present Value of Incomes 219
12.2.4 The Cross-sectional Income Distribution 220
12.2.5 Comparing Tax Structures 221
12.3 Welfare Comparisons 223
12.3.1 A Social Welfare Function 224
12.3.2 The Welfare Premium from Progression 225
12.3.3 Changes in Tax Parameters 226
12.4 Conclusions 228

13 Income Taxation and the Time Period **231**
13.1 The Simulation Model 234
13.1.1 Income Profiles 234
13.1.2 Income Tax Structures 236
13.2 Annual Incomes Over the Life Cycle 237
13.2.1 Taxation and Redistribution 237
13.2.2 Tax Disproportionality 238
13.3 Increasing the Accounting Period 240
13.3.1 Taxation and Redistribution 241
13.3.2 Progressivity and the Time Period 241
13.3.3 Taxation and Re-ranking 243
13.4 Cross-sectional Comparisons 245
13.5 A Simplified Income Mobility Process 248
13.5.1 Longer Time Periods 249
13.6 The Timing of Tax Structure Changes 251
13.6.1 Inequality and a Tax Switch 252
13.7 Conclusions 253

14 Mobility and Social Welfare **257**
14.1 Social Welfare and Mobility 259
14.1.1 A Dynamic Process 259
14.1.2 The Social Welfare Function 259
14.2 Some Numerical Simulations 262
14.2.1 The Simulation Strategy 262
14.2.2 Changes in Mobility and Welfare 263

List of Figures

List of Tables

Acknowledgements

This book brings together a number of (substantially revised) recent papers in the area of income distribution, rather than presenting a systematic or comprehensive treatment. It can be seen in some ways as a sequel to my earlier *Dynamics of Income Distribution* (1985) and *Income, Inequality and the Life Cycle* (1992). Several of the chapters in this book are based on jointly written papers. Chapter 4 is based on Creedy, Lye and Martin (1996); chapter 8 is based on Creedy and van de Ven (1997); chapter 14 is based on Creedy and Wilhelm (1995) and chapter 15 is based on Borooah and Creedy (1998). I am very grateful to these collaborators. Chapters 2, 3, 5, 6, 9, 10, and 11 are based respectively on Creedy (1996b; 1994b; 1998; 1997b; 1994b; 1997c; 1996c). I am grateful for permission to use this work. The original research on the material in chapters 3, 7, 9, 10, 11 and 13 was carried out for the Strategic Analysis Unit of the New Zealand Treasury. I should particularly like to thank Michael Dunn, of the Inland Revenue Department, and Deirdre Ross and Matthew Brougham, of the Treasury, along with George Barker, Manager and Advisor at the Strategic Analysis Unit, for valuable discussions on these and related issues. Much of this work also appeared in Creedy (1997d).

I should also like to thank Kath Creedy for substantial editorial and word processing help in preparing the camera-ready copy of this book.

Part I

Introduction

Chapter 1

Introduction and Outline

This book brings together a number of studies concerned with the analysis of income distribution both in cross-sectional and lifetime contexts. It presents statistical models of income distribution and income mobility, examines the relationship between annual and lifetime distributions and considers the evaluation of tax and transfer systems, allowing for their effects on a range of poverty and inequality measures.

This book is divided into three parts. Part I contains introductory material while Parts II and III contain substantive contributions of the book. Chapter 2 completes the first part by providing an introduction to the measurement of inequality and poverty. First the Lorenz curve, an extremely useful device for providing a visual impression of an income distribution, is defined. Lorenz curves can give a partial ordering of income distributions in terms of their inequality; an ordering cannot be given when they intersect. A complete ordering of distributions requires specific measures of inequality. Two extensively used measures, the Gini and Atkinson measures, are described. The value judgements, summarised by social welfare functions, associated with these measures are examined. The welfare functions can be used to provide complete orderings of distributions. Partial welfare orderings of distributions using the Lorenz curve and the associated concept of the generalised Lorenz curve are then discussed. Finally, the chapter introduces several measures of poverty and illustrates their properties using hypothetical examples. Any comparison of distributions cannot escape value judgements.

1

For this reason the chapter concentrates on showing how such judgements can be made explicit, so that the implications of adopting alternative values can be examined.

Part II is concerned with cross-sectional analyses of income distribution. It begins in chapter 3 with a survey of a number of issues involved in making cross-sectional comparisons. Choices regarding the income unit and income concept, just like the inequality measure, depend on value judgements and should be made explicit. When using equivalence adult scales, there is no single method of producing scales which can be regarded as superior to others. Results for a variety of scales should be reported as it is not appropriate to take an average of a set of scales, or to report results only for extreme values. Some results may usefully be obtained, which are to some extent independent of the set of equivalence scales used, by performing a decomposition analysis based on additively separable measures. Equivalence scales can sometimes be avoided in comparing distributions by the application of sequential dominance tests, provided that the proportions of each household type in each distribution are the same; this is satisfied in comparisons of pre- and post-tax distributions for the same population.

Chapter 4 turns to the problem of modelling the form of the distribution of earnings. One approach is to regard the distribution as the outcome of some kind of random process; this involve the application of a form of the central limit theorem to the sum of random variables, or the analysis of the results of applying a transition matrix to an arbitrary initial distribution. Such models have been criticised on the grounds that they are 'purely statistical' and thereby have a negligible degree of economic content. Chapter 4 explores an approach to modelling the earnings distribution which involves both stochastic and economic components. Individuals' earnings are seen as resulting from a simple market supply and demand model in which individual earnings are deterministic, though the model can have multiple solutions. A stochastic error-correction mechanism is then imposed and the resulting form of the distribution of earnings is derived, where the distributional analogue of multiple equilibria in the deterministic form is multimodality. In particular the model can generate a variety of flexible functional forms.

An advantage of the approach is that changes in the form of the distribution over time can be modelled explicitly in terms of changes in commodity and labour market conditions since the parameters governing the characteristics of the distribution are shown to be functions of the underlying economic parameters of the model. This makes it possible to give a clearer economic interpretation of the distribution of personal income and the reasons for changes in inequality over time. For each individual, the number of hours of labour supplied is treated as the reciprocal supply associated with the demand for goods, or real income, while the demand for labour is a function of the real wage rate. Equilibrium earnings, the product of the wage rate and the number of hours worked, are derived as the root or roots of a cubic equation.

The approach is found to perform well using US data from the Current Population Survey in that they are able to capture the empirical characteristics of the earnings distribution better than the standard forms. The specification is extended to allow the structural parameters to depend on specified characteristics such as the experience and education of individuals. This provides a mechanism for understanding the effects of changes in both education and experience on the shape of the conditional earnings distribution.

Chapter 5 turns to the evaluation of alternative tax and transfer systems and the debate over the use of means-testing. It illustrates the use of several different criteria to evaluate alternative tax and transfer systems. In particular, means-tested versus universal transfer systems are compared. The analysis proceeds by using numerical examples involving a small number of individuals, in order to highlight the precise effects on incomes. The implications of fixed incomes and of endogenous incomes are examined. Comparisons between tax systems involve fundamental value judgements concerning inequality and poverty, and no tax structure can be regarded as unambiguously superior to another. Judgements depend on the degree of inequality aversion and attitudes to poverty. However, in those cases where means-testing is preferred, the desired tax, or taper rate applying to benefits, is only slightly less than the marginal tax rate applying to tax payers, and is substantially less than 100 per cent.

Chapter 6 is concerned with the role of poverty in social evaluation functions. The standard analysis of individual labour supply uses a utility function specified in terms of the consumption of goods, purchased with wage and non-wage income, and leisure. By next imposing a poverty level, the model can be used to examine the way in which alternative poverty measures change when the tax structure is altered. A criticism of this type of approach is that some individuals, facing a given wage rate and tax structure, choose a level of labour supply which places them below the poverty level. The idea behind a poverty line is that individuals are substantially worse-off as a result of being in poverty, compared with being just above the poverty line. It may therefore reasonably be asked why people would not make a strong attempt to avoid poverty if possible.

A major aim of chapter 6 is therefore to explore a labour supply model in which each individual's utility function depends on a threshold consumption, or poverty, level and where there is a strong utility premium to be gained by avoiding poverty. The implication is that it may be worthwhile for some individuals, who would otherwise be in poverty, to supply higher amounts of labour in order to avoid poverty. Over a range of wage rates, labour supply falls as the wage increases. Nevertheless, there may still be some 'working poor' and some who are not working who choose to remain in poverty even though they may be able to achieve the threshold consumption level by giving up virtually all their leisure. There are others who face a wage rate that is too low for them to be able to obtain net earnings above the threshold in any circumstances.

A motivation for the analysis relates to the use of a social welfare or evaluation function when poverty is thought to be important. The standard welfare function used in the optimal tax literature is specified in terms of individuals' utilities, making no allowance for poverty. It is not clear how a desire for poverty alleviation can be added to, or integrated into, the standard welfare function. In chapter 6, poverty is integrated fully into the social welfare function because it matters to individuals; that is, the poverty line is a basic component of individuals' utility functions. It is shown that in a special case (combining a particular cardinalisation of utility functions with unitary relative aversion to inequality), an abbreviated social welfare function can be found in which welfare per head is expressed in terms of average utility, less a cost of inequality (where both terms exclude the special deprivation suffered by those in poverty), less a cost of poverty. The latter is expressed as the product of the degree of deprivation and the headcount measure of poverty.

Chapter 7 turns to an analysis of the redistributive impact of indirect tax changes using cross-sectional data. A feature of the chapter is that it allows for households' demand responses to price changes, and constructs welfare measures based on compensating and equivalent variations for a range of income groups. The method involves the use of the linear expenditure system, estimated for each income group, and is applied to the major tax change introduced in New Zealand. The results confirm those of previous studies which found that indirect taxes did not have a substantially larger impact on low-income groups than on high-income groups. Furthermore, the introduction of the goods and services tax does not appear to be regressive. The basic method developed in chapter 7 is used in chapter 8 to examine the distributional effects of inflation in both Australia and New Zealand. The differential price changes associated with inflation can have distributional implications if there is a systematic tendency for the prices of those goods which form a higher proportion of the budgets of low-income households to increase relatively more than other goods. However, recent price changes are found to have a small impact.

Part III of the book moves to the analysis of income dynamics. It begins in chapter 9 with a survey of some of the problems involved in trying to collect and examine longitudinal income data. Although longitudinal data are often desirable, it is sometimes possible to use cross-sectional data on age and earnings to estimate simple models of age-earnings profiles. Indirect information concerning relative earnings mobility can often be obtained in the same way. Such models and estimates can be useful for the analysis of taxes and transfers over the life cycle, and particularly the analysis of alternative pension and superannuation schemes using simulation methods.

However, genuine longitudinal data are ideally desirable, and a useful source consists of data collected as part of the administration of income taxation.

Chapter 10 provides an introduction to some of the complex relationships between cross-sectional and lifetime income distributions. The chapter highlights the difficulties of making inferences about lifetime incomes using only cross-sectional data. A simple model is used to provide simulation results. It is shown that simple inferences about lifetime income distribution comparisons cannot be made on the basis of cross-sectional distributions alone, as is sometimes suggested.

Chapter 11 then examines income dynamics in New Zealand for males and females, using a special set of data collected by the Inland Revenue Department. Attention is given to the process of relative income movements within the income distribution and the systematic movements over age, for particular cohorts. A special pooling of information for a variety of cohorts observed over a three-year period is used. Both males and females are found to display some 'regression towards the mean', although the extent of this falls with age (until it is very low in the late forties and fifties) and then increases in the highest age groups. For males there is some negative serial correlation in relative proportional income changes from year to year, which shows no systematic variation with age. Hence individuals do not move systematically up or down through the income distribution. For females it is found that there is some negative serial correlation in the early years, but this gradually falls and the higher ages show slight positive serial correlation.

There is found to be a substantial amount of apparently 'random' relative movement from year to year within the income distribution. For males this is higher in the very young age groups; it falls with age but then rises in the older age groups. For females, it rises with age and then gradually falls. The relative movements generate a changing dispersion of annual income over the life cycle, as measured by the variance of logarithms. For men, the dispersion increases sharply in the first few years. It subsequently falls sharply and then gradually rises to a maximum around age 60 after which it falls again.

Systematic variations in the mean of log-income for males can be described by quadratic age effects and a linear time effect, such that more recent entrants to the labour force have slightly lower incomes (on average) than their older cohorts at comparable ages. For females, a cubic age profile is produced, with recent entrants experiencing slightly higher average incomes than older cohorts at comparable ages. The results for females, in particular the finding that there are cubic age effects, should be treated with caution in view of the substantial changes that have taken place in labour force participation and the changes in participation over the life cycle.

These results are used to specify a simulation model of lifetime incomes. A model is applied to a cohort of males aged 20 years in 1991. It is found that the model is able to reproduce to a large degree the complicated profile of the variation in the variance of logarithms of incomes over the life cycle. An important result is the finding that the present value of income, over the 45-year period from age 20 to age 65, displays less inequality than in any single year. A significant advantage of the simulation model is that it is able to capture the earnings dynamics using few parameters, all of which have a straightforward interpretation. Hence, it is possible to use the model to consider the effects of specific changes in the mobility process and the systematic variations over the life cycle.

Chapter 12 turns to the problem of evaluating income tax structures, in terms of their progressivity and effects on inequality, using alternative income concepts and accounting periods. It uses a simple simulation model to examine alternative measures. The analysis is extended in chapter 13, which uses the lifetime income simulation model of chapter 11. The income tax schedule typically displays increasing marginal rates, and there is a substantial amount of relative income mobility, along with a systematic variation in average incomes over the life cycle of the cohort. These factors mean that the accounting period may have an important impact on the summary measures used, but simulation methods are required in view of the intractability of an analytical approach.

The simulations show that progressivity and inequality measures can often move in opposite directions, both over time for annual accounting periods and as the length of period is gradually increased. The relationship between summary measures is complicated by the role of the aggregate tax ratio, in addition to the horizontal inequity that can result in the larger period framework. Some tax structures are found to produce an increase in progressivity as the time period increases, while others show less progressivity as the time period increases. In view of the very different shapes of the profiles, the ranking of tax structures, according to the degree of redistribution and of progressivity produced, is found to change as the time period increases.

Horizontal inequity, in terms of change in the ranking of individuals when moving from the pre-tax to the post-tax distribution, is found to increase as the accounting period increases. Not surprisingly, inequity is higher and increases more rapidly as the accounting period is increased for tax structures displaying more steeply rising rate structures.

The differences in progressivity and redistribution resulting from different income tax structures applied over the 45-year period from age 20 to 65 are compared with results obtained from cross-sectional data. It is found that inequality is lower in the life-cycle context than in cross-sections, although both progressivity and redistributive effects can be either higher or lower, depending on the particular structures and years being compared. The changes in the inequality of post-tax income resulting from the use of different tax structures are generally found to be lower in the life cycle compared with the cross-sectional results. The cross-sectional comparisons combine the effects of the changing distribution of pre-tax income with those of the tax structure changes. In addition, the cross-sectional framework ignores the horizontal inequity, revealed in the longer-period comparisons, for tax structures having increasing marginal tax rates. Comparisons are also made using a simpler process of relative income mobility, giving similar results to those obtained for the more complex process.

The analysis demonstrates that valuable information can be revealed by analyses which allow for a longer accounting period and the potentially misleading nature of cross-sectional comparisons. The use of a longer-period framework also involves a considerable increase in complexity; it is seen that the use of a longer period makes it necessary to consider explicitly a large range of relevant factors which are too easily ignored when using the simpler cross-sectional approach to measuring tax progressivity.

Chapter 14 turns to the question of evaluating changes in inequality and mobility. If there is no income mobility from one year to the next, so that relative incomes remain unchanged over time, a relative measure of inequality has the same value irrespective of the accounting period used to measure income. It is sometimes suggested that the existence of income mobility, even if it causes the inequality of annual income to increase over time, leads to lower inequality of a longer-period measure. However, any statement about changes in mobility and the relationship between short- and longer-period inequality needs to be highly qualified, particularly as different types of income mobility may be distinguished, not all of which are egalitarian. Furthermore, so long as individuals have concave utility of income functions, income variability over time imposes a welfare loss, which may or may not be compensated by a higher annual average income. Consequently the implications of income mobility for social welfare are not immediately clear.

Chapter 14 examines in detail the relationship between relative income mobility, inequality and social welfare. While mobility is often regarded as reflecting opportunities for improvement and responses to incentives, income variability *per se* reduces individuals' utility where utility functions are concave (reflecting variability aversion). The question of whether social welfare, defined in terms of a social welfare function reflecting inequality aversion and in terms of individuals' longer-period utility, can increase while mobility increases is far from straightforward. Furthermore, mobility is not a one-dimensional phenomenon, since one type of mobility (regression towards the mean) may be inequality-reducing, while another type of mobility (relative movements uncorrelated with incomes) contributes to an increase in inequality. Whether a change in the pattern of income mobility can produce an increase in social welfare while at the same time reducing long-period inequality and increasing short-period inequality is also problematic.

It is found using simulation methods that if the aversion to variability of individuals is sufficiently larger than the aversion to inequality of the social welfare function, it is not possible to achieve all three changes simultaneously. If inequality aversion exceeds variability aversion, a small range of variations can produce the three changes; these involve an increase in the extent of regression towards the mean combined with a sufficient increase in the random variability of proportionate changes. The former change contributes to the reduction in longer-period inequality while the latter change is required for shorter-period inequality to increase. A brief review of evidence for the US suggests that while annual inequality increased during the 1980s, the changes in mobility required to offset this increase did not appear to take place.

Finally, the aim of chapter 15 is to incorporate poverty persistence in a measure of aggregate poverty over two periods. This is achieved by decomposing a class of poverty measures into two components, covering those temporarily in poverty and those in poverty in both periods. An additional weight is then added to the permanent component in forming an aggregate poverty measure over both periods; this weight reflects the degree of poverty-persistence aversion of the policy maker. It is found that the effect on the aggregate poverty measure of mobility between the categories of permanent and temporary poverty are not unambiguous (except in the special case of the headcount poverty measure). Simulations are used in order to investigate the relationship between poverty and mobility. The effects of two different types of mobility (random proportional income changes and a systematic regression towards or away from the median) are isolated.

Available evidence suggests that poverty persistence is an important phenomenon, so there is a clear need to allow for such persistence in measuring aggregate poverty. For example, given the observed correlation between unemployment and poverty, the increasing extent of long-term unemployment in many countries suggests that poverty persistence may also be increasing. The link with unemployment also suggests that there may well be a regional dimension to aggregate poverty, given an aversion to poverty persistence. The results demonstrate the need to have information about the process of income dynamics, in order to design appropriate policies to alleviate poverty.

Chapter 2

Measuring Inequality and Poverty

Many studies of the distribution of income are motivated by the idea that inequality is in some sense a 'bad' thing. Concern is therefore usually with the question of whether a change in income distribution, perhaps brought about by a tax change, represents an 'improvement'. This involves the introduction of ethical value judgements. For example, suppose that $60 is to be divided among three people who are regarded as identical in all other respects. In comparing the distribution (10, 20, 30) with the alternative of (5, 27, 28), there are no logical or specific economic arguments that can be used; different judges will take different views according to their ethical views regarding equity, and there is no sense in which judgements can be thought of as being correct or incorrect.

Value judgements cannot be avoided in any attempt to describe a change in income distribution in terms of improvement or deterioration. The role of the economist is therefore not to pass judgement but to examine the implications of adopting a variety of value judgements. The problem is to find ways of specifying different value judgements and to work out the implications of such values for comparisons of income distributions. The extensive research on inequality measures that has been carried out over the last quarter-century has been motivated by the desire to relate the measures explicitly to value judgements. This approach has produced an extensive and often technical literature.

This chapter provides an introduction to a small number of inequality and poverty measures, concentrating on those which have received most attention. The emphasis is on the link between the measures and evaluation of the income distribution involving value judgements.

First, section 2.1 introduces a basic method of presenting income distributions, the Lorenz curve, along with the Gini measure of inequality which is based on the Lorenz curve. Section 2.2 describes another inequality measure, the Atkinson measure, which is derived directly from an explicit value judgement. Section 2.3 investigates the implications of the inequality measures for the trade-off between total income and its inequality, or what is often referred to as the trade-off between equity and efficiency.

The use of explicit value judgements, and their associated inequality measures, makes it possible to provide unequivocal comparisons between any pair of income distributions. Much attention has, however, been given to the question of whether there is a broad range of agreement about a change being an improvement, using only a minimum of assumptions about value judgements. For example, when would a change in income distribution be approved by a large number of people who share only a few simple principles? A flavour of the sort of results that can be obtained is given in section 2.4. Section 2.5 turns to the concept of poverty and begins by discussing alternative approaches to measurement, using hypothetical examples. Section 2.6 presents a diagrammatic approach to poverty that is similar to the Lorenz curve, and section 2.7 considers the behaviour of several poverty measures using hypothetical examples.

A certain amount of technical discussion is used, although every attempt has been made to keep this to a minimum. For more extensive and technical treatments, see the surveys by Cowell (1977), Jenkins (1991a), Lambert (1993a, b) and Creedy (1996).

In practice, it is important to consider the difficult questions of how to measure income, whose income should be included (involving the definition of the income unit) and whether or not there are any relevant non-income differences between individuals that should be taken into account. The following discussion abstracts from these issues and simply assumes that there are no non-income differences, that the unit of analysis is the individual, and that money income in a given period is the appropriate variable to measure.

2.1 The Lorenz Curve and the Gini Measure

This section introduces the Lorenz curve, which provides a valuable method of summarising income distribution data. It provides a convenient descriptive tool and is fundamental when welfare comparisons are being made. A measure of inequality, the Gini measure, is based directly on the Lorenz curve; this measure is also presented.

2.1.1 The Lorenz Curve

Suppose that information is available about the incomes of a number of individuals. The first stage is to arrange the individuals in ascending order according to their incomes. Then, moving from the poorest to the richest individual, the Lorenz curve plots the proportion of people against the corresponding proportion of total income obtained by those people.

For example, in the first example involving three people given above, where the incomes (in ascending order) are 10, 20, 30, the poorest person (one-third of the people) has a proportion 10/60 of total income. The poorest two-thirds of the group have $(10 + 20)/60 = 1/2$ of the total income, while moving to the richest person obviously implies that all the people have 100 per cent of the income.

This does not give many points for plotting a diagram, but in practice there are many individuals to be considered. Suppose there are N individuals whose incomes are denoted y_i for $i = 1, ...N$, and they are ranked in ascending order such that $y_1 < y_2 < ... < y_N$. The Lorenz curve shows diagrammatically the relationship between the proportion of people with income less than or equal to a specified amount, and the proportion of total income obtained by those individuals. The proportion of people whose income is less than the kth income in the list is given by k/N. The corresponding proportion of total income is expressed as $\left(\sum_{i=1}^{k} y_i \right) / \sum_{i=1}^{N} y_i$. For example, when

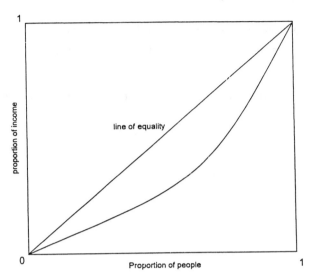

Figure 2.1: The Lorenz Curve

$k = 1$ the associated proportion of people is $1/N$ while the proportion of total income is $y_1/(N\overline{y})$ where $\overline{y}$ denotes the arithmetic mean income level.

Typically the Lorenz curve looks like the curve shown in Figure 2.1. When incomes are unequal, the fact that they are ranked in ascending order means that the proportion of people is always below the proportion of total income, except when $k = N$. Hence, the curve lies below the diagonal line shown.

The extreme case of inequality is where everyone has nothing, except one person. If everyone except person N has a zero income, then $\sum_{i=1}^{k} y_i$ is zero for all $k < N$. This case of extreme inequality therefore produces a curve that follows the bottom and right-hand edge of the box. If everyone has the same income, $y_i = \overline{y}$, then for all k the proportion of total income is $k\overline{y}/N\overline{y} = k/N$ and is equal to the corresponding proportion of people; the Lorenz curve in this case of complete equality is the diagonal line shown.

2.1.2   Comparisons Between Distributions

Any Lorenz curve lies between the diagonal line, representing complete equality of incomes, and the bottom and right-hand sides of the box, representing the extreme of inequality where only one person has all the income. Any distribution having a Lorenz curve that is closer to the diagonal of equal incomes than another distribution, over its whole range, can therefore be said to be unambiguously more equal. For example, returning to the three-person case involving \$60, the distribution (10, 20, 30) may be compared with the alternative of, say, (10, 25, 25). The latter gives the finding that the poorest two-thirds of people have a proportion 35/60 of total income, which is more than the corresponding value of 1/2 for the first distribution. Hence, the second distribution has a Lorenz curve that is closer to the diagonal of equal distribution.

This comparison appears to be somewhat mechanical, rather than being based on fundamental ethical judgements or value judgements. However, it is linked to a particular value judgement that seems to receive wide support and can be expressed as follows. Any transfer of income from a richer to a poorer person that leaves the identity of the richer person unchanged is regarded as an improvement. This is called the 'principle of transfers'. The two distributions discussed in the previous paragraph satisfy this principle because the distribution (10, 25, 25) is obtained from (10, 20, 30) by taking \$5 from the third person and giving it to the second person. Similarly, the distribution (15, 20, 25) is judged on this principle, and thus by the Lorenz curves, to be more equal than the first, as is (15, 15, 30).

In general, if distribution B can be obtained from distribution A by a series of such transfers, then B is judged to be more equal than A and has a Lorenz curve that is closer to the diagonal than that of A. However, it should be recognised that the value judgement embodied in the principle of transfers does not receive unanimous support; some people may not agree with the above judgement of the various distributions even though they may dislike inequality. How would this principle rank the two distributions (10, 20, 30) and (5, 27, 28) mentioned above? The second distribution cannot possibly be obtained from the first by a series of transfers from rich to poor, although total income is unchanged. Similarly, the first distribution cannot be obtained from the second by a series of transfers from rich to poor. Hence, in terms of the Lorenz curves, there is not an unequivocal comparison because they intersect each other. The second distribution appears to be more equal than the first at the top end of the distribution, but less equal at the lower end. Hence the broad value judgement embodied in the principle of transfers cannot produce an overall comparison in this case. In general, if two Lorenz curves intersect, there is a problem in making an unequivocal ranking of the two distributions in terms of their inequality. Further criteria, in the form of more specific value judgements, need to be brought to bear on the comparison in such a case.

2.1.3   The Gini Measure of Inequality

It has been suggested that the Lorenz curve allows an unambiguous inequality comparison of income distributions, using only the principle of transfers, when the curve for one distribution lies entirely outside that of another distribution. If Lorenz curves intersect, no overall comparison is possible without introducing more detailed ethical judgements. However, it is often required to rank distributions when they intersect, and even for those which do not intersect, some measure of the extent of the difference is required. For such purposes it is necessary to produce a single summary statistic which measures inequality.

The Gini inequality measure, G, is related directly to the Lorenz curve. It is therefore defined in this section, although the explicit value judgements that lie behind its use are discussed later. Its aim is to produce a measure of the extent to which the Lorenz curve departs from the line of equality. Various 'distance' measures could be devised, but the Gini measure is defined as the area enclosed by the diagonal and the Lorenz curve, expressed as a proportion of the area below the diagonal. This relationship ensures that the value of the Gini coefficient lies between zero (for complete equality) and one (for extreme inequality). The area below the diagonal is equal to 1/2, given that the height and base are both unity. Therefore G is twice the area enclosed by the Lorenz curve and the diagonal. However, in practice this approach does not give a convenient way to calculate the Gini measure because the calculation of areas is cumbersome. It is possible to show that an alternative analytical way of expressing the Gini measure is the following:

$$G = 1 + \frac{1}{N} - \frac{2}{N^2} \sum_{i=1}^{N} (N + 1 + i) \left(\frac{y_i}{\bar{y}} \right) \qquad (2.1)$$

This expression shows that the Gini measure depends on the ranking of individuals' incomes, as well as their size, because of the term $(N + 1 + i)$.

2.2 Atkinson's Measure

The Gini measure was introduced directly in terms of an area from the Lorenz curve diagram. Another way of producing an inequality measure is to begin by specifying the explicit value judgements regarding inequality held by someone making comparisons. These values are summarised using a mathematical relationship called a social welfare function. This function is described below, after which the Atkinson measure is defined.

2.2.1 The Social Welfare Function

One way of specifying a judge's value judgements about the distribution of income is to use a mathematical formula which is used to evaluate the overall influence of different incomes. A general value judgement that covers a wide range of possibilities is that an income distribution should be judged in terms of the incomes of each individual: a function that reflects this broad view is said to be 'individualistic'.

Consider the use of a function which involves the sum of some function of individuals' incomes. This type of social welfare function, where 'social welfare' is W, is written as:

$$W = \sum_{i=1}^{N} H(y_i) \qquad (2.2)$$

Here $H(y_i)$ represents the value attached to individual i's income in evaluating the distribution. It is referred to as the 'social value' of i's income, and should not be confused with i's own welfare or utility function. The term social welfare has thus to be treated with much caution. It is not meant in any way to describe the total welfare of a society, despite the impression that might be given by the use of the words 'social welfare'. It is simply the term given to the function by which a judge is regarded as evaluating the income distribution, and represents the value judgements of that person. In some ways it might be called instead an 'income distribution evaluation function'.

A distribution with a higher value of W is judged by the decision-taker to be an improvement over a distribution giving a lower value. The form of the function H reflects the inequality aversion of the decision-taker or individual making the judgements. For example, consider the extreme case when a judge has no aversion whatsoever to income inequality and evaluates alternative distributions purely by the total income involved. Hence the distribution involving three people, given by $(1, 1, 60)$, would be regarded as an improvement over the distribution $(20, 20, 20)$, because the former has a higher value of total income. In this case $H(y)$ is simply equal to y.

Another extreme type of judgement occurs when a person has such a high degree of aversion towards inequality that each income distribution is evaluated according only to the income of the poorest person. Hence, when incomes are in ascending order, $H(y_1) = y_1$ and $H(y_i) = 0$ for $i > 1$. Such a judge would be prepared simply to confiscate the incomes in excess of y_1 of the other $N - 1$ people. Thus the distribution $(10, 11, 12)$ would be judged inferior to the distribution $(12, 20, 30)$, for example.

Value judgements between these two extremes can be represented by a form of $H(y)$ that is concave. Concavity means that if an amount, Δy, is taken from a rich person with income y_2, and given to a poorer person with income y_1, the increase in 'social welfare' associated with the higher income of the poor person is greater than the decrease from the reduction for the rich person. Hence the new distribution is regarded by the judge as an improvement. Concavity therefore represents a mathematical expression of the principle of transfers, giving a precise measure of the effect of such transfers. The degree of concavity of $H(y)$ gives a direct measure of the degree to which the judge is averse to inequality.

2.2.2 The Measure of Inequality

A cornerstone of Atkinson's (1970) approach to the measurement of inequality is the linking of the welfare function in equation (2.2) with the concept of the *equally distributed equivalent* level of income, y_e. This is defined as the level of income which, if obtained by everyone, produces the same 'social welfare' as the actual distribution. Again, it must be stressed that this does not mean that total utility or wellbeing is in any sense the same in the two situations; it means rather that a judge ranks the distribution where everyone has y_e as being no better or worse than the actual distribution. Hence y_e is defined by:

$$W = \sum H(y_i) = NH(y_e) \qquad (2.3)$$

The Atkinson inequality measure, A, can now be defined. It is the proportional difference between arithmetic mean income and the equally distributed equivalent level. Hence:

$$A = \frac{\bar{y} - y_e}{\bar{y}} \qquad (2.4)$$

In practice, it is necessary to specify an explicit form for $H(y)$ that is capable of reflecting a range of value judgements. Atkinson used:

$$H(y) = \frac{y^{1-\varepsilon}}{1 - \varepsilon} \qquad \text{for } \varepsilon \neq 1$$

$$H(y) = \log y \qquad \text{for } \varepsilon = 1 \qquad (2.5)$$

The relationship between $H(y)$ and y is thus concave, reflecting the judgement that an increase in incomes at higher ranges of the distribution contributes less to W, or social welfare, than an equal increase in lower incomes. A measure of concavity, based on the extent to which the slope of $H(y)$ falls as y increases, can be shown to equal the parameter ε. Thus ε is a measure of relative inequality aversion. Combining (2.3) and (2.5) gives:

$$y_e = \left\{ \frac{1}{N} \sum_{i=1}^{N} y_i^{1-\varepsilon} \right\}^{1/(1-\varepsilon)} \qquad (2.6)$$

The value of y_e can therefore be directly calculated given a set of incomes. The value is sensitive to the value of ε used. If $\varepsilon = 0$ then A is zero whatever the range of incomes, and if ε is infinitely large, then A is equal to 1.

In view of the fact that the choice of ε reflects a value judgement, it is usual in investigating income distributions to report results for a range of values of ε, extending from a low of about 0.1 to a high of 2 or 3, which represents a considerable aversion to inequality. One way to view the size of ε is to consider judgements about the effect of taking \$1 from a richer person, giving some of this to a poorer person and destroying the rest. Suppose that one person has twice the income of another. When $\varepsilon = 0$, then the judge would only approve of the transfers if \$1 is given to the poorer person. But it can be shown that when ε takes the values 0.5, 1, 2 and 3 respectively, the amounts of \$0.71, \$0.50 and \$0.13 must be given to the poorer person from the \$1 taken from the richer person, in order for the resulting distributions to give the same value of W. This way of assessing the implications of ε is called the 'leaky bucket' experiment because it relates to the extent to which leaks are tolerated in attempting to transfer income between individuals.

2.3   Equity and Efficiency

The previous section explained how a measure of inequality can be defined using an explicit statement, in mathematical form, about value judgements used. The value judgements are summarised by a form of income distribution evaluation function called the social welfare function. The function was expressed in terms of the incomes of all individuals in the distribution. Although a judge may be averse to inequality, it is widely recognised that any attempt to make incomes more equal, for example by using a system of taxes and transfers, is likely to affect individuals' behaviour. In particular, the incentive for individuals to work is reduced, so that the total income may fall. The welfare function reflects this type of effect because it is expressed in terms of all incomes. But it is useful to be able to express the value judgements in terms of the willingness to trade total, or average, income for equality. This issue is examined in the present section.

2.3.1   The Atkinson Measure

It is possible to express social welfare in terms of the two summary measures $\overline{y}$ and A. This is particularly useful as it enables the implied trade-off between the two objectives of raising average income and reducing its inequality to be seen directly. From the definition of A in equation (2.4):

$$y_e = \overline{y}\left(1 - A\right) \tag{2.7}$$

so that substituting into (2.3) gives welfare per person expressed in terms of $\overline{y}$ and A as:

$$W = H\left[\overline{y}\left(1 - A\right)\right] \tag{2.8}$$

This way of writing the welfare function is called the 'abbreviated welfare function'. However, it is usual to write W simply in terms of the equally distributed equivalent income, as in (2.7), rather than $H\left(y_e\right)$. This is because the nature of the trade-off between equity and efficiency is the same for both forms. Welfare is given just by multiplying arithmetic mean income by $1 - A$, where the latter can be interpreted as a measure of equality (since the maximum value that A can take is 1). Another way of looking at this is to write $W = \overline{y} - \left(\overline{y}A\right)$, and the term $\overline{y}A$ can be interpreted as the 'cost' of inequality.

2.3.2   Social Indifference Curves

The parameter ε reflects the concavity of the function H. A very useful feature is that ε also affects the convexity of a social indifference curve showing combinations of y_i and y_j for persons i and j for which W is constant. The slope, or marginal rate of substitution between y_i and y_j, depends only on the ratio of incomes and not on their absolute levels. Furthermore, this holds for any two individuals in a population and does not depend on their ranks in the distribution, or on the incomes of other individuals.

An indifference curve is shown in Figure 2.2, where B is the point representing the incomes y_1 and y_2. This curve is symmetrical about the 45° line

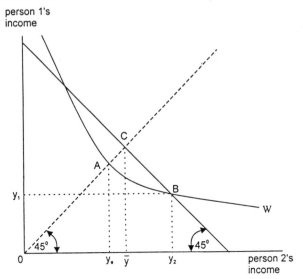

Figure 2.2: A Social Indifference Curve

through the origin because of the assumption that there are no non-income differences between individuals. This can be seen by differentiating W totally with respect to, say, incomes y_1 and y_2. The slope of the indifference curve is thus given by:

$$\left.\frac{dy_i}{dy_j}\right|_W = \left(\frac{y_i}{y_j}\right)^\varepsilon \tag{2.9}$$

A value of $\varepsilon = 0$ gives an indifference curve through B which coincides with the 45° line through B and C, so that total income is constant along the indifference curve. This reflects the absence of any aversion to inequality, and no leaks would be tolerated in making transfers between the individuals. An infinitely high value of ε would give an L-shaped indifference curve, which reflects extreme aversion; the judge would be indifferent between (y_1, y_2) and $(y_1, y_2 - (y_2 - y_1))$. The extent of aversion to inequality is therefore reflected in the shape of the indifference curve in relation to these two extremes. For the two-person case the equally distributed equivalent income is obtained from point A, which has equality in incomes and is on the indifference curve through B, so that the Atkinson inequality measure is the ratio AC/OC.

2.3.3 The Gini Measure

Attempts have also been made to relate the Gini measure to explicit value judgements. It was found that it is not consistent with an individualistic social welfare function of the type used above. Nevertheless, social welfare functions have been proposed which are consistent with the use of the Gini measure. Sen (1973) proposed a 'pairwise maximin' criterion according to which the welfare level of any pair of individuals is equal to the income of the poorest of the two. He then showed that average welfare across all pairs is equal to $\overline{y}\,(1-G)$. The abbreviated social welfare function therefore takes precisely the same form as that based on the Atkinson inequality measure. Welfare is expressed as the product of the arithmetic mean income and the degree of equality (defined as one minus inequality); increasing both total income and its equality are regarded as desirable.

An alternative approach was suggested by Lambert (1993a), whereby each individual's utility depends on income and the income distribution, so that in general terms utility is $U\,(y,F)$. Lambert showed that, in considering the class of welfare functions, $W = U\,(y,F)\,dF\,(y)$, two separate cases give rise to an abbreviated welfare function involving the Gini measure. One case involves U reflecting relative deprivation while in the other case U is specified in terms of the rank position of each individual in the income distribution. For both specifications, welfare can be written as $\overline{y}\,(1-kG)$, where the parameter, k, is restricted to the range $0 < k < 1$.

It is possible to show that the marginal rate of substitution between any pair of incomes, implied by a Gini-based abbreviated welfare function, is constant and depends on k, N and the rankings of the two relevant individuals; it does not depend on their actual incomes. This contrasts with the results for the Atkinson inequality measure, reflecting the different perspectives of the two measures. The Atkinson measure is said to reflect the wastefulness of inequality (the rankings of the two individuals in the distribution do not matter and the same social welfare can be obtained with a lower mean income) whereas the Gini measure is said to reflect the unfairness of inequality.

2.4   Lorenz Curves and Welfare Comparisons

Section 2.1 introduced the Lorenz curve as a way of representing income distributions and showed that two distributions can be compared in terms of their inequality if one distribution has a Lorenz curve that lies entirely inside that of the other distribution. The value judgement behind this idea is the view that an income transfer from a richer to a poorer person that does not change their ranking is an improvement. Such a transfer shifts the Lorenz curve inwards towards the line of equality. The idea that inequality is reduced by rich-to-poor transfers is widely but not universally accepted.

Where Lorenz curves intersect and unequivocal comparisons cannot be made, particular summary measures of inequality can be used, such as Atkinson's measure. As shown above, this is linked to an explicit social welfare function. However, Atkinson (1970) also obtained a more general result involving Lorenz comparisons that has formed the starting point of many investigations. Consider the class of welfare functions discussed earlier and which take the form $W = \sum_i H(y_i)$, where H, reflecting the decision-maker's value judgements, is increasing and concave. The fact that H is increasing means that an increase in any y_i, with all other values unchanged, increases total welfare. The concave property implies that a transfer of \$1 from a richer to a poorer person increases social welfare.

The idea that such transfers increase social welfare has been referred to earlier as the principle of transfers. A simple but powerful result links Lorenz curves to the broad class of welfare functions. Atkinson showed formally that for distributions with equal means, Lorenz dominance, such that the Lorenz curve of distribution A lies entirely inside that of distribution B, implies that social welfare under A exceeds that under B for all welfare functions in the above class. This result provides the welfare interpretation of Lorenz comparisons which was mentioned above. It also holds if the dominating distribution has a higher arithmetic mean than the dominated distribution.

When the arithmetic means of the distributions differ, Shorrocks (1983) and Kakwani (1984) showed that the appropriate concept, for social welfare functions of the form discussed above, is that of the 'generalised Lorenz curve'. This relates the cumulative amount of income, rather than its proportion, to the corresponding proportion of people. When means differ, Atkinson's result stated above can be translated directly in terms of generalised Lorenz curves. Generalised Lorenz dominance can be used to establish welfare rankings in some cases where the Lorenz dominating distribution has the relatively smaller arithmetic mean. Furthermore, there may be cases where Lorenz curves cross, but the generalised Lorenz curves do not cross.

When Lorenz curves and generalised Lorenz curves cross, further restrictions need to be imposed on the welfare functions in order to make unequivocal comparisons. It is not always necessary, however, to make precise assumptions about the form of H, depending on the nature of the distributions being compared. Various conditions have been established in relation to the class of welfare functions which, in addition to being increasing and concave, reflect what is called the 'principle of diminishing transfers'. This is more specific than the principle of transfers, and requires that transfers at the lower end of the income distribution are valued more highly than those in the higher ranges. If two distributions have the same arithmetic mean and population, the following result applies. If the Lorenz curve for distribution B cuts that for A from above, and if the variance of B is less than that of A, it can be inferred that B has a higher welfare than A, under all welfare functions displaying the principle of diminishing transfers. For a complete summary of the results, see Lambert (1993a, b). It may be mentioned that the form of H used in developing the Atkinson inequality measure is itself a special case of a function displaying the principles of diminishing transfers.

2.5 Measuring Poverty

A concern for poverty involves giving special attention to the bottom of the income distribution, in a way that is quite distinct from concern for inequality. People are concerned about poverty because they believe that there is a level of income below which people suffer some form of deprivation; conversely, being above the threshold income confers a special benefit. The idea of a threshold or 'poverty level' is therefore a central feature of poverty studies. It should, however, be recognised that this poverty level is imposed by the person making the poverty judgement; it involves a clear value judgement. In other words the poverty level is not usually viewed as a characteristic of individuals' preferences that is, at least in principle, an objective measure (which may differ between individuals).

Hence there will inevitably be some debate about the appropriate poverty line to use when measuring poverty, because different judges cannot be expected always to share the same precise value judgements. However, even if there is agreement about the poverty line, judges may take different views about aspects of poverty and hence the way in which it should be measured. In using a particular measure of poverty, it is useful to relate the statistical measure directly to basic value judgements, although this is not an easy thing to do. It is worth noting that most approaches to poverty measurement are described as being 'non-welfarist', in that they make no attempt to refer directly to the welfare of individuals. In particular, they are based simply on income comparisons.

2.5.1   The Headcount Poverty Measure

One view is that the major deprivation associated with being in poverty is caused simply by being below the poverty line, so that other considerations are secondary. Those who take this view are likely to have the objective of minimising the number of people found below the poverty line (subject to the usual constraints imposed on the tax and transfer system). The associated measure of poverty is the well-known 'headcount' measure; this is simply the proportion of the population found below the poverty line.

More formally, suppose that there are N individuals with incomes of y_i $(i = 1, ..., N)$, arranged in ascending order so that $y_1 < y_2 < y_3 < ... < y_N$. If y_p is the poverty level, suppose that $g(y_i | y_p)$ takes the value of 1 if $y_i \leq y_p$, and is 0 otherwise. The headcount poverty measure, H, can therefore be written as:

$$H = \frac{1}{N} \sum_{i=1}^{N} g(y_i | y_p) \qquad (2.10)$$

This measure reflects only the incidence of poverty, but there are other dimensions to poverty which other judges may regard as very important. An additional dimension is the intensity of poverty, reflected in the difference, or poverty gap, between income and the poverty line. Finally, some judges may have concern for the inequality of poverty. These three aspects are discussed in more detail below.

2.5.2 Hypothetical Populations

A useful way to highlight the various approaches to poverty measurement and the value judgements involved is to consider hypothetical populations. Suppose that there are 10 individuals, with incomes given as in the first row of Table 2.1. These incomes are ranked in ascending order. In order to abstract from the debate regarding the poverty line itself, suppose that all judges agree that the deprivation from poverty occurs with an income less than or equal to $10. Then the first four individuals are in poverty, so that $H = 0.4$.

Suppose that $5 is available to alleviate poverty. The policy question therefore concerns the appropriate way of spending the $5. The aim of minimising poverty by using the $5 can mean different things to different policy makers. One alternative dominates if the major aim is to minimise the number of people in poverty, that is, the headcount measure. This policy would give $2 to person 4 and $3 to person 3. This gives the distribution shown in the second row of Table 2.1 and raises persons 3 and 4 above the poverty line, thereby halving the number of people in poverty. The implication is that if resources available to alleviate poverty are scarce, a focus on the headcount measure involves helping the relatively better-off poor people rather than those right at the bottom of the distribution.

Not everyone would share this policy prescription and the value judgement behind it. In the distribution in the second row of Table 2.1, there is a larger gap between the lower two individuals and the rest of the population. This may be regarded as undesirable by some people. An alternative approach would be to focus help on the very poorest members of society (while

Table 2.1: Alternative Income Distributions

Distr. no.	Incomes of Persons:									
	1	2	3	4	5	6	7	8	9	10
1	4	6	8	9	12	15	20	25	30	35
2	4	6	11	11	12	15	20	25	30	35
3	7	8	8	9	12	15	20	25	30	35
4	6	7	8	11	12	15	20	25	30	35

retaining the same ranking of individuals by, for example, not raising person 1 above person 2). This view might involve giving $3 to the poorest and $2 to the next poorest, producing the distribution shown in the third row of Table 2.1. This has no effect on the number of people in poverty. Hence those judges who are concerned with the very poorest members of the population would not measure poverty using a headcount measure, but would use a measure that reflected the extent to which some people are below the poverty line.

A further alternative policy, preferred perhaps by some judges, may involve a compromise between the aim of helping the very poor and trying to reduce the number of people in poverty, by giving $2 to both persons 4 and 1, and the remaining $1 to person 2. This raises the relatively richer person, of those in poverty, above the poverty line and gives the distribution shown in the final row of Table 2.1.

The major implication is that there is clearly no policy which can be regarded as 'correct' or 'efficient' without reference to the basic value judgements involved.

2.6   TIP Curves

In examining inequality, considerable use is made of the Lorenz curve and associated generalised Lorenz curve. This section presents a very similar diagrammatic device for examining the main poverty features displayed by an income distribution, for a given poverty level. This is the TIP curve, introduced by Jenkins and Lambert (1997). The acronym refers to the three important characteristics of poverty, the 'Three "I"s of Poverty', which are incidence, intensity and inequality.

In defining the TIP curve, it is useful to redefine the function, $g\left(y_i | y_p\right)$, so that it indicates not only whether an individual is below the poverty line, y_p, but also the absolute 'poverty gap', or the extent to which y_i falls below y_p. Thus let:

$$
\begin{aligned}
g\left(y_i | y_p\right) &= y_p - y_i \quad \text{for } y_i \le y_p \\
&= 0 \quad\quad\quad \text{for } y_i > y_p
\end{aligned}
\tag{2.11}
$$

Suppose, as before, that the N individuals in the population are ranked in ascending order so that $y_1 < y_2 < ... < y_N$. The TIP curve is obtained by plotting the total poverty gap per capita against the corresponding proportion people. In other words, plot:

$$
\frac{1}{N} \sum_{i=1}^{k} g\left(y_i | y_p\right) \text{ against } \frac{k}{N} \text{ for } k = 1, ..., N
\tag{2.12}
$$

Consider the distribution in the first row of Table 2.1. The poorest $\frac{1}{10}$ of the population is responsible for a poverty gap per capita of $\frac{6}{10}$; the poorest $\frac{2}{10}$ produce a poverty gap per capita of $\frac{10}{10}$; the poorest $\frac{3}{10}$ produce a poverty gap per capita of $\frac{12}{10}$, and so on. The corresponding TIP curve is shown in Figure 2.3 where, in order to focus on the lower end of the distribution, only part of the horizontal axis is shown. The headcount poverty measure, H, which reflects the incidence of poverty, is shown by the horizontal distance, OH. The total poverty gap per capita reflects the intensity of poverty and is measured by the height, AH. Hence, the slope AH/OH indicates the average poverty gap among the poor.

The slope of the non-horizontal section of the curve at any point is the poverty gap at that point, since the slope of the straight line joining points for the $(k-1)$th and kth persons is given by:

$$
\frac{\frac{1}{N} \sum_{i=1}^{k} g\left(y_i | y_p\right) - \frac{1}{N} \sum_{i=1}^{k-1} g\left(y_i | y_p\right)}{\frac{k}{N} - \frac{k-1}{N}} = g\left(y_k | y_p\right)
\tag{2.13}
$$

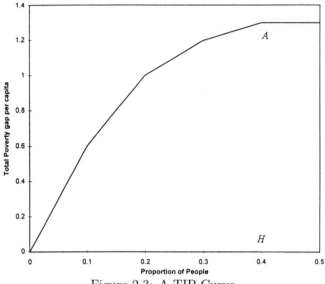

Figure 2.3: A TIP Curve

The extent to which the poverty gap falls as income rises is therefore reflected in the flattening of the TIP curve as it moves towards point A. Hence, the extent of inequality among the poor is shown by the concavity of the section OA of the TIP curve. If all those below y_p have the same poverty gap, then the section OA of the curve is simply a straight line with a slope equal to the common poverty gap.

In the extreme case where everyone is in poverty, the TIP curve is a straight line from the origin to the point $(y_p, 1)$ and therefore has a slope equal to the poverty line; and in the other extreme where no one is in poverty, the TIP curve simply follows the horizontal axis. Hence, just as in the case of the Lorenz curve, the TIP curve lies between two extremes. It was pointed out above that if the Lorenz curve for one distribution lies unambiguously closer to the line of equality than that of another distribution, the former distribution can be said to be more equal for all inequality measures satisfying the principle of transfers. In the case of the TIP curve, it can be shown that if the curve for one distribution lies closer to the horizontal axis than for another distribution, then the former displays less poverty for any measure that is based on poverty gaps.

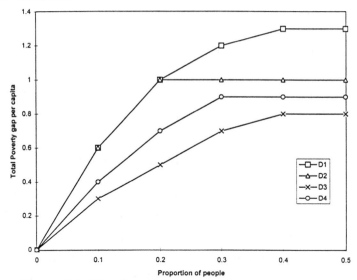

Figure 2.4: TIP Curves for Alternative Distributions

The TIP curves for all four distributions given in Table 2.1 are shown in Figure 2.4. The fact that distribution 2 has the lowest headcount measure is clearly shown in the figure. However, the headcount measure is not a member of the class of all measures that could be based on poverty gaps, since it completely ignores the poverty gaps. Distribution number 3 is unequivocally closer to the horizontal axis which represents the extreme of zero poverty, so it can be concluded that all judges who regard aggregate poverty as depending in some way on poverty gaps would judge this to have the lowest poverty (assuming that they all agree on the value of the poverty line, here set equal to 10). Distribution number 1 clearly has the highest poverty (though both 1 and 3 have the same headcount measure).

It is also possible to produce corresponding TIP curves based on poverty gaps expressed as a proportion of the poverty line, or normalised poverty gaps, $(y_p - y_i)/y_p$. This produces a diagram within a box having height and width of unity, just as the Lorenz curve. Extreme poverty is then represented by the leading diagonal, with slope of 45 degrees. Jenkins and Lambert (1997) show how several poverty measures can be related to areas within the diagram. Dominance of such normalised TIP curves implies that all measures based on normalised poverty gaps would give the same ordering of distributions. TIP curves are therefore valuable for poverty comparisons in the same way that Lorenz curves, and generalised Lorenz curves, are valuable for inequality comparisons. The following section considers specific poverty measures that are based on normalised poverty gaps.

2.7 Alternative Poverty Measures

In the previous section, the idea of a normalised poverty gap was introduced. This is simply the poverty gap divided by the poverty line, or $g\left(y_i \,|y_p\right)/y_p$. While it is very difficult to make a direct translation between value judgements and poverty measures (except perhaps in the case of the headcount measure), this section considers a class of poverty measures defined in terms of such gaps.

Consider the set of poverty measures, P_α, defined by:

$$P_\alpha = \frac{1}{N} \sum_{y_i \leq y_p} \left(\frac{y_p - y_i}{y_p}\right)^\alpha \tag{2.14}$$

where α is a parameter to be set by the user. This is the class of poverty measures introduced by Foster *et al.* (1984). Substitution into (2.14) shows that when $\alpha = 0$, the poverty measure, P_0, is equal to the headcount measure. When $\alpha = 1$, the corresponding poverty measure is equal to the headcount measure multiplied by $G = 1 - \mu_p/y_p$, where μ_p is the arithmetic mean income of those in poverty. Hence $P_1 = P_0 G$ depends on both the proportion of people in poverty and the extent to which, on average, those people fall below the poverty line. It is also equivalent to the right hand vertical intercept of the corresponding normalised TIP curve.

When $\alpha = 2$, the corresponding poverty measure depends also on the inequality of those in poverty, as measured by the coefficient on variation, η_p^2. It can be shown that:

$$P_2 = P_0 \left\{ G^2 + (1 - G)^2 \eta_p^2 \right\} \tag{2.15}$$

Table 2.2: Summary Measures of Poverty and Inequality

Distr. no	P_0	P_1	P_2	Gini
1	0.4000	0.1300	0.0570	0.346
2	0.2000	0.1000	0.0520	0.324
3	0.4000	0.0800	0.0180	0.312
4	0.3000	0.0900	0.0290	0.318

Table 2.2 shows the values of these three poverty measures for each distribution of Table 2.1. As can be seen from the formulae given above, these measures arise essentially from differences in the weighting that a judge may wish to attach to the extent to which individuals are found to be below the poverty line. Table 2.2 also shows the Gini inequality measure of each distribution.

The value of P_0, the headcount measure, is obviously minimised for the second distribution, and has the intermediate value of 0.3 for the fourth 'compromise' distribution. However, the third distribution has the lowest values of P_1 and P_2, along with the lowest overall inequality measure. Although distribution 2 involves a halving of the P_0 measure, distribution number 3 produces a much greater reduction in the other measures of poverty, while leaving P_0 unchanged.

2.7.1 Absolute and Relative Poverty Lines

The above examples involve differences in the incomes of only those below the poverty line, which remains fixed at $10 in all comparisons. However, suppose the distribution of income changes from the first row of Table 2.1 to the following:

$$\left[\begin{array}{cccccccccc} 4 & 6 & 11 & 11 & 15 & 18 & 25 & 30 & 35 & 38 \end{array} \right]$$

This is the same as the distribution in row 2 of Table 2.1, except that the incomes of the non-poor have generally increased. The general level of prices is assumed to be the same in each case. The question then arises of whether a judge of poverty would apply a different poverty line in examining the new distribution. This involves the issue of whether poverty is regarded in an 'absolute' or a 'relative' sense. Those who judge poverty in terms of a fixed or absolute 'basket of goods' would continue to use a poverty line of $10. Those who view deprivation in relative terms would wish to allow for the fact that the poorest members of society appear to have lagged behind the others. The arithmetic mean income in the first distribution is $16.4 while in the above new distribution it is $19.4. Applying the percentage increase in average incomes to the poverty level raises it to just above $11. Hence persons 3 and 4 continue to be in poverty when using a relative approach while they are considered to have escaped poverty when an absolute approach is used. Again, there is no correct way to proceed; value judgements play a central part in the comparisons. The poverty levels, using a relative approach with $y_p = 11$, are 0.4, 0.1117, 0.0620 respectively for measures P_0, P_1 and P_2, with a Gini of 0.336.

2.7.2   The Time Period of Analysis

The above comparisons are all entirely 'static' in the sense that judgements were being made on the basis of the income distribution and associated poverty measures of only a single year. However, dynamic considerations may also play an important role. In particular, some judges may be especially concerned by the extent to which some people remain in poverty over a long period. They may be somewhat less concerned by the poverty measure within each period, so long as those in poverty are able to escape quickly. Such judges will attach a higher priority to measures which encourage income mobility and remove 'poverty traps' (such as very high marginal tax rates associated with means-tested benefits, which may provide adverse work incentives).

Consider, for example, the income distribution shown in the first row of Table 2.1 and suppose that this is the distribution in year 1. Several alternative distributions for year 2 are shown in Table 2.3. The question of how a judge would rank the outcomes depends not only on the poverty measure used within each year, but on the extent to which additional weight is given to the existence of 'long-term poverty'.

Table 2.3: Alternative Income Distributions for Year 2

Distr. no	Incomes of Persons:									
	1	2	3	4	5	6	7	8	9	10
1	4	6	12	15	8	9	20	25	30	35
2	12	15	20	25	4	6	8	30	9	35
3	4	6	11	11	12	15	20	25	30	35

In the first example in Table 2.3, all the single-period poverty measures are unchanged because the only change is that persons 3 and 5 have changed places, along with persons 4 and 6. However, the poorest two people continue to be poor in both periods. In the second example in Table 2.3, there is rather more 'changing places' from one year to the next. The single-year poverty measures are still all the same as in the first year, but no one is in poverty for more than one year. In the third example, the income distribution is exactly the same as the second row of Table 2.1, and has the associated single-period poverty measures taken from Table 2.2. In this case, persons 1 and 2 continue to be in poverty in both periods. There is much more rigidity in the income distribution, but persons 3 and 4 have just escaped poverty in the second period. There is no unequivocal answer to the question of which year 2 distribution is preferred. They would be ranked differently by different judges who take different views not only about the way within-period poverty is judged, but also about the dynamics.

2.8 Conclusions

The purpose of this chapter has been to provide a brief introduction to inequality and poverty measures, emphasising the link between the measures and value judgements. First the Lorenz curve, as an extremely useful device for providing a visual impression of an income distribution, was defined. It was seen that Lorenz curves can give a partial ordering of income distributions in terms of their inequality; an ordering cannot be given when they intersect. A complete ordering of distributions requires specific measures of inequality. Two extensively used measures, the Gini and Atkinson measures, were described. The social welfare functions associated with these measures, particularly the abbreviated forms involving the arithmetic mean and inequality, were examined. The welfare functions can be used to provide complete orderings of distributions. The Lorenz curve and the associated concept of the generalised Lorenz curve were then used to provide partial welfare orderings of distributions. Alternative poverty measures were then introduced and their properties examined using hypothetical examples. Any comparison of distributions cannot escape value judgements. For this reason the chapter has concentrated on showing how such judgements can be made explicit, so that the implications of adopting alternative values can be examined.

Part II

Cross-sectional Comparisons

Chapter 3

Cross-sectional Comparisons

The distribution of income has a central role in many different types of economic and social study, so there are many approaches to its analysis. A large group of users includes those wishing to make social evaluations and who are concerned directly with measuring inequality and poverty. Some members of this group will wish mainly to study changes over time or compare countries using descriptive measures, while others will attempt to model tax and transfer systems, or evaluate the redistributive effects of a range of government policies. Policies may be introduced for other purposes, for example to stimulate saving and investment, but nevertheless have significant redistributive effects. These types of evaluation are usually necessarily based on outcomes (the observed distribution) rather than processes (such as opportunities for social mobility).

This chapter discusses some of the issues involved in making income distribution comparisons using cross-sectional data. Section 3.1 discusses the types of data used. Section 3.2 examines some issues relating to the unit of analysis, and section 3.3 discusses the construction of equivalence scales. The appendix provides some further references to the literature. First, however, some of the basic conceptual issues which arise in any income distribution study are briefly raised.

Any project involving the use of income distribution data must first make decisions about the following three inter-related concepts: these are the unit of analysis (or income recipient), the time period, and finally the measure of income. Income is derived from a variety of sources, including employment, rents and dividends, interest, capital gains and a variety of transfer payments, not all of which are taxable. The relative importance of the different sources varies over the life cycle. The choice of income concept will in part be influenced by the decision regarding the time period of analysis, and vice versa. For example, many transfer payments, such as unemployment or sickness benefits and state pensions, have an insurance element and a redistributive element, so that their redistributive impact cannot be examined using only annual information. Furthermore, as the length of time over which income is measured is increased, the opportunities are increased for changes to take place in the unit of analysis through household formation, marriage, divorce, births and deaths.

In considering the unit of analysis, a closely related, but often neglected, issue relates to the question of whether comparisons are to be made between or within generations. Since households often consist of members of different generations, many analyses compound two types of redistribution. Intergenerational transfers may be made within the family (or household) or via the tax and transfer system, and complicated off-setting changes may take place. For example, state pensions and other social insurance components may reduce intra-family inter-generational transfers, and the same may apply to student loans, making overall comparisons over time very complex.

The choices of income concept, time period and unit of analysis depend crucially on the nature of the basic questions motivating the use of the income distribution data. It is seldom possible to make an objective decision about the three related choices: value judgements play a crucial role. Too often the value judgements underlying the analysis are left implicit. It is thus important to examine the implications of adopting alternative clearly stated value judgements. Such values may relate not only to the measurement of inequality of any specified distribution. Any given inequality of income measured over several time periods may be associated with different degrees and types of relative earnings mobility, and some people may regard a certain type and extent of mobility as desirable in itself. Mobility is examined in Part III of this book.

3.1 Types of Data

The majority of studies of inequality and poverty are based on comparisons of static distributions of annual (or sometimes shorter period) incomes at different points in time or between different countries. The data used have typically been collected for other purposes than the measurement of poverty or inequality. For example, data are often obtained from the process of collecting income taxation, while another source is the income data in household expenditure surveys. The former usually have very large samples, and the unit of analysis is the tax unit, which corresponds more closely with the nuclear family than with the household. The assumption of equal sharing of resources (discussed below) is more appropriate for the nuclear family than the household. However, tax data necessarily exclude those below the tax threshold, so are of little use for poverty analyses.

A further problem with tax unit data is that changes in tax units (arising from marriage or divorce) within the year can lead to a certain amount of double counting, which may overstate the number of low incomes. Household expenditure surveys, while smaller, typically use a more comprehensive definition of income and contain information about transfer payments and imputed rents (but often not capital gains or income in kind). They also contain more information relating to the 'needs' of households, but the assessment period is usually for a short period such as a 'normal' week rather than a year. Furthermore, there is systematic non-response among the elderly and understatement of income from self-employment and investments. Household surveys necessarily exclude people who are institutionalised and homeless.

These problems of using data collected for other purposes to examine income distribution issues arise in all industrialised countries. A systematic comparison has been made by the *Luxembourg Income Study* (LIS), which has assembled data sets from a variety of countries and edited them in order to produce data which are more suitable for international comparisons. For detailed comparisons, see the papers collected by Smeeding *et al.* (1990). An evaluation of the transfer systems in various countries using LIS data is reported in Mitchell (1991).

Household survey data are now available on computer tape or disks. This allows researchers to examine alternative income concepts and income units and to carry out extensive analyses, in particular allowing for selected decompositions. For examples of the types of result that can be obtained from extensive decomposition analyses, see Borooah *et al.* (1991), Jenkins (1992) and Coulter *et al.* (1991).

3.2   The Unit of Analysis

3.2.1   Individuals and Households

In assessing distributional outcomes there is, as suggested above, no single definition of the income unit that is most appropriate in all situations, and the choice will often involve a value judgement. However, the effects of many labour market policies, and policies regarding subsidies for education and training, for example, are most appropriately examined in terms of individuals. The inequality of pay within and between occupational or educational groups is a perennial subject of concern, and the individual is the relevant unit.

An important subject which requires further investigation is the nature of the link between the personal and household or family distributions of income. There have been significant changes in the labour force participation by women, in the retirement behaviour of men, in the timing of births and in the extent to which births take place outside marriage. Increased labour market participation by, and higher earnings for, women may have different implications for the personal and the household income distributions. A reduction in the inequality of pay of both men and women, and a reduction in male-female pay differentials, would not necessarily reduce the inequality of household income. People may have quite different attitudes to these distributions: for example, some may be very concerned about inequalities in the labour market and would stress labour market policies, being less concerned with households. A more complete understanding of the relationship between the two distributions would therefore provide valuable information. For a discussion of the literature and an analysis of Australian data, see Saunders (1994); an analysis of UK data is presented by Parker (1994).

3.2.2   Intra-household Income Sharing

It is not surprising that a concern for inequality and poverty has led investigators towards the household or family as the unit of analysis, since there are very many people living in households who do not receive any income from employment. To concentrate only on pay inequalities would exclude a large proportion of the population, and would be of little interest to those whose main concern is poverty. The standard assumption used in such studies is one of equal sharing within the household. None of the major household surveys contains explicit information about consumption by particular members of the household.

The nature of any bias in poverty measurement arising from the assumption of equal sharing is not immediately clear. For example, if a 'headcount' measure of poverty is used, an equal-sharing assumption could lead to an upward bias. Here, all members of a household are included among the poor, whereas some members may in practice appropriate a larger share of household resources and escape poverty. With a 'poverty gap' measure, however, the conventional approach will more clearly provide a lower limit to the extent of poverty. In the context of a developing country with a single subsistence good, Haddan and Kanbur (1990) showed that inequality and poverty levels are understated using the equal-sharing assumption.

There have been some small-scale surveys that attempt to examine intra-household income sharing, including Brannen and Wilson (1987) and Pahl (1983, 1989). Piachaud (1982) is a rare study which attempts to allocate the expenditure on different goods to the various household members.

Some studies have used an assumption of 'no sharing' in order to consider the extreme of the possible range of outcomes; these include Townsend (1979) and Atkinson (1991). In these studies social transfers and occupational benefits and earnings are simply attributed to the person who receives them. This extreme is obviously unrealistic, but a slight modification has been suggested by Fuchs (1986) and Jenkins (1991b), involving 'minimum sharing'. In this approach, the difference between actual household income and 'equivalent' income is divided equally among the children, while each adult's income is adjusted accordingly. Hence each adult's adjusted income is the individual income multiplied by the ratio of the number of adults to the number of equivalent adults in the household. Each adult contributes in equal proportions to the children, and gets equal benefits from any economies of scale. Suppose there are two adults with the father earning $800 and the mother earning $200, with two children. With equivalence scales for male and female adults and children respectively of 1, 0.8 and 0.3, the equivalent household size is 2.4. The approach would assign $800(2/2.4) = \$666.67$ to the father and $200(2/2.4) = \$166.67$ to the mother, with $(1000 - 666.67 - 166.67)/2 = \$83.33$ to each child.

An alternative approach was suggested by Lazear and Michael (1986), which assumes equal sharing among adults and among children, but estimates an allocation between parents and children. The basis of the allocation rule is the idea that there are some goods which are consumed only by adults, combined with an assumption that the ratio of expenditure on these items to total adult expenditure does not depend on the number of children in the household. This assumption enables the ratio to be obtained using data for childless couples (allowing for other measurable characteristics such as occupation and education). Income shares are then equated to expenditure shares. Using US data, Lazear and Michael found that inequality is increased and more children are in poverty, compared with the standard assumption of equal sharing. For further developments of this kind of approach, see Deaton and Muellbauer (1986) and Gronau (1991).

An alternative method of allocating income within the household has been suggested by Borooah and McKee (1994), who assume that adults distribute resources to the children according to their needs as reflected in equivalence scales. Their approach is based on a simplified version of Sen's 'cooperative conflict' model. Cooperation is required to increase the total amount of resources, and this is reflected in the needs of children being met, while conflict arises over the division of the remaining amount between the adults. Borooah and McKee also estimated a non-market component of household resources by imputing hours worked on various activities and attaching an assumed wage rate to those hours. They found that both measured inequality and poverty are lower when allowance is made for household production. In addition, measures are lower with unequal sharing of 'full' income than with equal sharing of income obtained from market activities only.

Given the rather strong assumptions underlying the equal-sharing rule and the alternatives discussed above, and the sensitivity of results concerning poverty and inequality, it would be useful to obtain more direct information. It should also be recognised that some goods can be regarded as 'public goods' within the household. For a treatment of the income measure, see also Travers and Richardson (1993).

An early study of income sharing is Young (1952). On the importance of sharing in developing countries, see Sen (1984). A comparison of the equal-sharing assumption using households and families as the income units is by Johnson and Webb (1989). For the feminist literature concerned with income sharing in the context of poverty, see Glendinning and Millar (1987), Brannen and Wilson (1987), Edwards (1981) and Wilson (1987). On estimating the allocation between parents and children, see also Lazear and Michael (1988) and Gronau (1988).

3.2.3 Leisure and Household Production

The question of intra-household income sharing is also related to the wider question of how the household's income or resources should be measured. In particular, the standard analyses of inequality using household data ignore the allocation of time by household members between leisure and household production activities, such as cooking, cleaning and household maintenance. Household members typically provide different inputs into such activities. Recognition of these aspects suggests that any individual's 'full' income consists of the following components: the share of that individual's money income; the share obtained from other members' money incomes; the value of the individual's leisure; and the share of the output both from the individual's and from other household members' household production. The number of items which need to be valued and allocated within households is very large, and requires detailed information on the use of time, which is not available in the large-scale household surveys.

A survey of time use in the UK is reported in Gershuny *et al.* (1988). Time-use surveys have also been carried out in the US and Australia; see Australian Bureau of Statistics (1988) and Juster and Stafford (1991). In order to overcome the problem that time-use surveys are typically on a smaller scale, Jenkins (1991b) has suggested, following Fuchs (1986), that data sets may be merged by matching respondents to time budget surveys with individuals in the household expenditure surveys using information on personal characteristics contained in both surveys.

It is also worth bearing in mind that transfers also take place between households, often within families, about which very little information is available. Such transfers are largely between generations, and may well be influenced by, for example, the extent to which age pensions and health care for the elderly and support for those in higher education are financed by general taxation. Individuals may substitute private transfers for public transfers financed by taxation.

3.3   Equivalence Scales

3.3.1   Alternative Approaches

The extensive literature on the measurement of inequality and the progressivity of taxation is almost all concerned with groups of individuals whose only relevant differences are their incomes. It is usually suggested that the same methods can be applied to households by first dividing household income by an appropriate equivalence scale rate which depends on the size and composition of the household. Such an adjustment will change the relative incomes of households and may lead to some re-ranking when households are arranged in ascending order of income. It is worth noting that the standard approaches will thus be in terms of the inequality or redistribution of 'equivalent' income; but in practice such redistribution may be very difficult to achieve and may not be revenue-neutral in terms of actual income.

An equivalence scale rate can be expressed as the ratio of the money that a household, with specified characteristics and facing a set of prices, needs in order to achieve a certain level of 'wellbeing', compared with the cost of achieving the same level of wellbeing by a household with a 'reference' set of characteristics facing a 'reference' set of prices. The specification of the scales involves choices about all the elements of the cost ratio including: the characteristics of individuals and households which are regarded as relevant; the meaning attached to 'wellbeing'; and the relevant prices (it is not obvious that all households face the same prices as the 'reference household'). It is therefore not surprising that many different scales and several methods of construction have been devised.

Most scales have been produced using econometric methods applied to household budget data, based on a utility maximising model. Wellbeing is thus seen as utility, and the cost of achieving a specified level of utility is obtained from the relevant indirect utility function after estimation of the model's parameters, assuming that all households face the same prices. Not surprisingly, estimates vary according to the type of utility function and data used. However, estimated scales are often taken from one study and applied to other data, for perhaps quite different time periods and countries, to make judgements about inequality and poverty. Such econometric estimates are sometimes described as being more objective than other approaches, but it is far from clear that scales which may be appropriate for examining household demands are also appropriate for making social evaluations of income distributions.

There are technical issues relating to the identification of the scales, and strong identifying restrictions have to be imposed. Income and expenditure are treated as being the same in the cross-sectional studies but the difference may vary systematically with income. Furthermore, the estimates do not usually allow for household production and the use of time: this problem gives rise to similar issues to those discussed above in the context of intra-household income sharing. Furthermore the choices of relevant characteristics such as age, gender, disability and so on and of the function relating scales to characteristics are made by the econometrician, but these are not necessarily appropriate in social evaluation exercises.

Other fundamental issues remain. For example, the household choices observed in budget studies are necessarily highly constrained and may not reveal social values. Also, the expenditure patterns reflect parents' (constrained) assessments of the welfare of children, and these may not reflect social valuations. A basic criticism, made strongly by Pollack and Wales (1979), is that the approach regards children as imposing costs in relation to their needs, but it does not allow for any benefits arising from children. To the extent that people choose to have children, there is a revealed preference which is ignored in the estimates, so that the estimated scales have little value in the context of welfare comparisons.

Alternatively, scales have been produced using the so-called subjective approach associated with Kapteyn and van Praag (1976). This method produces estimates based on what people say about the income levels which they judge would produce alternative levels of welfare. The levels of welfare are specified in terms of a scale from 'very bad', through 'sufficient' to 'very good', and the scales are converted into numerical scores. The equivalence scales are then produced using an assumed form of utility function. In addition to the various technical problems of estimation, the same problems of interpretation arise as with the econometric approach. For a survey of subjective scales, see Bradbury (1989).

The earliest equivalence scales were produced using what is called a 'budget standard', which involves the judgements of 'experts' concerning the dietary and other needs of individuals. The selection of goods to be included, the appropriate quantities, the relevant prices and of course the characteristics of individuals are all made by the 'experts'. The use of such scales is suggested by Bradshaw *et al.* (1987) and Bradshaw (1991), who argue that the approach makes all judgements explicit.

Investigators have also used scales based on those used as part of the government system of social assistance, particularly the set of rules determining eligibility for means-tested social transfers. It is sometimes suggested that these represent scales based on a social consensus, but the high level of political debate concerning adjustments to such scales provides little support for the idea that they receive widespread approval. The 'budget standard' and 'social assistance' scales also focus on poverty; it is far from clear that they would be appropriate for the assessment of broader aspects of inequality. Faced with this array of different approaches, it is perhaps not surprising that some investigators have taken a pragmatic attitude. This has sometimes involved taking an average of alternative scales, or simply adopting a set of scales such as those suggested by OECD publications on social indicators. The relevant value judgements being made are thus far from clear.

3.3.2 Sensitivity of Results

The above summary has argued that there is no objective way of producing equivalence scales which can be used to evaluate distributional outcomes; value judgements are inevitably required and so, given the wide variety of views, there is no consensus. However, this diversity would not matter if evaluations of income distributions were insensitive to the choice of scale rates used. An analysis of alternative scales has been carried out by Buhman *et al.* (1988) using data from the *Luxembourg Income Study* database. For convenience, they specified a set of scale rates using a simple formula whereby the scale is equal to the number of persons in the household raised to a power, say q. This constant elasticity form ignores the characteristics of individuals, but provides a reasonable description of rates in use: the subjective scales give values of q about 0.2 while the OECD scale gives a value of about 0.7. A value of 1 corresponds to the use of per capita incomes while a value of 0 involves no adjustment to household incomes at all. It was found that as q is increased, measured inequality at first decreases and then increases in a systematic way.

   In an extensive analysis of a range of inequality and poverty measures (producing analytical results), Coulter *et al.* (1992) have demonstrated that the U-shaped result of Buhmann *et al.* (1988) is robust, and applies to all the measures considered. The implication of this strong finding is that it is not appropriate to produce a single set of results based on one set of scales, or even a range of results which purport to cover the extremes. A full sensitivity analysis should be carried out. For further discussion, see also Atkinson *et al.* (1994) and Bradbury (1994).

3.3.3   Decomposition Analysis

Faced with the sensitivity of inequality measures to equivalence scales, another strategy is to produce decomposition analyses. Overall comparisons can be decomposed into comparisons of distributions for various household types considered separately. The within-group inequality measures would not be affected by the equivalence scale used; only the between-group component is affected. The need to use inequality measures that are decomposable led Coulter *et al.* (1992, 1994) to suggest that greater use should be made of the generalised entropy class of measures. Consider Atkinson's (1970) measure of inequality, given by:

$$I = 1 - \left[\frac{1}{N}\sum_i (y_i/\mu)^{1-\varepsilon}\right]^{1/(1-\varepsilon)} \quad \varepsilon \neq 1 \qquad (3.1)$$

where y_i (for $i = 1, ..., N$) is the equivalent income of the ith household; μ is arithmetic mean income; and ε is the measure of constant relative inequality aversion.

Although this measure cannot be decomposed, the following transformation can be decomposed into terms which capture the contribution to inequality of the sub-populations, with a remainder term which measures the inequality between sub-populations:

$$J = \left[(1 - I)^{1-\varepsilon} - 1\right] \qquad (3.2)$$

This belongs to the class of generalised entropy measures. The following decomposition is then available:

$$J = \sum_{j=1}^{m} q_k^{1-\varepsilon} p_k^{\varepsilon} J_k + J_B \qquad (3.3)$$

where

q_k is the share of group k in total equivalent income;

p_k is the population share of group k;

J_k is the within-group inequality measure for group k; and

J_B is the 'between-group' measure.

The between-group measure, J_B, is calculated by replacing each unit's equivalent income with the arithmetic mean equivalent income for the relevant sub-population. This eliminates the within-group inequality without affecting the totals. The analysis of poverty, rather than inequality, is more awkward. Although many poverty measures can be written as functions of decomposable inequality measures, a different equivalence scale may change the composition of those counted as poor, so the within-group measures may also be influenced by the scales used.

3.3.4 Dominance Conditions

The use of a set of equivalence scales and an explicit measure of inequality, or poverty, will enable two distributions to be ranked unequivocally. However, strong value judgements are needed in the choice of inequality or poverty measure and in the choice of equivalence scales. There will inevitably be differences of opinion about such basic issues. This problem has motivated the study of conditions under which one distribution may be said to 'dominate' another, from a social welfare point of view, avoiding the need for equivalence scales and using a minimum set of value judgements. It may be easier to find agreement about the smaller set of judgements.

Dominance conditions for homogeneous populations (where income is the only relevant difference between individuals) have been established following the pioneering work of Atkinson (1970). These conditions involve additively separable social welfare functions and the use of Lorenz curves and generalised Lorenz curves; see chapter 2. Atkinson and Bourguignon (1987) deal with differences in household composition. They consider a general class of social welfare functions in which total welfare is a sum of the welfare within each household type (distinguished by size and composition). Their approach requires first that there is agreement about how to rank household types in decreasing order of their needs. Secondly, it must be agreed that an extra dollar given to a person is more highly valued (in producing social welfare) for someone from a more needy compared with a less needy household group, with a given income, and the marginal social value decreases with income.

Without imposing any further value judgements, Atkinson and Bourguignon established that one distribution can be regarded as superior to another if a specified sequence of generalised Lorenz curve comparisons is satisfied. This involves starting with the most needy group, and successively combining relatively less needy groups. If the generalised Lorenz curve for the most needy group for one distribution is above that of the same group in the other distribution (for, say, before- and after-tax comparisons), then add the next most needy group and make the same comparison, until the whole population is included.

More formally, consider the case of m population groups and suppose the social welfare function is written:

$$W = \left(\frac{1}{N}\right) \sum_{k=1}^{m} \sum_{i=1}^{n_i} U_k\left(y_{ik}\right) \tag{3.4}$$

and the following two restrictions are agreed:

(i) $U_k\left(y\right)$ is strictly increasing and concave, so that more is judged to be good, and rich to poor transfers within each group are judged to be good.

(ii) For each $k \leq m - 1$, $U_k'\left(y\right) - U_{k+1}'\left(y\right) > 0$ and decreasing in y.

It is not necessary to specify a cardinalisation of the U_k functions. First, rank household in order, $j = 1, ..., m$ so that $j = 1$ for the 'most deserving' household type. One distribution dominates another (say post- and pre-tax and transfer distributions) if and only if there is generalised Lorenz dominance for the j most needy sub-populations, for each $j = 1, ..., m$. Thus, check generalised Lorenz dominance for group 1, and if the post-tax curve lies above the pre-tax curve add the next group, for $j = 2$. Then check the generalised Lorenz curves for the combined group of 1 and 2, and so on.

The standard Lorenz curve traces the relationship between the proportion of total income and the proportion of people, whereas the generalised Lorenz curve traces the cumulative income of the poorest $100p$ per cent of the population, expressed per capita of the whole population, against the percentage of people. Hence for incomes $y_1 < y_2 < ...y_N$, with $p = j/N$, the Lorenz curve is defined by:

$$L(p) = \sum_{i=1}^{j} y_i / (N\mu) \qquad (3.5)$$

The generalised Lorenz curve is defined by:

$$GL(p) = \mu L(p) = \sum_{i=1}^{j} y_i / N \qquad (3.6)$$

The major problem with this procedure is, however, that it can only be applied to situations in which the two populations being compared have the same proportions of each household type. Atkinson (1992) has extended the approach to deal with poverty comparisons; see also Jenkins and Lambert (1993).

3.3.5 Further Studies

On welfare aspects of equivalence scales, see Sen (1982) and Bradbury (1992). On econometric estimates see Deaton and Muellbauer (1980), Blundell and Lwebel (1990) and McClements (1978). Subjective scales are examined by Hartog (1988). For comparisons of alternative estimates, see Coulter *et al.* (1992), and on the sensitivity of results to the choice of scales see also Jenkins (1991b). Some studies, such as Kakwani (1986) and the Central Statistical Office (1990), concluded that the choice of scale has little effect on redistribution and inequality measures, but these studies have in fact used a narrow range of scales. On the generalised entropy measure of inequality, see Cowell and Kuga (1981) and on its decomposition, see Shorrocks (1984); Jenkins

(1988) provides a further example of its use. On re-ranking of households using equivalence scales, see Nolan (1985). On the impact effects of taxes where there are differences in household composition, see also Lambert (1994a, b).

3.4   Conclusions

This chapter has provided a limited introductory survey of issues and studies concerning the statics of income distribution. Choices regarding the income unit and income concept, along with summary measures of inequality and poverty, depend on value judgements. These should be made explicit, and a variety of results should be produced where possible. When using equivalence scales, there is no single method of producing equivalence scales which can be regarded as superior to others; they all involve value judgements. Results for a variety of equivalence scales should be reported; it is not appropriate to take an average of a set of scales, or to report results only for extreme values.

Some results may usefully be obtained, which are to some extent independent of the set of equivalence scales used, by performing a decomposition analysis based on additively separable measures. Equivalence scales can sometimes be avoided in comparing distributions by the application of sequential dominance tests, provided that the proportions of each household type in each distribution are the same; this is satisfied in comparisons of pre- and post-tax distributions for the same population.

Chapter 4

A Model of Income Distribution

There is a substantial literature seeking to explain the form of the distribution of earnings in terms of the outcome of some kind of random process.
Approaches involve the application of a form of the central limit theorem
to the sum of random variables, or the analysis of the results of applying a
transition matrix to an arbitrary initial distribution, in terms of the characteristic vector corresponding to the unit root of the matrix. In each case the
'final' distribution is independent of the initial distribution. These include
the famous 'law of proportionate effect' of Gibrat, discussed by Aitchison
and Brown (1957) and Brown (1976) as a possible genesis of the lognormal
form, and the alternative model of Champernowne (1953) which produces the
Pareto distribution; see also Mandelbrot (1960), Klein (1962), Hart (1973),
and Shorrocks (1975b). For a useful non-technical discussion see Phelps
Brown (1977, pp.290-294).

These models have, perhaps not surprisingly, been criticised on the grounds
that they are 'purely statistical' and thereby have a negligible degree of economic content; see in particular Mincer (1970) and Lydall (1979, pp.233-236).
Lydall (1976, p.19) has argued, for example, that 'this type of stochastic theory is ... not scientific in the usual sense. The "explanation" which it offers
is at a very superficial level and does not explain any of the real factors -
economic or other - which are responsible for the shape of the distribution'.

This chapter explores an approach to modelling the earnings distribution which involves both stochastic and economic components. Individuals' earnings are seen as resulting from a simple market supply and demand model in which individual earnings are deterministic, though the model can have multiple solutions. A stochastic error-correction mechanism is then imposed and the resulting form of the distribution of earnings is derived, where the distributional analogue of multiple equilibria in the deterministic form is multimodality. In particular the model generates a flexible functional form described as the generalised gamma distribution. Special cases of this general distribution include the gamma, exponential and Weibull distributions as well as the power distribution. An advantage of the approach is that changes in the form of the distribution over time can be modelled explicitly in terms of changes in commodity and labour market conditions since the parameters governing the characteristics of the distribution are shown to be functions of the underlying economic parameters of the model. This makes it possible to give a clearer economic interpretation of the distribution of personal income and the reasons for changes in inequality over time.

The basic model is introduced in section 4.1, which describes the labour demand and supply components and the stochastic specification. In view of the exploratory nature of the analysis, the model is very simple. However, it is rich enough to generate a distribution of personal earnings from first principles which is sufficiently flexible to capture a range of observed distributional characteristics. Section 4.2 describes the method of estimation, where both least squares and maximum likelihood methods are discussed. The generalized gamma distribution is applied in section 4.3 to estimating the distribution of alternative earnings models.

4.1 The Model

4.1.1 Labour Demand and Supply

Consider a market in which all individuals are assumed to be in the labour force. Individual i's real earnings are denoted y_i, which are by definition the product of the wage rate per hour which the individual can obtain, w_i, and the number of hours worked, n_i. Thus:

$$y_i = w_i n_i \tag{4.1}$$

The individual's labour supply may of course be derived using a standard utility-maximising approach in which the arguments of the utility function are consumption and leisure. For present purposes it is convenient to adopt the approach discussed by Robbins (1930) which exploited the reciprocal nature of labour supply in terms of the demand for goods, or real income. Suppose that the individual's demand for goods can be expressed as the following simple function of the real wage, the reciprocal of which represents the price of goods in terms of labour:

$$x_i^d = \alpha_i - \beta_i w_i^{-1} \tag{4.2}$$

The associated labour supply function is therefore given by:

$$n_i^s = x_i^d / w_i \tag{4.3}$$

The labour demand function facing the individual can be viewed as resulting from profit maximising, such that the optimal solution involves the demand for labour being expressed as a function of the real wage. For a linear labour demand schedule, the relationship is represented as:

$$n_i^d = \delta_i - \gamma_i w_i \tag{4.4}$$

It is required to solve these equations for the individual's real income, y_i. This can be done as follows. Use the demand function in (4.2) to express w_i in terms of x_i^d, so that $w_i = \beta_i / (\alpha_i - x_i^d)$, and substitute the result into (4.3) to give:

$$n_i^s = x_i^d (\alpha_i - x_i^d) / \beta_i \tag{4.5}$$

This is in fact the 'offer curve' of the individual, since it expresses the supply of labour directly in terms of the demand for goods: this has the typical 'backward-bending' shape of standard offer curves. In equilibrium, the supply of labour given by (4.5) must equal the demand as in (4.4), where in the latter, w_i is also expressed in terms of x_i^d. This equilibrium condition gives, after some rearrangement, the following cubic, writing $x_i = x_i^d$:

$$x_i^3 - 2\alpha_i x_i^2 + (\alpha_i^2 + \beta_i \delta_i)x_i - (\beta_i \delta_i \alpha_i - \gamma_i \beta_i^2) = 0 \qquad (4.6)$$

In this model real consumption is equivalent to real earnings since there is no role for savings, so it is only necessary to substitute for $y_i = x_i$ in (4.6) to obtain the equation for earnings. Hence:

$$y_i^3 - 2\alpha_i y_i^2 + (\alpha_i^2 + \beta_i \delta_i)y_i - (\beta_i \delta_i \alpha_i - \gamma_i \beta_i^2) = 0 \qquad (4.7)$$

This summarises the equilibrium properties for the ith individual in the market. There may be a unique equilibrium when (4.7) has a single real root, or multiple equilibria when it exhibits two or three real roots. In cases where there are three real roots, two of the equilibria can be shown to be stable; and if there are two real roots, only one is stable.

It can also be shown that the equilibrium wage rate corresponds to the root or roots of a cubic equation: substitute for x_i^d in (4.3) using (4.2), and equate the result to the labour demand given by (4.4). The equilibrium properties of the determination of a price, in this case the price of labour per hour, rather than the product of price and quantity, in this case real earnings, have been examined in detail in Creedy and Martin (1993, 1994).

The above supply and demand model is obviously very simple, but for present purposes it is sufficient for demonstrating how such an economic model can be used as the basic component of a distributional model. Further complications may provide a more detailed foundation for the functions used, and may even change the order of the polynomial in (4.7). A further possibility is that the equilibrium real wage may not be expressed as the root (or roots) of a polynomial, but it would be possible to rewrite the condition as a polynomial using a Taylor series expansion. The major elements of the approach followed below would thus remain unchanged, and examples of alternative specifications are discussed later in this section.

4.1.2 The Stochastic Specification

The analysis so far is deterministic and describes the equilibrium properties of the level of earnings of an individual, with a specified demand function for goods (real earnings) and facing a demand function for labour. If some joint distribution of the parameters $\alpha_i, \beta_i, \delta_i, \gamma_i$, were specified, it would in principle be possible to examine the implied distribution of real earnings, though this would be extremely complex and some method of handling the multiple equilibria would be required. It is most unlikely that any analytical expression for the distribution could be obtained following such an approach. Furthermore, it would in some sense simply be 'pushing back' the explanation of the form of the distribution one stage, in that some rationale for the joint distribution of the parameters among individuals would be required.

The present approach is instead based on the view that the parameters of each individual's demand and supply functions are subject to random or stochastic 'shocks' which lead to movements of earnings away from their equilibrium values. However, earnings are subsequently assumed to return or 'error correct' to their values which held before the shocks. Given the possibility of multiple equilibria, even small shocks can lead to large jumps in the value of real earnings over time. A standard representation of such a stochastic process involves the following expression, written in terms of the proportionate change in the individual's real earnings:

$$\frac{dy_i}{y_i} = -\left(y_i^3 - 2\alpha_i y_i^2 + (\alpha_i^2 + \beta_i \delta_i)y_i - (\beta_i \delta_i \alpha_i - \gamma_i \beta_i^2)\right) dt + \sigma_i dZ_i \quad (4.8)$$

Here Z_i is a Wiener process with the property that dZ_i is normally distributed as $N(0, dt)$ and σ_i is the standard deviation of dy_i/y_i which for simplicity is assumed to be constant; however, more elaborate specifications can be accommodated. For further details of this type of process, see Cox and Miller (1984).

The formulation in (4.8) applies to each individual in the market. Its continued application, following the approach described below, would generate the form of the probability density of each individual's earnings resulting from changes over time in response to the stochastic shocks. The informational requirements of such an approach are of course enormous, and ultimately it is required to generate the distribution of real earnings defined over all individuals. Thus to continue to allow for such a large degree of heterogeneity would not be helpful.

This difficulty can be overcome by introducing an assumption of population homogeneity. Thus the random shocks applying to individuals are assumed to be drawn from essentially the same distribution: this assumption is of course precisely the same as that used by all the stochastic process models mentioned above. Furthermore, the individuals are homogeneous to the extent that they have the same demand and supply functions. However, it will be shown below that some heterogeneity can be introduced by allowing some of the structural parameters to be functions of various characteristics such as labour market experience and education. At any moment in time, individuals are affected by quite different shocks; they are simply assumed to originate from the same distribution. This simplification makes it possible to drop the individual subscripts from equation (4.8) and to regard the resulting distribution as applying over all individuals in the market. The form of the distribution will be seen to depend on the precise nature of the demand and supply schedules and the characteristics of the Wiener process. The only distributional assumption made in the model is that of the normality of dZ.

If the density function of real income is written as $f(y)$, then (4.8) gives rise to the following Kolgomorov forward equation (see Cox and Miller, 1984):

$$\frac{\partial f}{\partial t} = \frac{\partial}{\partial y}\left(y^4 - 2\alpha y^3 + (\alpha^2 + \beta\delta)y^2 - (\beta\delta\alpha - \gamma\beta^2)y\right) + \frac{1}{2}\frac{\partial^2}{\partial y^2}\left(\sigma^2 y^2\right) \quad (4.9)$$

This is a partial differential equation which has the solution:

$$f(y) = \exp\left[h(y, t; \theta) - \eta(t; \theta)\right], 0 < y < \infty \quad (4.10)$$

where θ is a vector of parameters which, in turn, are functions of the structural parameters $\alpha, \beta, \delta, \gamma$, and $\eta(t; \theta)$ is the normalizing constant given by:

$$\eta(t; \theta) = \ln \int \exp\left[h(y, t; \theta)\right] dy \quad (4.11)$$

The function $h(y, t; \theta)$ is a general expression which unfortunately has no closed form solution. This means that it is not possible to derive an analytical solution of the transitional density $f(y)$ except for some very special cases of the model given above; for a general discussion of the problems, see Soong (1973). This form of $f(y)$ in (4.10) is known as a transitional distribution since it describes the evolution over time of the distribution of earnings from an initial equilibrium distribution after a change in the parameters of the demand and supply functions caused by some shock.

This process will converge to the 'stationary' distribution, which is obtained by setting $\partial f / \partial t = 0$ in (4.9). This is the approach followed below. Thus, it must be acknowledged that the same type of issue arises here as with all the other types of stochastic process models, namely that of the speed of adjustment. Critics of the stochastic models have argued that any observed distribution is unlikely to be an equilibrium distribution, so that the results of such processes cannot strictly be applied. In addition, Shorrocks (1975b) has used numerical simulation methods, finding that the 'half life' of such processes is typically many 'periods'.

A substantial advantage of the stationary distribution is that, unlike the transitional distribution, the stationary distribution can in general be derived analytically. By setting $\partial f / \partial t = 0$ in (4.9), this converts the partial differential equation into an ordinary first-order differential equation which can be solved by standard integration methods to yield a closed form solution. For a general solution of the stationary distribution for general specifications corresponding to (4.8), see Creedy and Martin (1994). For the stochastic differential equation in (4.8), the stationary density, $f^*(y)$, is:

$$f^*(y) = \exp\left[-\int^{y} \frac{2s^2 - 4\alpha s + 2(\alpha^2 + \beta\delta) - 2(\beta\delta\alpha - \gamma\beta^2 + 2\sigma^2)s^{-1}}{\sigma^2} ds - \eta^*\right]$$

After integration this becomes:

$$f^*(y) = \exp\left[-\frac{2y^3/3 - 2\alpha y^2 + 2(\alpha^2 + \beta\delta)y - 2(\beta\delta\alpha - \gamma\beta^2 + 2\sigma^2)\ln(y)}{\sigma^2} - \eta^*\right]$$

$$(4.12)$$

or, more compactly:

$$f^*(y) = \exp\left[\theta_1 \ln(y) + \theta_2 y + \theta_3 y^2 + \theta_4 y^3 - \eta^*\right], 0 < y < \infty \qquad (4.13)$$

where the θs are functions of the structural form parameters, obtained by comparing coefficients in (4.12) and (4.13), and:

$$\eta^* = \ln \int_0^\infty \exp\left[\theta_1 \ln(s) + \theta_2 s + \theta_3 s^2 + \theta_4 s^3\right] ds \qquad (4.14)$$

The distribution given by (4.13) is the generalized gamma. Creedy and Martin (1994) have shown that the same form applies in the context of price distribution models, using a simple general equilibrium model similar to that used here. It can be unimodal, which corresponds to the situation where the economic model given by (4.1) - (4.4) contains a unique equilibrium. Unlike the standard gamma distribution proposed by Salem and Mount (1974) to describe income distributions, this generalised gamma can also be multimodal. This situation arises when the model has multiple equilibria whereby the modes of the density correspond to the stable equilibria and the anti-mode corresponds to the unstable equilibrium. The flexibility of the generalised gamma distribution to model alternative empirical earnings distributions arises from the inclusion of the higher-order terms, which enable such properties as skewness and kurtosis to be modelled adequately. Marron and Schmitz (1992) give an example of a distribution displaying multimodality.

The above approach can be applied to a single cross-section of earnings, or to a time series of cross-sections. In the latter case the parameters may be regarded as functions of exogenous variables which change over time. An advantage of this framework is that it provides a method of modelling the influence of macroeconomic variables on the personal distribution of earnings. This also introduces the interesting possibility that the form of the distribution of earnings could change in distinct ways, while the underlying generating process is unchanged. This represents a potentially fruitful area of future research.

A comparison of (4.12) and (4.13) shows that the five structural parameters $(\sigma, \alpha, \beta, \gamma, \delta)$ cannot all be recovered from the θ_is. The emphasis in the present chapter is on the form of the distribution and hence the distributional parameters θ, so the lack of identifiability of the structural parameters is not considered to be a problem. However, as shown below, it is possible to discriminate between alternative classes of structural models through tests on the form of the distribution.

4.1.3 Alternative Specifications

The theoretical model discussed above involves linear demand and supply functions. However, alternative specifications can be explored. For example, suppose that the goods demand function is rewritten as:

$$w_i = \alpha_i + \beta_i \ln(x_i^d) \tag{4.15}$$

Notice that when using a non-linear specification of equation (4.2), it is simpler to write w as a function of x^d. This provides a tractable formulation in view of the need to solve the model for y. Combining (4.15) with (4.1), (4.3) and (4.4) gives real earnings as the root or roots of:

$$y_i + \gamma_i \beta_i^2 \left(\ln(y_i)\right)^2 + \beta_i(2\gamma_i\alpha_i - \delta_i) \ln(y_i) + (\gamma_i\alpha_i - \delta_i)\alpha_i = 0 \tag{4.16}$$

which corresponds to (4.7). This gives rise to a stationary distribution of the form:

$$f^*(y) = \exp\left[\theta_1 \left(\ln(y)\right)^3 + \theta_2 \left(\ln(y)\right)^2 + \theta_3 \ln(y) + \theta_4 y - \eta^*\right], 0 < y < \infty \tag{4.17}$$

where the θ_is are functions of the structural parameters. This is a generalised lognormal distribution.

Another example consists of specifying the labour demand function in reciprocal form as:

$$n_i^d = \delta + \frac{\gamma}{w_i} \tag{4.18}$$

When combined with equations (4.1) to (4.3), this gives rise to a quadratic of the form:

$$y_i^2 - y_i(\gamma + \alpha) + (\delta\beta + \gamma\alpha) = 0 \tag{4.19}$$

Alternatively, if (4.2) is replaced by:

$$x_i^d = \alpha + \beta w_i \tag{4.20}$$

and is combined with equation (4.4), the following quadratic results:

$$\gamma y_i^2 - y_i(\delta\beta - \beta^2 + 2\alpha\gamma) + \alpha(\delta\beta + \gamma\alpha) = 0 \tag{4.21}$$

Finally, the combination of equation (4.18) and (4.20) leads to the linear form:

$$y_i(\beta - \delta) + (\alpha\delta - \beta\gamma) = 0 \tag{4.22}$$

An interesting feature of this equation is that the resulting distribution is the standard gamma distribution which is a special case of (4.13) with $\theta_3 = \theta_4 = 0$. The generalised gamma distribution also contains as special cases a number of other distributions which have been used in the empirical modelling of earnings distributions: the exponential distribution ($\theta_1 = \theta_3 = \theta_4 = 0$), the Weibull distribution ($\theta_2 = \theta_4 = 0$), and the power distribution ($\theta_2 = \theta_3 = \theta_4 = 0$). Where each distribution has been used in the past, a special estimation method has been devised, as in Salem and Mount (1974). The present approach thus has the substantial advantage of nesting several distributions which can therefore be consistently estimated and compared. In the case of the generalised lognormal distribution, as with the generalised gamma distribution, it is possible to devise theoretical models with give rise to special cases. For example the standard lognormal distribution arises when $\theta_1 = \theta_4 = 0$, and the gamma distribution when $\theta_1 = \theta_2 = 0$.

4.2   Estimation Methods

This section presents procedures for estimating the theoretical income distributions derived above. Two cases need to be distinguished depending upon whether the structural form parameters $\alpha, \beta, \delta, \gamma$, are constant or are functions of individual characteristics. In the former case, the derived earnings distribution is referred to as an unconditional distribution, whilst for the latter, a set of conditional distributions are estimated. These cases are discussed in turn below. The generalised gamma distribution given by (4.13) represents a special case of the generalised exponential family. For further discussion of estimation, see Creedy and Martin (1997).

4.2.1 The Unconditional Distribution

From the discussion above, a general form of the density for y is:

$$f^*(y) = \exp\left[\sum_{i=1}^{M} \theta_i \psi_i(y) - \eta\right] \tag{4.23}$$

where $\psi_i(.)$ is some general function depending on the density type, M is the number of terms in the density depending on the specification of the model, and η is the normalizing constant which is given by:

$$\eta = \ln \int \exp\left[\sum_{i=1}^{M} \theta_i \psi_i(y)\right] dy \tag{4.24}$$

The $\psi_i(.)$ in the case of the generalised gamma income distribution are $\psi_1(y) = \ln(y)$, $\psi_2(y) = y$, $\psi_3(y) = y^3$, and $\psi_4(y) = y^3$, by comparison with (4.13). In the case of the generalised lognormal distribution, the $\psi_i(.)$ are $\psi_1(y) = (\ln(y))^3$, $\psi_2(y) = (\ln(y))^2$, $\psi_3(y) = \ln(y)$, and $\psi_4(y) = y$, by comparison with (4.17).

For a sample of observations on earnings, $y_1, y_2, ..., y_N$, maximum likelihood estimates are obtained by choosing the θ_is to maximise the log-likelihood function:

$$\ln L = \sum_{j=1}^{N} \sum_{i=1}^{M} \theta_i \psi_i(y_j) - N\eta \tag{4.25}$$

Standard iterative optimisation routines can be used to determine the θ_is which maximise (4.25). In maximising (4.25), the normalising constant η in (4.24) can be determined numerically using Gaussian quadrature routines.

Suppose instead that earnings data are available in the form of a frequency table. Lye and Martin (1993) introduced a least-squares approach for estimating the parameters in (4.23) when the data are grouped, motivated by the least-squares estimator of the Pareto distribution suggested by Johnson and Kotz (1970, p.235). The distinguishing feature of the least-squares estimator proposed by Lye and Martin (1993) is that it is based on frequencies. The error terms are therefore more likely to satisfy the assumption of independence than in the approach of Johnson and Kotz, which uses cumulative frequencies. Let the number of classes of equal width be K, with midpoints y_k, $k = 1, 2, ...K$, and define O_k as the observed frequency corresponding to the kth class interval. The expected frequency in the kth group, E_k, can be written as:

$$E_k = \phi^{-1} \exp\left[\sum_{i=1}^{M} \theta_i \psi_i(y_k)\right] \tag{4.26}$$

where ϕ is the normalising constant and values are assumed to be concentrated at the class midpoint.

The least-squares estimator consists of defining a logarithmic linear regression relationship between the observed frequency O_k and the expected frequency E_k, as given by (4.23). Letting v_k be an error term, the regression equation is:

$$\ln(O_k) = \ln(E_k) + v_k \tag{4.27}$$

The ratio, O_k/E_k, is assumed to be lognormally distributed with unit mean, so that the estimates are constrained to be non-negative. Substituting (4.26) into (4.27) gives:

$$\ln(O_k) = -\ln \phi + \sum_{i=1}^{M} \theta_i \psi_i(y_k) + v_k \tag{4.28}$$

The parameters can be estimated using a standard ordinary least-squares procedure. Since the sampling theory of the estimators has not been fully worked out, conventional formulae to compute standard errors and hence test statistics are not reported below. Instead, a goodness of fit measure based on a chi-square statistic is calculated in order to compare models.

Denoting least-squares estimators by ˆ, the estimate of the kth frequency is:

$$\hat{E}_k = \psi^{-1} \exp\left[\sum_{i=1}^{M} \hat{\theta}_i \psi_i(y_k)\right] \tag{4.29}$$

where:

$$\psi = \frac{1}{N} \sum_{k=1}^{K} \exp\left[\sum_{i=1}^{M} \hat{\theta}_i \psi_i(y_k)\right] \tag{4.30}$$

In the case where the required maximum likelihood software is not available, the least-squares estimator discussed above can also be used by grouping the data into a frequency table. Since there is a loss of information from grouping, some loss of efficiency relative to the maximum likelihood estimator can be expected from using the least-squares estimator.

4.2.2   The Conditional Distribution

In the estimation procedures discussed so far, individuals are assumed to be homogeneous. To allow for heterogeneity, assume that associated with the jth individual is a set of characteristics given by the vector z_j. In terms of the economic model presented above, this amounts to allowing the structural parameters to be functions of the variables in z. Examples that would help determine the earnings of individuals would be the level of education and experience.

Maximum-likelihood parameter estimates of the heterogeneous earnings model when the data are ungrouped are obtained by maximising the log likelihood function:

$$\ln L = \sum_{j=1}^{N} \sum_{i=1}^{M} \theta_i(z_j) \psi_i(y_j) - \sum_{j=1}^{N} \eta_j \tag{4.31}$$

where the normalizing constant is:

$$\eta_j = \ln \int \exp \left[\sum_{i=1}^{M} \theta_i(z_j)\psi_i(y) \right] dy \tag{4.32}$$

The main difference between (4.32) and (4.24) is that the former needs to
be computed for each individual in the sample at each iteration. Thus the
algorithm is computationally burdensome, especially for large data sets.

4.3 Applications

This section applies the equilibrium earnings model to both unconditional
and conditional distributions of earnings, and the results are compared with
existing distributional specifications. The data are from the 1987 March Sup-
plement (Annual Demographic File) of the United States Current Population
Survey (CPS) which contains information on individual earnings and labour
market characteristics in 1986. The total sample is 4,927 individuals. Since
there is a bunching at the top end of the distribution caused by an upper
limit on hours worked, 104 individuals are removed from the sample used in
this chapter. The earnings variable is a measure of weekly earnings obtained
as the product of hours per week and wages per hour.

4.3.1 The Unconditional Earnings Distribution

Maximum-likelihood estimates of the structural parameters for the unconditional generalised gamma earnings distribution in (4.13) are given in Table 4.1, along with estimates of the standard gamma distribution where
$\theta_3 = \theta_4 = 0$. The asymptotic standard errors, shown in parentheses, are
based on the inverse of the Hessian matrix. In addition, the results of the
generalised lognormal distribution as given by (4.17) and the standard lognormal distribution where in (4.17) $\theta_1 = \theta_4 = 0$, are reported. Inspection of
the standard errors in the case of the generalised gamma distribution shows
that the estimates of θ_1 and θ_2 are statistically significantly different from
zero, although those of θ_3 and θ_4 are not. More important, however, is an
overall measure of the model's performance. This is achieved by the Akaike
Information Criterion (AIC) reported in Table 4.1. This is computed as AIC

Table 4.1: The Unconditional Earnings Distribution: MLE Estimates.

Parameter	Gen. Gamma	Gamma	Gen. Lognorm.	Lognorm.
θ_1	2.0298	2.4365	-0.1604	
	(0.1556)	(0.0698)	(0.1929)	
θ_2	-4.9953	-6.8078	-0.7728	-1.3882
	(1.0931)	(0.1471)	(1.3183)	(0.0361)
θ_3	-0.5772		1.1212	-3.2810
	(1.0888)		(3.2684)	(0.0586)
θ_4	-0.1813		-5.7674	
	(0.4079)		(3.3140)	
ln L	-39.9708	-50.3252	-39.1348	-318.9790
AIC	43.9709	52.3252	43.1348	320.9790

$= -\ln L + K$, where K, the number of estimated parameters, acts as a penalty for the inclusion of additional parameters. The result in Table 4.1 shows that the generalised gamma distribution is preferred to the gamma distribution as the AIC is minimized for the generalised gamma distribution. Furthermore, inspection of the AIC for the generalised lognormal distribution shows that this distribution also performs very well; indeed, it is difficult to distinguish between the two generalised forms.

The results using the least-squares estimator are given in Table 4.2 for the same four types of distribution given in Table 4.1. The data are grouped into 21 cells, with the first cell having a mid-point of $100, the second a mid-point of $200, and so on. The chi-square statistics shown in Table 4.2 indicate that both of the generalised distributions perform significantly better than their standard forms even when the loss of degrees of freedom is taken into account. The superiority of the generalised distributions are further highlighted in Table 4.3, which gives the actual and expected frequencies from the alternative models.

Table 4.2: The Unconditional Earnings Distribution: Least Squares Estimates.

Parameter	Gen. Gamma	Gamma	Gen. Lognorm.	Lognorm.
Constant	8.7108	5.1751	-9.4945	-3.2895
θ_1	5.6220	4.2579	-0.8121	
θ_2	-14.7650	-8.2186	-5.6642	-1.9856
θ_3	3.2468		-10.1307	-3.4505
θ_4	-0.3946		6.2802	
χ^2 stat.	45.0612	133.9298	46.4094	110.6682
d.o.f.	9	11	9	11

Table 4.3: Actual and Expected Frequencies: Least Squares Estimates.

Group midpoint	Actual	Gen. Gamma	Gamma	Gen. Lognorm.	Lognorm.
100	17	17	21	17	14
200	180	206	179	193	276
300	598	536	443	533	657
400	785	764	663	776	817
500	729	800	754	813	772
600	650	702	720	708	636
700	622	553	611	553	487
800	428	408	474	404	359
900	301	288	344	284	258
1000	162	198	237	194	183
1100	129	134	156	132	130
1200	77	90	99	89	91
1300	77	60	61	60	65
1400	44	41	37	40	46
1500	24	27	22	28	33

4.3.2 The Conditional Earnings Distribution

In order to illustrate the way in which further heterogeneity may be introduced, suppose that the demand for labour is affected by the labour market
experience, t, and education of individuals, h, measured in terms of years
of schooling. The constant term, δ, in the labour demand function can be
specified as a function of these variables. This can be seen to imply that the
terms θ_1 and θ_2 in the stationary distribution are functions of those variables.
Suppose that, following the standard use of a quadratic experience profile,
the relevant functions can be written as:

$$\theta_1 = \delta_0 + \delta_1 h_n + \delta_2 t_n + \delta_3 t_n^2$$

$$\theta_2 = \gamma_0 + \gamma_1 h_n + \gamma_2 t_n + \gamma_3 t_n^2$$

Maximum-likelihood estimates of the conditional earnings model are given in
Table 4.4. The asymptotic standard errors, shown in parentheses, are based
on the inverse of the Hessian matrix.

   Increases in both education and experience shift the earnings distribution
to the right so that, on average, people with higher education and more
experience have higher earnings levels. Furthermore, the dispersion increases
with experience.

4.4 Conclusions

This chapter has explored the integration of a simple economic model of
labour supply and demand with a stochastic process which causes shocks to
the structural form of the model. For each individual, the number of hours
of labour supplied was treated as the reciprocal supply associated with the
demand for goods, or real income, while the demand for labour was a function
of the real wage rate. Equilibrium earnings, the product of the wage rate
and the number of hours worked, were derived as the root or roots of a cubic
equation. An error-correction process was then used to derive the stationary
distribution associated with the model. This was found to be a generalised

Table 4.4: The Conditional Earnings Distribution: MLE Estimates.

Variable	Parameter	Gen. Gamma
Constant	δ_0	1.6201
		(0.4669)
h	δ_1	-0.0019
		(0.0329)
t	δ_2	0.0846
		(0.0442)
t^2	δ_3	-0.0016
		(0.0006)
Constant	γ_0	-18.3953
		(1.4232)
h	γ_1	0.8770
		(0.0727)
t	γ_2	0.2878
		(0.0996)
t^2	γ_3	-0.0040
		(0.0015)
	θ_3	-3.0728
		(1.6999)
	θ_4	0.0570
		(0.4717)
	ln L = 775.5155	AIC = 795.5155

gamma distribution. An alternative specification of the structural form of the model produced a generalised lognormal distribution.

The generalised distributions have the advantage of nesting other special cases, such as the standard gamma or lognormal, which have been used in the statistical analysis of income distribution, depending on particular assumptions about the structural form. A special feature of these generalised distributions, in contrast with their standard forms, is that they can display multimodality corresponding to multiple equilibria in the structural form of the economic model. Furthermore, the parameters can be allowed to vary over time, so that the model has the potential to allow for macroeconomic changes to alter the form of the personal distribution of earnings.

It was possible to use estimation methods developed for the generalised exponential distribution, which encompasses generalisations of the gamma and lognormal distributions. These models were found to perform well using US data from the Current Population Survey in that they were able to capture the empirical characteristics of the earnings distribution better than the standard forms. The specification was extended to allow the structural parameters to depend on specified characteristics such as the experience and education of individuals. This provided a mechanism for understanding the effects of changes in both education and experience on the shape of the conditional earnings distribution.

Chapter 5

Comparing Transfer Systems

This chapter discusses alternative approaches to the evaluation of income tax and transfer systems, concentrating on the question of whether transfers should be universal or means-tested. The emphasis is on income testing, so that, in the examples given, non-income differences between individuals are treated as being irrelevant. Hence categorical or state-dependent benefits are also ignored; for broad discussions of means-testing versus universal benefits, see Atkinson (1995) and Mitchell *et al.* (1994). Analyses using specific models or approaches include Besley (1990), Kesselman and Garfinkel (1978), Sadka *et al.* (1982), Lambert (1988) and Creedy (1996).

Those on the different sides of the debate have different value judgements and different basic frameworks of analysis. In very broad terms, the advocates of means-testing typically argue that the primary concern of a transfer system should be to alleviate poverty, so that universal benefits are judged to be wasteful and involve an excessive level of gross government revenue. Schemes are compared using several measures of 'target efficiency' which reflect the extent to which transfer payments are concentrated on the poor; on target efficiency measures, see Beckerman (1979) and Mitchell (1991). Target efficiency measures are not concerned with the extent to which poverty is actually reduced by a tax and transfer system and, despite the terminology, have nothing to do with economic efficiency. The framework of reference is usually one in which the distribution of income before taxes and transfers is fixed independently of the tax system in operation. Analyses of poverty are typically 'non-welfarist' in that they are based on summary measures involving the income distribution, rather than the distribution of utility.

On the other hand, advocates of universal benefits argue that taxes and transfers have a much wider redistributive role than poverty alleviation implies. The framework of analysis is more closely related to the 'optimal tax' literature, in which labour supply plays a crucial role. Hence, great stress is placed on the incentive effects arising from the high marginal tax rates involved in means-testing. Evaluation of alternative systems is usually 'welfarist' and based on the use of social welfare or evaluation functions defined in terms of individuals' utilities. The proponents of universal benefits usually argue that an emphasis on the gross level of government revenue is not appropriate in a tax and transfer system.

It is not obvious how alternative tax and transfer systems may be compared, where it is required to allow for both poverty and inequality in a social evaluation function. Atkinson (1987) has suggested that in this case a lexicographic ordering could be used, in which primary concern is attached to poverty reduction while schemes giving rise to the same degree of poverty (however measured) are compared using the type of welfare function used in the optimal tax literature. This approach allows for the use of both welfarist and non-welfarist measures in the evaluation procedure, since poverty measures are non-welfarist.

In this chapter, the various issues involved in evaluating tax and transfer systems are discussed using simple numerical examples involving a small number of individuals. Such examples help to illustrate the contrasts between systems and evaluation approaches. Two basic cases are considered. In section 5.1, the pre-tax distribution is assumed to be fixed. Section 5.2 turns to a framework in which the distribution of wage rates is fixed, but the labour supply and hence income of each individual varies in response to changes in the tax system. A flexible tax and transfer scheme, allowing for the complete range between universal benefits and means-testing with 100 per cent marginal tax rates (as in a minimum income guarantee), is presented. Section 5.3 discusses further numerical examples obtained using the model of section 5.2.

Table 5.1: Alternative Tax and Transfer Schemes

No	y	Net income with:			
		A	B	C	D
1	10	30	20	28.33	36.15
2	20	30	40	31.66	42.31
3	60	56	56	56	66.92
4	100	92	92	92	91.54
5	200	182	182	182	153.0
P_0	0.4	0.4	0.2	0.4	0.2
P_1	0.25	0.1	0.1	0.1	0.0192
P_2	0.1625	0.025	0.05	0.0257	0.0018
G	0.472	0.375	0.386	0.377	0.290
$A\,(0.5)$	0.199	0.116	0.123	0.116	0.068

5.1 Fixed Pre-tax Incomes

This section examines four alternative tax and transfer schemes using numerical examples involving just five individuals. This highlights the use of alternative criteria.

5.1.1 Four Alternative Tax Structures

Table 5.1 presents details of five hypothetical individuals under four different tax and transfer schemes. These are 'pure' transfer systems, so that gross revenue from taxation is exactly matched by gross expenditure on transfer payments. In schemes A, B and C the gross revenue raised by income taxation is 30, and the transfer payment systems are such that only those in poverty, judged by pre-tax income, receive benefits and none is raised above the poverty line. The individuals are ranked in ascending order of their incomes and it is assumed that the poverty level is equal to 40, so that individuals 1 and 2 are in poverty before taxes and transfers. The alternative schemes are as follows.

In scheme A, the income tax is such that the tax paid $T\,(y)$ on an income of y is given by:

$$
\begin{aligned}
T\left(y\right) &= 0 && \text{for } y \leq 20 \\
&= 0.10\left(y - 20\right) && \text{for } y > 20
\end{aligned}
\tag{5.1}
$$

Hence there is a single marginal tax rate of 0.10 applied to income measured in excess of a tax-free threshold of 20. In addition, there is a minimum income guarantee (MIG) such that those individuals with incomes, after the deduction of income tax, below 30 have their net incomes brought up to 30. This is usually referred to as a 'fully integrated' MIG.

In scheme B the income tax is the same as in A, but the transfer payments are designed in order to minimise the number of people with net income below the poverty line; that is, the headcount poverty measure is minimised. In C, the income tax is the same as in A but the transfer system has means-tested or 'tapered' benefits. Those with $y < 50$ receive a basic benefit of 25 which is reduced at a rate of $2/3$ of pre-tax income. Hence net income, z, is given by:

$$
z = 25 + y\left(1 - \frac{2}{3}\right)
\tag{5.2}
$$

This transfer system, given the pre-tax income distribution, exactly exhausts the 30 raised from income taxation imposed on the three richest individuals.

In scheme D, there is a universal benefit, or social dividend, of 30 which is received by all individuals. Income taxation is imposed at a fixed proportional rate on all income. With a gross revenue requirement of 150, the tax rate required is 0.3846. Hence there is a linear income tax system with net income given by:

$$
z = 30 + y\left(1 - 0.3846\right)
\tag{5.3}
$$

5.1.2 Comparisons Among Tax Structures

For each of the four tax and transfer schemes, Table 5.1 shows the net incomes along with several measures of poverty and inequality. The poverty measures are obtained using the class of measures of defined by:

$$P_\theta = \frac{1}{N} \sum_{y_i \le y_p} \left(1 - \frac{y_i}{y_p}\right)^\theta \qquad (5.4)$$

where y_p denotes the poverty line and θ is a parameter. This is the class of poverty measures proposed by Foster *et al.* (1984). It can be shown that P_0 is the headcount measure giving the proportion of people with $y \le y_p$, P_1 depends on the average income of those in poverty relative to the poverty line, and P_2 depends also on the coefficient of variation of those in poverty. The two inequality measures used are the Gini coefficient, G, and the Atkinson measure for a relative inequality aversion coefficient of 0.5, $A(0.5)$.

In comparing the four structures, it can first be argued that the gross revenue raised by income taxation is rather an arbitrary measure to take as a criterion. The linear income tax can be administered in two ways; either everyone is taxed at the proportional rate of 0.3846 in order to produce gross revenue of 150, or revenue is only obtained from those with incomes above the arithmetic mean, in which case the gross revenue is effectively 55.38 rather than 150. These have the same effect if there are no administrative costs of collecting taxation or of administering benefits. In practice the administrative costs of the various structures would be expected to vary, and it may be that they vary in proportion to the total (gross) revenue raised and disbursed.

The structures A to C all have target efficiency measures of 100 per cent, reflecting the fact that only those who have $y < y_p$ are better off after taxes and transfers and none has a net income exceeding the poverty line. However, poverty is not eliminated in any of the schemes, according to any of the poverty measures; the elimination of poverty is discussed below.

If target efficiency is thought to be a fundamental criterion, then the linear income tax of D is automatically ruled out. This criterion is essentially negative: it simply argues that a scheme is 'bad' if transfers payments bring recipients above the poverty line. A choice has to be made among structures A, B and C. This depends on which poverty measure reflects the value judgements of whoever is making the evaluation. The MIG of structure A would be chosen if P_2 is used. Although structure B is designed to minimise P_0

it does badly according to P_2. However, all three structures have the same value of P_1. Hence those who argue that the alleviation of poverty is the only legitimate role of a transfer system would be indifferent between the three structures A to C if they also hold value judgements which imply the use of the measure P_1. However, there may be people who attach primary importance to poverty reduction, but who have some aversion to inequality more widely perceived. This suggests the application of a lexicographic approach; that is, a primary aim is to minimise poverty (for a given measure) and a secondary aim is then to minimise inequality among schemes which achieve the minimum poverty level. Here the choice depends on value judgements which are involved in the choice of inequality measure. Thus schemes A and C, the MIG and the modified MIG with tapered benefits, continue to tie when both P_1 and Atkinson's measure (with inequality aversion coefficient of 0.5) are used, but the MIG dominates if the Gini measure is used along with P_1.

The linear income tax of structure D performs badly from the point of view of target efficiency since person 2's net income is above the poverty line and person 3 has a higher net income than gross income. Indeed, all those with $y < \bar{y}$ in this scheme are better off. It does not, however, eliminate poverty because the net income of person 1 is below y_p. Some people may believe that target efficiency is unimportant as it does not reflect the extent to which poverty is actually reduced. Table 5.1 shows that the linear income tax has lower poverty measures P_1 and P_2 than any of the other schemes. If P_0 is used, then D ties with B, but the lexicographic approach results in D being chosen because it has lower inequality measures. A concentration on inequality reduction as a sole criterion would, not surprisingly, give a preference for the linear income tax.

In comparing the four structures of Table 5.1, there is therefore no single scheme that can automatically be regarded as superior to any other. The evaluation inevitably involves value judgements, and such values involve complex issues relating to views about both poverty and inequality. Although the term target 'efficiency' has been used in the literature, the use of such measures really has nothing to do with economic efficiency or the actual amount of poverty reduction but involves the value judgement that transfers to the non-poor are 'bad', as are excessively generous payments to the poor. Efficiency considerations cannot really be applied in this context of a fixed pre-tax income distribution.

5.1.3 Zero Poverty Comparisons

The above discussion involved cases where value judgements were summarised by a lexicographic approach in which concern for poverty dominates, while inequality considerations are used to choose among systems which generate the same poverty level. Comparisons of inequality, for given poverty levels, may depend on the precise level of poverty achieved. The question arises, for example, of whether the comparisons would be affected if poverty were eliminated altogether. Such comparisons are shown in Table 5.2, for the minimum income guarantee and the linear income tax schemes, A and D respectively, modified as follows in order to reduce poverty to zero.

In order to eliminate poverty with structure A, it is necessary to raise gross revenue of 50 from those above the tax-free threshold, so that a MIG can operate such that for $y \leq 40$, net income is brought up to 40. This requires the choice of tax rate, t, such that, for $y \geq 20$:

$$T(y) = t(y - 20) \tag{5.5}$$

and revenue is equal to 50. With a total taxable income arising from the three richest individuals of 300, this is achieved with $t = 0.1667$.

The linear income tax must give the poorest person a net income of 40. This is achieved with a social dividend of say, a, and a marginal tax rate applied to all income of t; hence:

$$40 = a + 10(1 - t) \tag{5.6}$$

The government's budget constraint also requires that the social dividend can be financed from income taxation, so that:

$$a = t\overline{y} \tag{5.7}$$

Table 5.2: Comparisons with No Poverty

| | | Net income with: | |
No.	y	A	B
1	10	40.00	40.00
2	20	40.00	45.61
3	60	53.33	68.01
4	100	86.67	90.41
5	200	170.00	146.41
G	0.472	0.315	0.264
$A(0.5)$	0.199	0.082	0.056

with $\bar{y} = 390/5$. The two simultaneous equations (5.6) and (5.7) can be solved to give $a = 34.41$ and $t = 0.44$.

The imposition of these schemes give the net incomes and inequality measures shown in Table 5.2. It can be seen that the poorest four people are better off with the linear income tax, which involves heavier taxation of the richest person. Both inequality measures are lower for structure D, the linear income tax. However, a judge who regards it as 'bad' to bring person 2's net income above 40 (the poverty line) would prefer the minimum income guarantee. Hence some value judgements favour A, while others favour D. The value judgements involved in the choice of tax structure are essentially those involving interpersonal comparisons. A comparison which simply dismissed D because the marginal tax rate, t, is much higher than in A would appear to be arbitrary.

These examples help to illustrate how different value judgements can be applied to alternative tax structures. For further treatment of this case using a continuous income distribution, see Creedy (1995). However, the assumption that the pre-tax distribution of income remains constant, so that there are no incentive effects, is rather restrictive. With such an assumption it is possible always to eliminate inequality and, provided average income exceeds the poverty line, simultaneously to eliminate poverty. In practice, however, it may not be possible to eliminate poverty. The tax and transfer system may affect incentives so that the attempt to increase transfers is self-defeating. It is therefore necessary to consider such incentive effects.

5.2 Fixed Wage Rates

This section presents the framework used to compare the effects of tax and transfer schemes where individuals face fixed wage rates rather than fixed incomes. First, the basic results concerning labour supply in the case of constant elasticity of substitution (CES) preferences are presented in the absence of a tax scheme. Secondly, a modified form of minimum income guarantee is introduced, with the flexibility to handle the range between a linear tax and means-testing using 100 per cent marginal tax rates.

5.2.1 CES Utility Functions

This subsection introduces incentive effects by supposing that each individual faces a fixed pre-tax wage rate but can vary the proportion of time spent in work. It is assumed initially that each individual has the same tastes, described by the CES form of utility function, and chooses the consumption of goods, c, and the proportion of time spent in leisure, h, in order to maximise utility, $U(c, h)$, given by:

$$U = \left\{ \alpha c^{-\rho} + (1 - \alpha) h^{-\rho} \right\}^{-1/\rho} \tag{5.8}$$

where $\rho > -1$ and $0 < \alpha < 1$. The elasticity of substitution, σ, is given by $1/(1 + \rho)$. The marginal rate of substitution of leisure for consumption is given by:

$$\left. \frac{dc}{dh} \right|_U = - \left(\frac{1 - \alpha}{\alpha} \right) \left(\frac{h}{c} \right)^{-(1+\rho)} \tag{5.9}$$

Utility must be maximised subject to a budget constraint that requires the value of consumption to be equal to net (after tax and transfer) income. In the simplest case, where there are no taxes or transfers, the price index is set equal to unity and the individual has a fixed non-wage income of g, this constraint requires that:

$$c = w(1 - h) + g \tag{5.10}$$

Hence interior solutions are obtained by equating (5.9) and the rate of substitution between c and h along the budget line, which in the absence of taxes is $-w$, giving c in terms of h:

$$c = h \left[\left(\frac{1-\alpha}{\alpha} \right) \frac{1}{w} \right]^{-\sigma} \tag{5.11}$$

Substituting (5.11) in (5.10) and rearranging gives h as:

$$h = \Psi M \left(\frac{1-\alpha}{w} \right)^{\sigma} \tag{5.12}$$

where M is 'full income', the income obtained when all time is devoted to labour, and is equal to $w + g$, and Ψ is given by:

$$\Psi = \left[\alpha^{\sigma} + w \left(\frac{1-\alpha}{w} \right)^{\sigma} \right]^{-1} \tag{5.13}$$

This tangency solution only applies when w is above a minimum wage, w_L, for which the individual works, that is for which $h < 1$. Using (5.12) this is found to be:

$$w_L = g^{1+\rho} \left(\frac{1-\alpha}{\alpha} \right) \tag{5.14}$$

For those who work, earnings are given by $w(1 - h)$ or:

$$y = w \left[1 - \Psi M \left(\frac{1-\alpha}{w} \right)^{\sigma} \right] \tag{5.15}$$

These results can be modified to allow for a tax and transfer system by suitable adjustment of the non-wage component and the wage rate, and suitable allowance for further kinks in the budget constraint; this is discussed in the next subsection for a modified minimum income guarantee. In the simplest case, that of the linear income tax, w is replaced by $w(1 - t)$ and g is replaced by a.

In examining the relationship between labour supply, $1 - h$, and the wage rate (or the net of tax wage rate), two cases need to be distinguished. If $\sigma > 1$, labour supply increases continually as the wage rate increases, so the wage elasticity of labour supply is positive once w exceeds w_L. If $\sigma < 1$, labour supply eventually falls as the wage increases, so that (with w on the

vertical axis and $1 - h$ on the horizontal axis of a diagram) the labour supply
curve can become 'backward-bending'. If the non-wage income is zero, only
the backward-bending part of the supply curve is relevant when $\sigma < 1$.
Empirical results suggest a value less than unity. For discussion of the CES
in optimal tax calculations, see Stern (1976).

Care needs to be taken in the calibration of the model, in addition to the
choice of the elasticity of substitution. For example, it is known that as σ
approaches unity, (5.8) approaches the Cobb-Douglas form and α indicates
the proportion of time spent working, in the absence of non-wage income and
taxation. If $g = 0$, the Cobb-Douglas case implies that h is independent of
the wage rate faced. When non-wage income is positive, as in the case of a
tax and transfer system, labour supply always increases as the net wage, w,
increases (once w_L is exceeded, of course), and there is a linear relationship
between y and w, unlike the nonlinear expression in (15.14). The appropriate
value of α in the CES case depends on the units in which w is measured. In
the no-tax case, with $g = 0$, the re-arrangement of (5.12) gives:

$$
\alpha = \left[1 + \left\{ \left(\frac{h}{1-h} \right) w^{\sigma-1} \right\}^{1/\sigma} \right]^{-1}
\tag{5.16}
$$

It is therefore possible to specify a particular wage for which it is desired that
labour supply should take a certain value, for a given value of the elasticity of
substitution. These three variables can be substituted into (5.16) to obtain
the required value of α. For example if $s = 0.7$ and it is required that $h = 0.3$,
when $w = 80$, the solution for α is 0.9564.

5.2.2   A Modified Minimum Income Guarantee

A wide variety of alternative tax systems can be modelled by specifying a
modified form of the minimum income guarantee, involving means-testing in
the form of a taper. Consider the tax structure given by:

$$
\begin{aligned}
\text{benefit} &= s\,(a - y) \quad \text{for } y \leq a \\
\text{tax} &= t\,(y - a) \quad \text{for } y > a
\end{aligned}
\tag{5.17}
$$

Hence for those who pay tax $(y > a)$ the tax system is just like the

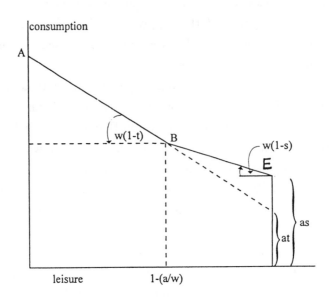

Figure 5.1: The Budget Constraint

familiar tax function having a single marginal rate and tax-free threshold. For those with $y \leq a$, a benefit is received such that if $y = 0$ the individual receives the amount sa, and the benefit is withdrawn at a marginal rate of s for each unit of income. This system is very useful for present purposes because it allows for the standard MIG at one extreme, where $s = 1.0$, and for the linear income tax (with a social dividend or universal benefit) when $s = t$.

The nonlinear budget constraint produced by (5.17) has interesting implications for labour supply behaviour. The convex budget constraint is shown in Figure 5.1 as the line ABE. At point B, the value of net income is equal to the threshold income level, a. As w increases the budget constraint pivots about the point E. For very low values of w (below w_L, given by substitution into (5.14) with g replaced by ta), corner solutions are appropriate and no labour is supplied. As the wage is increased, two alternatives arise. One alternative, which occurs for very high values of s, is that the individual does not work for low wage rates, but at some wage rate, $w = w_m$, jumps directly to the section AB of the constraint. The wage rate w_m is such that an indifference curve is simultaneously tangential to the section AB and touches the corner, E, of the constraint. In this case (depending on the tax parameters and the utility function), the individual never simultaneously works and receives transfer payments.

The second alternative is such that as the wage increases from $w = w_L$, the individual moves away from the corner, E, along the section BE of the constraint, thereby both earning some wage income and receiving means-tested transfer payments. Then at some wage, w_s, the individual jumps to the section AB; this occurs at a wage such that there is an indifference curve that is tangential to both sections AB and BE simultaneously. Hence the point B is never chosen in practice.

The values of the wage thresholds, w_m and w_s, are given by the roots of the relevant equations obtained by writing the conditions under which either a tangency and corner solution are simultaneously attained, or two tangency positions are attained. However, these equations are nonlinear and therefore do not give rise to explicit solutions for the values of w_m and w_s. The values may be calculated for any set of preferences and tax parameters using an iterative procedure, such as Newton's method. In the Cobb-Douglas case, the value of w_s can be obtained explicitly; see Creedy (1994, 1996). Lambert (1985b, 1988) used this type of modified minimum income guarantee with Cobb-Douglas preferences, but did not consider the possibility associated with the threshold, w_m.

5.3 Numerical Examples

The analysis of the modified minimum income guarantee, when allowance is made for incentive effects, is much more awkward than when incomes are assumed to be fixed. First, a distribution of the wage rate for a given number of individuals must be specified. Then, in order to calculate the values of the tax parameters that are consistent with the assumption of a 'pure transfer' system, an iterative solution procedure must be used. It is first necessary to specify some value of the taper rate, s, and then to calculate, for a given tax rate t, the value of the tax threshold, a, which ensures that the government's budget constraint is satisfied; that is, the tax revenue must be sufficient to pay for the transfer payments. This stage has to be done using a numerical search procedure which involves repeated trial calculations for alternative values of the tax threshold, because no explicit algebraic solution is available. This is essentially because the labour supplies depend on the tax thresholds (along with the preference parameters), so that the threshold is required in order to calculate incomes. Only when incomes are available is it possible to check if the implied taxes and transfers exactly balance. Hence a trial and error process is needed.

The following examples are for a group of ten individuals, and their wage rates were selected at random from a lognormal distribution with mean and variance of logarithms of 4.5 and 0.5 respectively. The use of the lognormal distribution to specify wage rates is standard in optimal tax models. The number of individuals is higher than in the previous examples because non-convergence of the iterative sequence, used to obtain a for given t and s, can arise with very small numbers if, for a particular combination of t and s, one individual has a wage rate that is very close to the 'switching' wage, w_s. Each individual is assumed to have an elasticity of substitution, σ, of 0.7 and a value of α of 0.96. The poverty level is assumed to be 52.

5.3.1   Gross and Net Income Comparisons

The implications of the above assumptions for earnings in the case of a linear income tax are shown in Table 5.3 for tax rates of 0 and 0.3. The second column of the table shows the wage rates (obtained by selecting at random from the distribution specified above); these are used in all of the following examples. In the absence of any tax and transfer system ($t = 0$), it can be seen that the first three individuals are in poverty, with incomes below the threshold of 52. The case where $t = 0.3$ has been selected for illustration because this turned out to be the optimal linear income tax for the standard 'optimal tax' problem, where the social welfare or evaluation function involves the maximisation of:

$$W = \frac{1}{10} \sum_{i=1}^{10} \frac{U_i^{1-\varepsilon}}{1-\varepsilon} \qquad (5.18)$$

and ε, the constant relative inequality aversion coefficient, is set equal to 0.5. The welfare function (5.18) has an abbreviated form given by:

$$W = \overline{U} \left\{ 1 - A\left(\varepsilon\right) \right\} \qquad (5.19)$$

where $\overline{U}$ is arithmetic mean utility, and $A\left(\varepsilon\right)$ is, as before, Atkinson's inequality measure. It is well-known that the result of this kind of exercise depends on the cardinalisation of the utility function used.

Table 5.3 shows the extent to which the 'optimal' linear income tax has target inefficiency. In the pure transfer system considered here, all individuals below the arithmetic mean have net incomes above their gross incomes, and persons 3 to 5, who have gross wage incomes that would otherwise place them in poverty, have net incomes which bring them above the poverty line, even though in this case only those in poverty receive transfers.

The welfare function in (5.18) or (5.19) has, of course, no reference to poverty at all, and does not represent the social evaluation function of those who regard poverty minimisation as the primary requirement of a tax system. It would be a coincidence if the tax rate of 0.3 were also to minimise poverty. Table 5.3 shows that the first two individuals remain in poverty, so $P_0 = 0.2$. By increasing t is it not possible to reduce P_0 further, because the resulting increase in the social dividend, a, is accompanied by reductions in labour supply. However, increasing t somewhat does result in reductions in both P_1 and P_2, until the labour supply effects dominate, causing all measures to increase. These poverty measures are both minimised for the linear income tax system for $t = 0.45$.

The introduction of means-testing is designed to overcome the target inefficiency of universal schemes such as the linear income tax. Table 5.4 gives information about the gross and net incomes of each of the ten individuals under four different values of the taper rate, s. In each case the tax rate, t, is the same, at $t = 0.3$, in order to restrict the table to reasonable proportions.

Table 5.3: Linear Tax: Pre- and Post-Tax Incomes

No.	w	$t = 0$ y, z	$t = 0.3$ y	z
1	63.04	45.86	39.14	49.68
2	66.28	48.01	41.29	51.18
3	70.91	51.08	44.34	53.31
4	72.74	52.29	45.55	54.16
5	78.23	55.89	49.14	56.68
6	132.52	90.25	83.85	80.97
7	134.35	91.38	84.99	81.77
8	152.80	102.64	96.46	89.80
9	154.48	103.65	97.50	90.53
10	259.07	164.74	160.25	134.45

It can be seen that the combination of a taper rate of 0.55 with a tax rate of 0.3 does not entirely eliminate target inefficiency because individual number 5 is raised slightly above the poverty line of 52. When s is raised to 0.65, target efficiency is 100 per cent; transfer payments are concentrated only on those below the poverty line and no one in poverty is given 'excessive' transfers.

The target efficiency is, however, obtained at a cost which is much more apparent in this context of variable labour supplies than when pre-tax incomes are assumed to be fixed. Even though each case illustrated in Table 5.4 involves the first five individuals simultaneously working and receiving transfers, the elimination of target inefficiency is accompanied by an increase in the number of those below the poverty line; P_0 is obviously equal to 0.5 for the higher values of the taper rate. Hence in each case shown in the table, w_s is relevant rather than w_m. For the four values of s shown (and $t = 0.3$) the value of w_s takes values respectively of 102.01, 98.02, 92.32 and 84.81, while the corresponding values of w_L are 6.36, 14.03, 20.06 and 28.96.

The increase in the degree of targeting leads to the population being increasingly 'polarised' into two groups, because the targeting has its major effect on the labour supply of those facing relatively low wage rates. Indeed, as s is increased, the pre-tax incomes of those who face the tax rate, $t = 0.3$,

Table 5.4: Modified MIG: Pre- and Post-Tax Incomes: $t = 0.3$

No.	w	$s = 0.35$		$s = 0.55$	
		y	z	y	z
1	63.04	37.90	49.63	31.68	47.85
2	66.28	40.04	51.02	33.81	48.81
3	70.91	43.09	53.00	36.84	50.18
4	72.74	44.29	53.79	38.04	50.72
5	78.23	47.89	56.12	41.64	52.33
6	132.52	84.21	80.37	85.52	78.19
7	134.35	85.35	81.17	86.67	78.99
8	152.80	96.83	89.21	98.18	87.05
9	154.48	97.87	89.93	99.23	87.78
10	259.07	160.66	133.88	162.16	131.84
No.	w	$s = 0.65$		$s = 0.75$	
		y	z	y	z
1	63.04	27.29	45.75	21.22	42.28
2	66.28	29.40	46.49	23.31	42.80
3	70.91	32.42	47.55	26.29	43.55
4	72.74	33.62	47.96	27.48	43.85
5	78.23	37.20	49.22	31.03	44.73
6	132.52	86.20	77.05	87.01	75.70
7	134.35	87.36	77.86	88.17	76.51
8	152.80	98.89	85.93	99.73	84.60
9	154.48	99.93	86.66	100.77	85.33
10	259.07	162.95	130.77	163.88	129.51

actually increase. This is explained by the fact that the threshold value, a, that can be supported by the tax system falls as s increases (for given t). The use of target efficiency as a criterion by which to judge a tax and transfer system, by entirely ignoring the outcomes in terms of either poverty or inequality, would appear to be rather narrow. The simplicity of the argument, when expressed in the context of a fixed pre-tax income distribution, disappears when incomes are endogenous.

5.3.2 Poverty and Social Welfare Comparisons

Turning to the evaluation of schemes in terms of outcomes rather than targeting, Table 5.5 shows summary measures for a range of values of the taper,
s, and the marginal tax rate, t. The summary measures are the three poverty
measures defined above, and the values of an abbreviated social welfare function of the form $W = \overline{U}\left(1 - I_U\right)$, where I_U denotes a measure of inequality
of utility. The measures $W\left(A\right)$ and $W\left(G\right)$ denote values of W obtained
using respectively the Atkinson inequality measure (with inequality aversion
of 0.5 as above) and the Gini measure for I_U. The basic value judgements
involved in the use of the Gini measure in an abbreviated welfare function
of this type were explored by Sen (1973). The case where $s = t$ refers to the
standard linear income tax which has universal transfers.

First, consider the used of only the social evaluation function defined
without any reference to poverty, as in the standard 'optimal' tax problem.
Here, with the modified minimum income guarantee scheme, the problem is
to find the optimal combination of s and t (with the associated value of a
being determined by the revenue constraint). Hence the search is over two
dimensions rather than a single dimension of the linear income tax considered above. It can be seen from Table 5.5 that $W\left(A\right)$ is maximised for the
combination of $s = 0.35$ and $t = 0.3$. When the Gini measure is use, $W\left(G\right)$
is found to be maximised for the combination of $s = 0.55$ and $t = 0.5$. Table
5.5 obviously reports only a very small number of the combinations that had
to be examined, involving a very much finer grid division. Calculations revealed that the optimal linear income tax rate in the case of the Gini-based
evaluation function is 0.55.

Hence a concentration on the distribution of utility would give support
to a degree of means-testing of transfer payments, with the taper rate being
slightly higher than the income tax rate applied to those with gross incomes
above the threshold, a. Investigations show that this result, support for a
taper rate applying to transfers, depends on both the assumed distribution
of wage rates and the degree of inequality aversion in the social evaluation
function. For higher values of ε the linear income tax dominates the modified

minimum income guarantee; this is not surprising as more weight is attached to the lower range of the distribution. When a much larger population is used (consisting of several thousand random drawings from a lognormal wage rate distribution), the linear tax again appears to dominate.

The question then arises of how a primary concern for poverty would evaluate the outcomes of the different systems. Table 5.3 shows how the increase in the taper, s, for given marginal tax rate, t, increases each of the measures of poverty. However, increasing t for a given value of s can, over a range, reduce each of the poverty measures. This means that, for higher values of the taper, there are combinations of s and t which give lower poverty measures than the corresponding values obtained with a linear tax with $t = s$; consider the values of P in Table 5.5 for the taper rates of 0.55 and above. Nevertheless, the tax system producing the minimum overall level of poverty depends on the specific poverty measure used. There are many combinations giving rise to a value of P_0 of 0.2; so that the adoption of a lexicographic approach would give the same result as the direct application of the social welfare function, of the previous paragraph, which ignores poverty. However, it can be seen from the table that either the use of P_1 or P_2 gives support for a linear income tax with a marginal tax rate of 0.45.

5.3.3 Heterogeneous Preferences

The above comparisons were made under the assumption, usually made in 'optimal tax' studies, that all individuals have the same preferences; they differ only in that each individual faces a different wage rate. However, it is possible to repeat the above calculations allowing the values of α to vary over individuals. If α is thought to increase with w, this means that those with higher wages systematically also have a lower preference for leisure. This in turn means that the distribution of wage income is more widely dispersed than in the examples shown above and the poverty measures are higher (except for very high values of t in the linear income tax). It is found that the use of universal transfers (as in the linear income tax) is even more likely to dominate the use of means-testing, when a social evaluation function

Table 5.5: Poverty and Social Welfare

s	a	t	P_0	P_1	P_2	$W(A)$	$W(G)$
0.35	71.41	0.30	0.2	0.0064	0.0002	36.0086	32.0125
0.45	66.17	0.30	0.3	0.0091	0.0004	35.9303	32.1112
	68.94	0.40	0.2	0.0053	0.0002	35.8742	32.4084
	31.36	0.45	0.2	0.0044	0.0001	35.7766	32.4654
0.55	61.09	0.30	0.4	0.0201	0.0012	35.7065	32.0083
	64.07	0.40	0.4	0.0104	0.0005	35.6821	32.4164
	65.59	0.50	0.2	0.0068	0.0002	35.4612	32.5606
	36.17	0.55	0.2	0.0065	0.0002	35.2546	32.5174
0.65	55.69	0.30	0.5	0.0443	0.0042	35.2540	31.6057
	58.77	0.40	0.5	0.0293	0.0020	35.2565	32.1266
	60.64	0.50	0.5	0.0202	0.0011	35.0664	32.3831
	61.13	0.60	0.5	0.0178	0.0009	34.6051	32.3052
	39.48	0.65	0.5	0.0197	0.0010	34.2250	32.0976
0.75	49.30	0.30	0.5	0.0823	0.0137	34.3840	30.6707
	52.38	0.40	0.5	0.0646	0.0085	34.4020	31.3003
	54.52	0.50	0.5	0.0523	0.0056	34.2373	31.6825
	55.54	0.60	0.5	0.0464	0.0044	33.8176	31.7415
	55.04	0.70	0.5	0.0493	0.0050	32.9795	31.3134
	40.45	0.75	0.5	0.0556	0.0063	32.2925	30.8078
0.85	42.79	0.30	0.5	0.1098	0.0280	33.2811	29.4345
	43.46	0.40	0.5	0.1255	0.0316	32.5788	29.2730
	45.76	0.50	0.5	0.1101	0.0243	32.4139	29.7772
	47.27	0.60	0.5	0.1000	0.0200	32.0255	30.0068
	47.65	0.70	0.5	0.0974	0.0190	31.2743	29.8047
	46.06	0.80	0.8	0.1190	0.0240	29.7964	28.7849
	37.29	0.85	0.9	0.1669	0.0352	28.4780	27.6555

of the form of (5.19), or its equivalent using the Gini inequality measure, is applied. If the alternative assumption is made that the preference for leisure increases with the wage rate, then the distribution of wage income is much more compressed and poverty is very much less than in the above examples. The social welfare comparisons between schemes are little affected, however.

5.4 Conclusions

This chapter has illustrated the use of different criteria used to evaluate alternative tax and transfer systems. In particular, means-tested versus universal transfer systems were compared. The analysis proceeded by using numerical examples involving a small number of individuals, in order to highlight the precise effects on incomes. The implications of fixed incomes and of endogenous incomes, using CES utility functions, were examined. Comparisons between tax systems involve fundamental value judgements concerning inequality and poverty, and no tax structure can be regarded as unambiguously superior to another. Judgements depend on the degree of inequality aversion and attitudes to poverty. However, in those cases where means-testing is preferred, the desired tax or taper rate applying to benefits is only slightly less than the marginal tax rate applying to tax payers, and is substantially less than 100 per cent.

Chapter 6

Poverty with Threshold Consumption

The standard analysis of individual labour supply uses a utility function specified in terms of the consumption of goods, purchased with wage and non-wage income, and leisure. By next imposing a poverty level, the model can be used to examine the way in which alternative poverty measures change when the tax structure is altered; for examples, see Kanbur and Keen (1989), Kanbur *et al.* (1994) and Creedy (1997). A criticism of this type of approach is that some individuals, facing a given wage rate and tax structure, choose a level of labour supply which places them below the poverty level. The idea behind a poverty line is that individuals are substantially worse-off as a result of being in poverty, compared with being just above the poverty line. It may therefore reasonably be asked why people would not make a strong attempt to avoid poverty if possible. A major aim of this chapter is to explore a labour supply model in which each individual's utility function depends on a threshold consumption, or poverty, level and there is a strong utility premium to be gained by avoiding poverty.

The standard labour supply model also forms the basis of optimal tax analyses which use a social welfare function to represent the distributional views of the decision-taker, and which is usually expressed as a function of individuals' utilities. For several types of welfare function, an abbreviated form can be obtained in which social welfare per person is expressed in terms of average utility and a measure of inequality; see Lambert (1993a). This allows for the discussion of a trade-off between 'equity and efficiency', though it is recognised that the precise results depend on the cardinalisation of individuals' utility functions as well as the form of the social welfare function. In the case of Atkinson's (1970) inequality measure, I, its associated abbreviated social welfare function is simply written as $\bar{U}(1 - I)$. Hence welfare per person can be regarded as average utility less the 'cost of inequality', UI.

A problem arises when attempting to allow for poverty in any social evaluation. Several poverty measures are available, for example using the family of measures specified by Foster *et al.* (1984). But these have not been defined in the context of the overall evaluation of social welfare, and indeed they are 'non-welfarist' in that they are based on individuals' net incomes or consumption, rather than utility. The standard social welfare function cannot be manipulated to produce an abbreviated form expressed in terms of inequality and some measure of poverty.

In discussing this type of issue, Atkinson (1987) recognised that quite different criteria are often used in the evaluation of poverty and inequality. He considered starting directly from an abbreviated welfare function in which a cost of poverty, say P, might be deducted from average utility in the same way in which the cost of inequality is deducted, so that welfare per person is $U-(IU)-P$. Faced with the problem of specifying P, Atkinson suggested the possible use of a lexicographic approach in which the alleviation of poverty (however defined) has the first priority, and inequality reduction enters as a second concern. This allows different approaches to poverty and inequality to be used; see Atkinson (1987, p.761). This approach was adopted by Creedy (1997) in making 'equal poverty' comparisons of social welfare for a variety of tax and transfer systems.

A pioneering attempt to combine poverty and inequality in a social evaluation function was made by Lewis and Ulph (1988). Their objective was to have a social welfare function, 'in which poverty matters to society only because it matters to individuals' (1988, p.117). They took the view that if individuals are thought to be strongly deprived because of their failure to consume certain goods, this judgement should not be 'externally imposed' but should correspond to individuals' own views. Lewis and Ulph constructed

a model in which individuals have fixed incomes, but certain minimum out-
lays on some goods are required in order to avoid poverty. In their model no
individuals would choose not to purchase at least the minimum amount of
those goods if they could possibly do so. Lewis and Ulph were able to derive
logically distinct measures of inequality and poverty, and expressed social
welfare in terms of per capita income less the welfare loss from inequality
and poverty. An interesting result is that the welfare cost of poverty arises
as the product of the 'degree of deprivation' and the headcount measure of
poverty.

This chapter examines a simple extension of the standard labour supply
model in which a threshold consumption, or poverty, level is introduced at
the individual level as a component of the utility function. Hence, unlike the
Lewis and Ulph (1988) approach, individuals' incomes are endogenous and
the poverty level is expressed in terms of an index of consumption (rather
than looking at specific goods). In other words, rather than focusing on the
allocation of a fixed income among goods, the chapter concentrates on the
labour supply aspect, grouping all goods into a single index of 'consumption'. Labour supply is modelled in a framework in which, except in special
circumstances, individuals do not choose a level of labour supply, and hence
income, which places them in poverty, if they can avoid poverty without
giving up 'too much' leisure. This also contrasts with the Lewis and Ulph
(1988) model in which individuals never choose not to purchase those goods
which are required to avoid poverty.

The labour supply model is presented in section 6.1, after which section
6.2 derives the government's budget constraint for the case of a linear income tax. Social welfare or evaluation functions and poverty measures are
discussed in section 6.3. Simulation results are reported in section 6.4.

6.1 Labour Supply

6.1.1 The Utility Function

Suppose that an individual chooses consumption, c, and leisure, h, in order to maximise utility, $U(c, h)$, where the utility function takes the modified Cobb-Douglas form:

$$U(c, h) = f(c) + (1 - \alpha) \log h \qquad (6.1)$$

The form of $f(c)$ depends on whether the individual is in poverty, which by definition occurs when consumption falls below a threshold level, c_m. When $c < c_m$, the standard Cobb-Douglas function applies and:

$$f(c) = \alpha \log c \qquad (6.2)$$

There is a positive premium gained by avoiding poverty, such that when $c \geq c_m$, then:

$$f(c) = \alpha \log c + \gamma \qquad (6.3)$$

Leisure, h, is defined in terms of the proportion of available time, so that $0 \leq h \leq 1$. The introduction of the term γ is directly in the spirit of Lewis and Ulph (1988) and those who argue that a minimum consumption level is required in order to participate fully in society.

6.1.2 Interior Solutions

Suppose also that there is a linear income tax with a social dividend of a and a marginal tax rate of t. If the wage rate is w, then the budget constraint facing the individual is:

$$c = a + w(1 - h)(1 - t) \qquad (6.4)$$

The value of 'full income', M, defined as the maximum possible income (obtained with $h = 0$), is equal to $a + w(1 - t)$. Interior solutions to this problem take the familiar form given by:

$$c = \alpha M \tag{6.5}$$

$$h = \frac{(1 - \alpha) M}{w (1 - t)} \tag{6.6}$$

which hold for $w > w_s$, where:

$$w_s = \frac{a (1 - \alpha)}{\alpha (1 - t)} \tag{6.7}$$

In addition, gross earnings, y, are a linear function of the wage rate, given by:

$$y = \alpha w - \psi \tag{6.8}$$

where:

$$\psi = \frac{a (1 - \alpha)}{1 - t} \tag{6.9}$$

6.1.3 Avoiding Poverty

If $a \geq c_m$ nothing needs to be added to this standard solution because no one, including those who do not work, is in poverty. However, in the present framework such interior solutions hold only if $c > c_m$, which requires w to exceed a level of, say, w_H. Above this wage rate, labour supply is sufficient to ensure that net earnings are above the poverty line so that:

$$w_H = \frac{c_m - \alpha a}{\alpha (1 - t)} \tag{6.10}$$

If, however, $w_s \leq w < w_H$, the individual has to decide whether it is worthwhile increasing labour supply in order to raise net income, and hence consumption, up to the poverty line. This is only possible if $M \geq c_m$, that is, if $w \geq w_L$ where:

$$w_L = \frac{c_m - a}{1 - t} \tag{6.11}$$

For those with $w_H > w > w_L$ and $w > w_s$, labour supply has to be increased in order to ensure that $c_m = a + w(1-t)(1-h)$. This requires leisure to fall to:

$$h = 1 - \frac{c_m - a}{w(1-t)} \tag{6.12}$$

However, it is only worthwhile to increase labour supply if the resulting level of utility exceeds the utility that would otherwise be obtained in poverty; there is a trade-off because the extra utility has to be matched against the loss of leisure. Working extra hours in order to reach c_m gives a utility level of U^e, where:

$$U^e = \alpha \log c_m + (1-\alpha)\log\left\{1 - \frac{c_m - a}{w(1-t)}\right\} + \gamma \tag{6.13}$$

while utility in the (poverty generating) tangency solution, U^p, is:

$$U^p = \alpha \log(\alpha M) + (1-\alpha)\log\left\{\frac{(1-\alpha)M}{w(1-t)}\right\} \tag{6.14}$$

In order for $U^e > U^p$, the wage rate must exceed some level, say, w_m. It can be shown that w_m is given by the root of $\Phi(w) = 0$, with:

$$\Phi(w) = \alpha \log\left(\frac{c_m}{M}\right) + (1-\alpha)\log\left(1 - \frac{c_m}{M}\right) - (k - \gamma) \tag{6.15}$$

and:

$$k = \alpha \log \alpha + (1-\alpha)\log(1-\alpha) \tag{6.16}$$

It is clear that the value of w_m falls as γ increases; however, even for relatively large values of γ the value of w_s does not necessarily fall to w_L ($> w_s$). This means that it is possible to have some people who are working but nevertheless in poverty. For those with $w_m < w < w_H$, higher wage rates are actually associated with lower levels of labour supply.

Equation (6.15) is nonlinear, but it can be solved using Newton's method. Using an initial trial value of w, an adjustment, $\triangle w$ can be obtained using:

$$\triangle w = \frac{\Phi(w)}{\Phi'(w)} \tag{6.17}$$

where:

$$\Phi'(w) = -\frac{c_m(1-t)}{M^2}\left\{\alpha\left(\frac{c_m}{M}\right) - (1-\alpha)\left(1 - \frac{c_m}{M}\right)\right\} \qquad (6.18)$$

This process of adjustment can be continued until convergence is reached.

Another possibility needs to considered. Some individuals who have $w_L \leq w \leq w_s$ and who would otherwise not work at all may find it worthwhile working in order to escape poverty. However, not all those who could possibly avoid poverty would do so by supplying very large amounts of labour. The utility of those who decide to work and reach the threshold consumption level, c_m, is the same as U^e given above, but the alternative of not working and being in poverty, U_N^p, is simply $\alpha \log a$. It can be shown that $U^e > U_N^p$ if $w > w_n$, where w_n is given by:

$$w_n = \frac{c_m - a}{(1-t)\left[1 - \exp\left(\frac{\alpha \log(a/c_m) - \gamma}{1-\alpha}\right)\right]} \qquad (6.19)$$

This last possibility can, however, be ruled out if none of those below w_s could avoid poverty by working, that is if $w_L > w_s$. This applies if $a < \alpha c_m$. If the value of w_n from equation (7.28) exceeds w_s, above which individuals would anyway work, then the solution cannot be regarded as applicable and none of those below w_s find it worthwhile working to escape poverty.

6.1.4 Diagrammatic Form

The above labour supply model gives rise to two alternative types of relation between gross earnings, y, and the wage rate; y is often referred to as measuring labour supply in 'efficiency units'. These relationships are illustrated in Figure 6.1, where the top section refers to the case where the threshold wage w_n is appropriate. The line Ow_sC shows the relationship between y and w in the standard Cobb-Douglas case, but in the present model it is given by Ow_nABC. For wages between w_n and w_H, over the range AB, gross earnings are constant at $(c_m - a)/(1-t)$, which ensures a net income (consumption) of c_m. Hence labour supply falls as w increases over this range. To the extent that $w_n > w_L$, some individuals could avoid poverty by working very long hours, but choose not to do so.

(a)

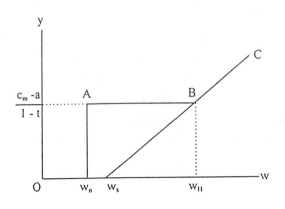

(b)

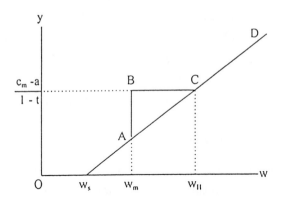

Figure 6.1: Labour Supply

The bottom section of the figure shows the situation where there are some 'working poor', who face a wage rate between w_s and w_m. The relationship between y and w follows the line marked Ow_sABCD. Here labour supply falls as w increases over the range BC. In case (a), all those in poverty consume only the social dividend, a, so that there is no dispersion in consumption among the poor. In case (b), there is some variation.

6.2 The Government Budget Constraint

The values of the social dividend, a, and the marginal tax rate, t, cannot be set independently because the income tax revenue must be sufficient to cover the cost of the social dividend and other specified non-transfer government expenditure. This section derives the form of the budget constraint facing the government.

Within the partial equilibrium framework used here, the distribution of wage rates is assumed to be fixed. As in most of the optimal tax literature, it is assumed that individuals have the same preferences and differ only in the wage rate they face. Hence the values of c_m and γ are also assumed to be common to all individuals. Hence there is a conventional minimum level of consumption on which all individuals agree. Consider first the case where $a > c_m$, which corresponds to the standard linear income tax case since the minimum consumption level is not relevant. Suppose that it is required to raise an amount, R, per capita for non-transfer purposes. The government budget constraint takes the form:

$$a + R = t\bar{y} \tag{6.20}$$

where $\bar{y}$ is arithmetic mean gross income given by:

$$\bar{y} = \int_{w_s}^{\infty} w\,(1 - h)\,dF\,(w) \tag{6.21}$$

and $F(w)$ denotes the distribution function of wage rates. Equation (6.21) can be written as:

$$\bar{y} = \alpha\bar{w}G_\psi\,(w_s) \tag{6.22}$$

where $\bar{w}$ is the arithmetic mean wage rate and:

$$G_\psi\left(w_s\right) = \left\{1 - F_1\left(w_s\right)\right\} - \frac{\psi}{\alpha\bar{w}}\left\{1 - F\left(w_s\right)\right\} \qquad (6.23)$$

The term $F_1\left(w\right)$ denotes the first moment distribution function of wages; that is, $F_1\left(w_s\right)$ is the proportion of total wages obtained by those with $w \leq w_s$. For further discussion of functions of the type shown in (6.23) in income tax and transfer models, see Creedy (1996).

When the minimum consumption level is relevant, that is when $a < c_m$, two cases need to be distinguished, as discussed above. First, in the case where some of those who would otherwise supply no labour find it worthwhile to work in order to avoid poverty, and all those with wage rates between w_s and w_H increase their labour supply to avoid poverty, then w_n is relevant. The gross earnings of those who just reach the poverty level are $\left(c_m - a\right)/\left(1 - t\right)$, and in this case arithmetic mean earnings are given by:

$$\bar{y} = \left(\frac{c_m - a}{1 - t}\right)\int_{w_n}^{w_H} dF\left(w\right) + \int_{w_H}^{\infty}\left(\alpha w - \psi\right)dF\left(w\right) \qquad (6.24)$$

where ψ is the same as in (15.9). This simplifies to:

$$\bar{y} = \left(\frac{c_m - a}{1 - t}\right)\left\{F\left(w_H\right) - F\left(w_L\right)\right\} - \alpha\bar{w}G_\psi\left(w_H\right) \qquad (6.25)$$

In the case where none of those below w_s find it worthwhile to work, but those between w_m and w_H increase their labour supply to avoid poverty, there are some working poor, and the form in (6.25) must be modified to:

$$\bar{y} = \int_{w_s}^{w_m}\left(\alpha w - \psi\right)dF\left(w\right) + \left(\frac{c_m - a}{1 - t}\right)\int_{w_m}^{w_H} dF\left(w\right) + \int_{w_H}^{\infty}\left(\alpha w - \psi\right)dF\left(w\right) \qquad (6.26)$$

and the first term can be expressed as:

$$\int_{w_s}^{w_m}\left(\alpha w - \psi\right)dF\left(w\right) = \alpha\bar{w}\left\{F_1\left(w_m\right) - F_1\left(w_s\right)\right\} - \psi\left\{F\left(w_m\right) - F\left(w_s\right)\right\} \qquad (6.27)$$

Both (6.25) and (6.26) are highly nonlinear since the various wage thresholds are functions of the tax parameters a and t, as is the term ψ. They can be solved using iterative methods, though it is necessary to solve each constraint for the value of the social dividend, a, for a specified marginal tax rate, t. This is because there is not a unique tax rate associated with any given social dividend. The evaluation of the various integrals required is conveniently carried out in the case where wage rates are lognormally distributed as $\Lambda\left(w|\mu, \sigma^2\right)$. The first moment distribution takes the form $\Lambda\left(w|\mu + \sigma^2, \sigma^2\right)$ and a polynomial approximation to the normal integral can be used.

6.3   Social Welfare and Poverty

6.3.1   The Social Welfare Function

Values of social welfare are usually examined for the well known welfare function:

$$W = \frac{1}{N}\sum_{i=1}^{N}\frac{U_i^{1-\varepsilon}}{1-\varepsilon} \qquad (6.28)$$

where ε denotes the degree of relative inequality aversion and N is the population size. In the standard case, where the poverty level does not enter U_i and therefore also does not enter the welfare function, it is known that (6.28) can be expressed as $\bar{U}\left(1 - I_\varepsilon\right)$, where I_ε is Atkinson's (1970) inequality measure, as discussed in the introduction. For the model described in section 6.1, where c_m is relevant, social welfare in (6.28) must depend in a complex way on c_m as well as the form of the distribution. It does not seem possible, for example by writing the indirect form of the utility function for each individual, to simplify (6.28) in order to get an expression involving both an inequality measure and a poverty measure. However, numerical results are given below for the direct evaluation of W using the resulting value of U_i for each simulated member of the population.

An explicit result is, however, available in the case where $\varepsilon = 1$ and the welfare function becomes $W = \sum_i \log U_i$ instead of the form in (6.28). In addition, consider the cardinalisation of the utility function such that, for those with $c \geq c_m$, the monotonic transformation $U_i' = gU_i^*$, where $g = \exp\gamma$

and $U_i^* = c_i^\alpha h_i^{1-\alpha}$, is used. In this case, the value of social welfare is, ignoring the constant term, expressed as:

$$W = \bar{U}^* (1 - I_1) - gP_0 \tag{6.29}$$

where I_1 is the Atkinson measure of inequality of U^*. This result, for a particular cardinalisation and welfare function, corresponds to a similar result found by Lewis and Ulph (1988) for their model. Social welfare is expressed in terms of the average utility, $\bar{U}^*$, defined such that the benefit of escaping poverty is excluded, less the 'cost of inequality', $\bar{U}^* I_1$, less the 'cost of poverty', gP_0. The latter is the product of the headcount poverty measure and the term g, which reflects the utility from which those in poverty are deprived. In commenting on their similar 'resurrection' of the headcount poverty measure, Lewis and Ulph (1988, p.129) make the argument that, 'none of the writers who have tried to incorporate the distribution of income among the poor into their measure of poverty, have adequately explained why this feature of income distribution should matter when measuring poverty (as distinct from inequality)'. Nevertheless, it is of interest to examine the behaviour of other commonly used poverty measures, described in the following subsection.

6.3.2   Poverty Measures

The following simulation results concerning labour supply and social welfare are supplemented by several poverty measures based on the family proposed by Foster *et al.* (1984). These measures are defined, in terms of net income or consumption rather than utility, as:

$$P_j = \sum_{c < c_m} \left(\frac{c_m - c}{c_m} \right)^j \tag{6.30}$$

Hence P_0 is the familiar headcount ratio. The measure P_1 is the product of P_0 and 1 minus the ratio of the arithmetic mean net income of those in poverty, $\bar{c}_p$, to the poverty line, that is:

$$P_1 = P_0 \left(1 - \frac{\bar{c}_p}{c_m} \right) = P_0 H \tag{6.31}$$

The measure P_2 reflects also the coefficient of variation of net income of those in poverty, η_p^2, such that:

$$P_2 = P_0 \left\{ H^2 + (1 - H)^2 \eta_p^2 \right\} \tag{6.32}$$

6.4 Simulation Results

The following simulation results were produced for 'populations' of 5,000 individuals, using values of μ and σ^2 respectively of 10 and 0.5, so that the arithmetic mean wage rate is 28,282. The value of α was set at 0.7, and several values of γ were used. The inequality aversion parameter, ε, was set to 0.8. In addition, it was assumed that non-transfer government revenue of 2,000 per person was required from tax revenue. The poverty level was set to 8,000. These simulations are obviously intended only to illustrate the main characteristics of the alternative frameworks. The computer programs are available from the author.

First, results for the standard linear income tax model, where there is no role for a poverty level in the utility functions (and thus also in the social welfare function), are shown in Tables 6.1 and 6.2. Each table shows selected results for the marginal tax rates over the range from 0.2 to 0.9, where the government budget constraint is satisfied at all times. The associated value of the social dividend is shown in Table 6.2, along with the wage rate above which individuals supply labour. It can be seen that the tax rates that minimise P_1 or P_2 are significantly higher than that for which P_0 is minimised. The optimal tax rate is found, from the final column of Table 6.2, to be approximately 0.45.

Corresponding results for the model presented in section 6.1 are shown in Tables 6.3 and 6.4. These results are for a value of γ of 0.2. Not surprisingly, the poverty measures in this case are substantially lower than those shown in Table 6.1, and arithmetic mean earnings are higher. The marginal tax rates that minimise the poverty measures are also higher in Table 6.3, and the minimising rates for each measure are much closer together. This result is not surprising, as can be seen from the wage thresholds shown in Table 6.4.

Table 6.1: Standard Linear Income Tax

t	P_0	P_1	P_2	$c_m/\bar{c}$	$\bar{y}$
0.20	0.1988	0.0487	0.0173	0.467	19113
0.25	0.1884	0.0414	0.0133	0.478	18727
0.30	0.1794	0.0350	0.0101	0.491	18304
0.35	0.1698	0.0297	0.0076	0.505	17842
0.40	0.1626	0.0253	0.0058	0.522	17337
0.45	0.1590	0.0219	0.0044	0.542	16780
0.50	0.1598	0.0193	0.0033	0.565	16168
0.55	0.1642	0.0176	0.0025	0.593	15492
0.60	0.1830	0.0171	0.0020	0.628	14743
0.65	0.2188	0.0186	0.0019	0.672	13910
0.70	0.2822	0.0243	0.0025	0.729	12981
0.75	0.3800	0.0382	0.0045	0.805	11921
0.80	0.5514	0.0730	0.0114	0.915	10728
0.85	0.7590	0.1508	0.0342	1.088	9342
0.90	0.9392	0.3034	0.1063	1.407	7681

Table 6.2: Standard Linear Income Tax

t	a	w_s	W
0.20	1826.1	978.2	6.3431
0.25	2676.6	1529.5	6.3596
0.30	3484.9	2133.6	6.3735
0.35	4237.1	2793.7	6.3841
0.40	4925.3	3518.0	6.3914
0.45	5543.8	4319.8	6.3951
0.50	6075.7	5207.8	6.3945
0.55	6511.5	6201.4	6.3889
0.60	6836.5	7324.8	6.3772
0.65	7033.4	8612.3	6.3583
0.70	7076.0	10108.5	6.3291
0.75	6953.1	11919.6	6.2878
0.80	6593.6	14129.2	6.2268
0.85	5951.5	17004.4	6.1341
0.90	4918.5	21079.1	5.9827

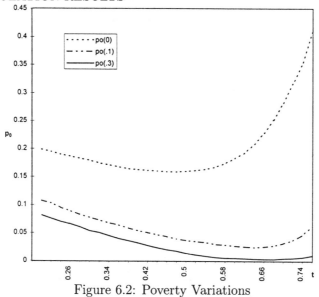

Figure 6.2: Poverty Variations

For the lower range of marginal tax rates, the threshold w_n is not relevant, so those in poverty include the 'working poor' as well as those whose wage rate is so low that they supply no labour. For the higher range of tax rates, w_n is relevant, so all those who are in poverty have exactly the same consumption, given by the social dividend, and $\bar{c}_p = a$, while $\eta_p^2 = 0$. The optimal tax in this case is, as expected, higher than in the standard case, and it is lower than the poverty minimising rates.

The threshold wage rate, w_m, falls as t increases, and when w_n becomes relevant it too falls until it reaches a minimum; this must occur at the same point at which P_0 is minimised. (For very high marginal tax rates and lower values of γ, the wage w_m again becomes the relevant threshold.) The value of $H = 1 - \bar{c}_p/c_m$ is minimised when the social dividend, $a = \bar{c}_p$, is maximised, so that $P_1 = P_0 H$ is not necessarily minimised at the same tax rate for which P_0 is minimised. The variation in each of the poverty measures with t is shown in Figures 6.2 to 6.4, for the standard model and for two values of γ, 0.1 and 0.3.

As γ increases, the poverty levels fall, the wage thresholds w_n and w_m fall (although w_s rises), average earnings and the social dividend increase.

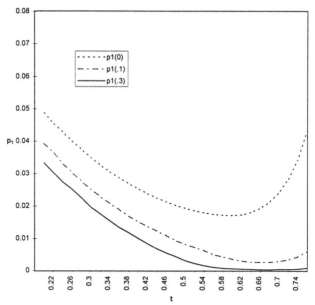

Figure 6.3: Poverty Variations

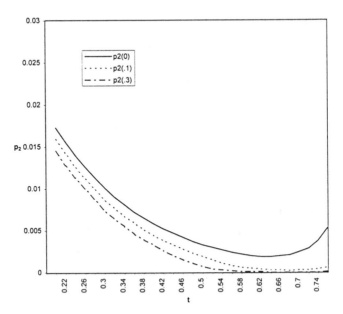

Figure 6.4: Poverty Variations

Table 6.3: Threshold Case: $\gamma = 0.2$

t	P_0	P_1	P_2	$c_m/\bar{c}$	$\bar{y}$
0.20	0.0898	0.0355	0.0151	0.464	19223
0.25	0.0756	0.0281	0.0111	0.475	18845
0.30	0.0626	0.0218	0.0080	0.487	18430
0.35	0.0504	0.0164	0.0056	0.501	17977
0.40	0.0380	0.0117	0.0036	0.517	17480
0.45	0.0290	0.0081	0.0023	0.536	16934
0.50	0.0204	0.0047	0.0011	0.558	16333
0.55	0.0134	0.0023	0.0004	0.586	15672
0.60	0.0086	0.0011	0.0001	0.619	14936
0.65	0.0062	0.0006	0.0001	0.660	14129
0.70	0.0082	0.0007	0.0001	0.711	13269
0.75	0.0182	0.0016	0.0001	0.772	12368
0.80	0.0484	0.0049	0.0005	0.843	11488
0.85	0.1392	0.0163	0.0019	0.923	10657
0.90	0.4200	0.0665	0.0105	1.039	9692

However, it was found that there is only a very small increase in the optimal tax rate; when γ doubles to 0.4, the increase in the optimal rate is less than one percentage point. With the specified poverty line of $c_m = 8,000$, it is not possible to eliminate poverty altogether with this type of linear income tax, though with $\gamma = 0.4$, the minimum headcount measure falls to 0.0016 (at the optimal tax rate it is 0.0094).

The above examples are all for a poverty line which remains fixed in absolute terms. The decline in average earnings as the tax rate increases gives rise to an increasing ratio of the poverty line to the post-tax value of average earnings. This increase is partly responsible for driving the increase in the poverty measures at high marginal tax rates. The effect of using a relative poverty line is that poverty eventually falls to zero as the marginal tax rate increases, though in this case poverty is eliminated by making everyone poorer.

Table 6.4: Threshold Case: $\gamma = 0.2$

t	a	w_n	w_s	w_m	w_H	W
0.20	1848.1	0.0	990.1	8580.4	11975.6	6.5196
0.25	2706.3	0.0	1546.4	8008.2	11629.7	6.5401
0.30	3522.9	0.0	2156.9	7413.6	11293.8	6.5576
0.35	4284.3	0.0	2824.8	6812.5	10991.1	6.5716
0.40	4982.9	0.0	3559.2	6215.9	10742.8	6.5820
0.45	5609.8	0.0	4371.3	5641.1	10579.6	6.5884
0.50	6159.3	5105.6	5279.4	0.0	10538.6	6.5905
0.55	6607.0	4610.3	6292.4	0.0	10714.6	6.5869
0.60	6949.9	4165.3	7446.3	0.0	11196.8	6.5772
0.65	7174.9	3917.8	8785.6	0.0	12153.4	6.5601
0.70	7275.7	4101.9	10393.9	0.0	13842.8	6.5336
0.75	7275.7	4922.3	12472.7	0.0	16611.4	6.4970
0.80	7194.4	6722.5	15416.5	0.0	21171.1	6.4478
0.85	7064.8	10123.6	20185.2	0.0	29091.9	6.3819
0.90	6733.3	19291.8	28857.0	0.0	46952.9	6.2695

6.5 Conclusions

A major purpose of this chapter has been to examine a labour supply model
in which a poverty level or threshold consumption level plays an integral
part. Individuals receive a utility 'premium' if they are able to raise their
net income up to or above the threshold level (or, correspondingly, can be
viewed as suffering a degree of deprivation if they fail to reach the threshold).
The implication is that it may be worthwhile for some individuals, who would
otherwise be in poverty, to supply higher amounts of labour in order to avoid
poverty. Over a range of wage rates, labour supply falls as the wage increases.
Nevertheless, there may still be some 'working poor' and some who are not
working who choose to remain in poverty even though they may be able
to achieve the threshold consumption level by giving up virtually all their
leisure. There are others who face a wage rate that is too low for them to be
able to obtain net earnings above the threshold in any circumstances.

A further motivation for the analysis relates to the use of a social welfare
or evaluation function when poverty is thought to be important. The stan-

dard welfare function used in the optimal tax literature is specified in terms of individuals' utilities, making no allowance for poverty. It is not clear how a desire for poverty alleviation can be added to, or integrated into, the standard welfare function. In this chapter, poverty is integrated fully into the social welfare function because it matters to individuals; that is, the poverty line is a basic component of individuals' utility functions. It was shown that in a special case (combining a particular cardinalisation of utility functions with unitary relative aversion to inequality), an abbreviated social welfare function could be found in which welfare per head is expressed in terms of average utility, less a cost of inequality (where both terms exclude the special deprivation suffered by those in poverty), less a cost of poverty. The latter is expressed as the product of the degree of deprivation and the headcount measure of poverty.

Within the present framework, the concern for poverty as a separate concept, using an individualistic Paretean social welfare function expressed in terms of individuals' utilities, arises because individuals do not like being in poverty themselves. However, each individual's utility is not affected by the existence of other people in poverty, just as it is not affected by the relative position of that individual in the income distribution. It would perhaps be of interest to extend the analysis to consider alternative tax structures, such as those involving the use of means-tested transfer payments.

Chapter 7

Indirect Tax Reform

This chapter examines the welfare changes imposed on different income (total expenditure) groups by changes in prices which arise from changes in indirect taxes. The approach is based on the use of the Linear Expenditure System (LES) which is applied to each income group separately, rather than being estimated for a 'representative household'. Estimation of the parameters of the LES for each income group is based on the expressions obtained by Frisch (1959) for the own-price and cross-price elasticities of demand for additive utility functions, of which the LES is a special case.

The method is used to examine the distributional effects of the change in the indirect tax system in New Zealand during the mid-1980s, carried out as part of a major package of tax reforms involving a flattening of the income tax structure, a large amount of base-broadening and a partial shift towards indirect taxation. An extensive analysis of the incidence of indirect taxes in New Zealand and the likely effects of the introduction of a Goods and Services Tax (GST) was carried out by Scott *et al.* (1985), along with supporting material by Broad and Bacica (1985). Their analysis involved a detailed study using the unit record data from the New Zealand Household Expenditure Survey.

For a range of income groups and household types, the authors mentioned above measured the impact effects of the changes by assuming full shifting of indirect taxes to consumers in the form of price rises. Hence, no attempt was made to allow for behavioural changes such as substitution between commodity groups or changes in labour supply behaviour by household members. The analysis necessarily used a partial equilibrium framework, so no allowance was made for changes in tax-exclusive goods prices or factor prices.

The following analysis adopts all the assumptions of the earlier study, with two exceptions. Consumer responses to price changes are modelled, and money measures of welfare changes (compensating and equivalent variations) are calculated for each income group. The conclusions of the earlier study were based on estimated profiles of indirect tax paid in relation to household income. The present study is, however, more limited in that it has not been able to examine different household types (by size, composition and age of head), and unit record data have not been used.

Section 7.1 derives the expressions for compensating and equivalent variations in the case of the Linear Expenditure System. As these results are well established, the discussion is brief in order to present the main results. A property of the LES is that, using a single set of parameters for a representative household, the compensating variation as a ratio of income falls as income increases if the price of 'necessities' increases by relatively more than the price of 'luxuries'. The present approach does not, however, use a single set of parameters but obtains a separate set for each income group. The method used to estimate the required parameters is described in section 7.2. Section 7.3 presents the results relating to the introduction of a Goods and Services Tax (GST) in New Zealand.

7.1 The Welfare Effects of Price Changes

7.1.1 The Linear Expenditure System

The utility function takes the form:

$$U = \sum_i \beta_i \log (x_i - \gamma_i) \tag{7.1}$$

with $x_i \geq 0, 0 \leq \beta_i \leq 1$. Furthermore, γ_i is committed expenditure on good i, and $\sum \beta_i = 1$. Maximisation subject to the budget constraint $y = \sum p_i x_i$

gives rise to the linear expenditure functions:

$$p_i x_i = \gamma_i p_i + \beta_i \left(y - \sum_j p_j \gamma_j \right) \tag{7.2}$$

or $x_i^* = \beta_i y^* / p_i$ where $y^* = y - \sum p_j \gamma_j$ is supernumerary income and $x_i^* = x_i - \gamma_i$ is supernumerary consumption of good i. The indirect utility function, $V(p, y)$, is obtained by substituting (7.2) into (7.1) and rearranging using $\sum \beta_i = 1$ to get:

$$V = \log \left\{ y^* \prod \left(\frac{\beta_i}{p_i} \right)^{\beta_i} \right\} \tag{7.3}$$

It is convenient to use $V^e = \exp(V)$, which is equivalent to writing the utility function in multiplicative form, so that:

$$V^e = \frac{(y - A)}{B} \tag{7.4}$$

where:

$$A = \sum_i p_i \gamma_i \tag{7.5}$$

and:

$$B = \prod \left(\frac{p_i}{\beta_i} \right)^{\beta_i} \tag{7.6}$$

The expenditure function, the minimum expenditure required to achieve U at prices p, $E(p, U)$, is thus given by:

$$E(p, U) = A + BU \tag{7.7}$$

7.1.2 Compensating and Equivalent Variations

Suppose that prices change from p_0 to p_1, as a result of the imposition of indirect taxes. The compensating variation is the difference between the minimum expenditure required to achieve the original utility level, at the new price, and the initial total expenditure. Hence:

$$CV = E\left(p_1, U_0\right) - E\left(p_0, U_0\right)$$

Substituting using (7.7) gives:

$$CV = A_1 + B_1 U_0 - y_0 \tag{7.8}$$

where subscripts refer to the set of prices used. After substituting for $U_0 = (y_0 - A_0)$, this can be rearranged to give:

$$CV = A_0 \left[\frac{A_1}{A_0} + \frac{B_1}{B_0}\left(\frac{y_0}{A_0} - 1\right)\right] - y_0 \tag{7.9}$$

The term A_1/A_0 is a Laspeyres type of price index, using the committed consumption of each good as the weight. If $\dot{p}_i$ denotes the proportionate change in the price of the ith good, then $p_{1i} = p_{0i}\left(1 + \dot{p}_i\right)$ and:

$$\frac{A_1}{A_0} = 1 + \sum_i s_i \dot{p}_i \tag{7.10}$$

where:

$$s_i = \frac{p_{0i}\gamma_i}{\sum_i p_{0i}\gamma_i} \tag{7.11}$$

The term B_1/B_0 simplifies to $\prod\left(p_{1i}/p_{0i}\right)^{\beta_i}$, which is a weighted geometric mean of price relatives. Expressing this in terms of the proportionate changes gives:

$$\frac{B_1}{B_0} = \prod_i\left(1 + \dot{p}_i\right)^{\beta_i} \tag{7.12}$$

It is therefore possible to use (7.9), with (7.10) and (7.12), to calculate the compensating variation, given a set of proportionate price changes and the coefficients β_i, along with the initial cost of committed expenditure for each good, $p_i\gamma_i$. An important feature of the results is that information about separate values of γ_i and p_i are not required.

The equivalent variation is the difference between the post-change total expenditure and the minimum expenditure required to achieve post-change utility at the pre-change prices. Hence:

$$EV = E\left(p_1, U_1\right) - E\left(p_0, U_1\right) \tag{7.13}$$

so that:

$$EV = y_1 - \left(A_0 + B_0 U_1\right) \tag{7.14}$$

Substituting for U_1 into (7.14) and rearranging gives:

$$EV = y_1 - A_0 \left[1 + \frac{B_0}{B_1}\left(\frac{y_1}{A_0} - \frac{A_1}{A_0}\right)\right] \tag{7.15}$$

which may be compared with (7.9). The two price indices may be obtained using (7.10) and (7.12), which require only information about the values of β_i and $p_{0i}\gamma_i$ in each income group, along with the price changes $\dot{p}_i$.

The approach used here involves the separate application of the LES to each total expenditure group, indexed by $k = 1, ..., K$, so it is necessary to add a k subscript to each of the terms used above. The following analysis uses $K = 9$ and $n = 60$, as in the Household Expenditure Survey, giving a total of 32,400 price elasticities and 540 total expenditure elasticities. This is obviously too much information to present here.

7.1.3 Comparing Tax Structures

In the following empirical analysis, separate parameters of the LES and therefore welfare changes are estimated for each of a range of different income, or total expenditure, groups. The price changes, $\dot{p}_i$, are regarded as arising from a change in the indirect tax structure. The above results are then used to calculate compensating and equivalent variations for each income group.

Some authors, including Kay (1980), Pazner and Sadka (1980), King (1983) and Pauwels (1986), have argued that the equivalent variation is superior to the compensating variation, particularly as the latter is defined for an arbitrary utility level rather than an arbitrary set of prices. However, Ebert (1995) argued, using an axiomatic approach, that no measure can be regarded as unambiguously superior to others and that value judgements are involved in the choice of measure. For this reason, both measures are reported below.

An advantage of the equivalent variation is that it can usefully be linked to the concept of 'equivalent income', introduced by King (1983). This is defined as the value of total expenditure, y_e, which at some reference set of prices, p_r, gives the same utility as the actual income. Hence, in terms of the expenditure function, equivalent income is given by:

$$y_e = E\left(p_r, V\left(p, y\right)\right) \qquad (7.16)$$

Comparisons of various tax structures based on the use of y_e therefore involve fixed reference prices, and using pre-change prices as p_r, it can be seen that $y_e = y - EV$.

The pre-change equivalent income is simply y and the proportionate change in equivalent income following a set of price changes is thus EV/y. If this ratio is the same for all households, then any relative measure of inequality of 'equivalent income' is unchanged as a result of the tax change. Hence, values of this ratio are reported below along with the absolute values of equivalent variations for each income group. This approach has the desirable property that an equal proportionate increase in all prices gives rise to the same ratio of welfare loss to total expenditure for each household; for example, a proportionate increase of x in all prices produces a CV/y ratio of x, and an EV/y ratio of $1/\left(1 + x\right)$, for each household.

This argument also shows that it is not appropriate to divide the equivalent variation by disposable income (that is, post-tax-and-transfer income) or even total pre-tax income, rather than total expenditure, when the aim is to examine the welfare changes for each household arising from a set of price changes. Some commentators argue that low-income households face a higher burden of indirect taxes than high-income households simply because the latter save relatively more. However, in the present context savings are irrelevant. It is also often forgotten that savings are ultimately spent. In considering differences in savings patterns among households, the real issue concerns the precise tax treatment of those savings. For example, it would be of interest to examine differential real rates of return obtained by savers in different income groups, but that is a separate question.

7.2   Estimation of the LES

This section describes the method used to estimate the required elasticities and parameter values for the linear expenditure function in each income (total expenditure) group. From the Household Expenditure Survey (HES), the average expenditure weights or budget shares for K total expenditure groups are available. These weights are arranged in the form of a matrix with K rows and n columns. The published budget shares from the 1993-4 HES for New Zealand, for nine total expenditure groups and 60 commodity groups, were used here. However, the analysis excludes the category 'net capital outlay and related expenditure' which is too unreliable and contains capital gains and losses.

Denote the midpoint of the kth total expenditure group by y_k $(k = 1, ..., K)$ and the budget share, or expenditure weight, for the ith commodity group and kth total expenditure group by w_{ki} $(i = 1, ..., n)$. Using the basic definition $w_{ki} = p_{ki}q_{ki}/y_k$, differentiation gives:

$$\dot{w}_{ki} = \dot{y}_k \left(e_{ki} - 1 \right) \qquad (7.17)$$

where $\dot{w}_{ki}$ denotes the proportional change in the budget share of the ith good resulting from the proportional change in total expenditure. Rearranging this result gives:

$$e_{ki} = 1 + \dot{w}_{ki}/\dot{y}_k \qquad (7.18)$$

As only cross-sectional data are available, these changes are obtained by moving from one total expenditure group to another, and changes, for $k = 2, ..., K$, were based on terms such as $\dot{y}_k = (y_{k-1}/y_k) - 1$, and $\dot{w}_{ki} = (w_{k-1,i}/w_{ki}) - 1$. Hence, although the 'dot' notation has been used, the calculated values are discrete changes, obtained by comparing values in adjacent total expenditure groups. In fact, the e_{ki} were calculated using (except for groups 1 and K) the average of the upward and downward changes.

The raw weights could not be used directly because they would give rise to numerous negative income elasticities. It was necessary first to obtain a smooth relationship between the weights and total expenditure. This was

carried out by estimating, for each commodity group, the following relationship:

$$w_{ki} = a_i + b_i \log(y_k) \qquad (7.19)$$

which generally provides a good fit; for further discussion of this type of
function to describe budget shares, see Deaton and Muellbauer (1980). The
estimated values from the fitted regression lines were then used to calculate
the income elasticities.

Having calculated the e_{ki}s, the corresponding values of β_{ki} were obtained
using the result for the linear expenditure system that the income (total
expenditure) elasticity is:

$$e_{ki} = \frac{\beta_{ki}}{w_{ki}} \qquad (7.20)$$

so that $\beta_{ki} = e_{ki} w_{ki}$.

From equation (15.2), the own-price elasticity of demand for the linear
expenditure system is:

$$e_{kii} = -\frac{\beta_{ki}}{p_i x_{ki}} \left\{ y_k - \sum_{j \neq i} p_j \gamma_{kj} \right\} \qquad (7.21)$$

This can be rearranged as:

$$e_{kii} = \frac{\gamma_{ki}(1 - \beta_{ki})}{x_{ki}} - 1 \qquad (7.22)$$

Consider the calculation of committed expenditure for each commodity
group (and income group). If a value of the own- price elasticity of demand
is available using extraneous information for each good at each income level,
equation (12.19) can be used, giving:

$$p_i \gamma_{ki} = \frac{y_k w_{ki}(1 + e_{kii})}{1 - \beta_{ki}} \qquad (7.23)$$

The required set of own-price elasticities may be obtained using the Frisch
(1959) result for additive utility functions. In particular, Frisch showed that:

$$e_{kii} = e_{ki} \left\{ \frac{1}{\xi_k} - w_{ki} \left(1 + \frac{e_{ki}}{\xi_k} \right) \right\} \qquad (7.24)$$

where ξ_k is the elasticity of the marginal utility of 'income', generally referred to as the Frisch parameter, in the kth group. In the case of the LES, it is known that $\xi_k = -y_k/y_k^*$, or the ratio of income to supernumerary income. This cannot of course be used to obtain values of ξ_k, because the committed expenditures must be known in order to obtain the supernumerary incomes.

The outstanding problem is that in using (7.24) it is required to have values of ξ_k for each income, or total expenditure, group. Unfortunately, estimates are not available, so it is necessary to specify a pattern using *a priori* assumptions. The linear expenditure system involves a minimum absolute value of unity, but the above result suggests that the absolute value is higher for lower income groups, for whom committed expenditure is expected to form a higher proportion of income. Frisch's own conjectures regarding the variation in ξ, along with the available evidence from other demand studies, were discussed at length in Cornwell and Creedy (1997), where it was suggested that a suitable specification for the variation in ξ_k with y_k is a modified double-log form. In the present context, following experimentation with alternative parameter values, the following specification was used:

$$\log\left(-\xi_k\right) = 17.5 - 2.2\log\left(y_k + 450\right) \qquad (7.25)$$

This gives values of ξ_k ranging from -19.73 for the lowest income group to -3.7 for the highest income group. Using this specification, the own-price elasticities for each income and commodity group were calculated. Sensitivity analyses were carried out by investigating the effects of different parameter values for the specification in (7.25), but the comparisons between tax structures shown above were not significantly affected.

The commodity groups used in the HES, in the order in which the price changes are listed above, are: (1) fruit; (2) vegetables; (3) meat; (4) poultry; (5) fish; (6) farm products, fats, oils; (7) cereals, cereal products; (8) sweet products, spreads, beverages; (9) other foodstuffs; (10) meals away from home, ready-to-eat foods; (11) rent; (12) mortgage payments; (13) payments to local authorities; (14) property maintenance goods; (15) property maintenance services; (16) other housing expenses; (17) domestic fuel and power; (18) home appliances; (19) household equipment and utensils; (20) furniture; (21) furnishings; (22) floor coverings; (23) household textiles; (24) household supplies; (25) household services; (26) men's clothing; (27) women's clothing; (28) children's clothing; (29) other clothing; (30) clothing supplies and services; (31) men's footwear; (32) women's footwear; (33) children's footwear; (34) other footwear; (35) footwear supplies and services; (36) public transport within New Zealand; (37) overseas travel; (38) road vehicles; (39) vehicle ownership expenses; (40) other private transport costs; (41) tobacco products; (42) alcohol; (43) medical goods; (44) toiletries and cosmetics; (45) personal goods; (46) pets, racehorses and livestock; (47) publications, stationery and office equipment; (48) leisure and recreational goods; (49) recreational vehicles; (50) other goods; (51) health services; (52) personal services; (53) educational and tuitional services; (54) accommodation services; (55) financial, insurance and legal services; (56) vocational services; (57) leisure services; (58) other services; (59) other outgoings; (60) superannuation contributions.

7.3   Changing Indirect Taxes

The tax change considered here consists of the abolition of a set of wholesale taxes combined with the introduction of a general consumption tax. As explained above, the direct tax and transfer structure is assumed to remain unchanged, so the analysis cannot be considered as an appraisal of overall tax reform in New Zealand. The calculation of the welfare measures, described in the previous section, requires the use of a set of price changes resulting from this tax structure change. As in the vast majority of partial equilibrium analyses, the taxes are assumed to be fully passed to consumers in the form of higher prices, but an immediate problem arises in the present context because the two types of tax (wholesale and consumption taxes) have very different tax bases. The calculation of price changes is described in the first subsection below, and this is followed by the empirical results.

7.3.1   The Indirect Tax System

Before the GST was introduced, a range of wholesale taxes existed, along
with taxes on alcoholic beverages, tobacco products, petroleum fuels and
motor vehicles. For present purposes, it is required to express these indirect
taxes in terms of *ad valorem* tax-exclusive rates on commodity groups that
correspond with those used by the Household Expenditure Survey, since the
latter data are used to calculate the required elasticities for a range of income
groups. This is not a straightforward exercise, as not all taxes are expressed
as *ad valorem* rates and there is not always a direct correspondence between
commodity groups.

For use with the framework presented in section 7.1, it is necessary to
convert tax rates into equivalent percentage price increases, so that it is
possible to examine the welfare loss associated with the imposition of these
rates (assumed to be fully passed on to consumers). Suppose that for any
particular good the tax-exclusive price is p_E, the tax-inclusive price is p_I and
the wholesale price is p_W.

A Wholesale Tax

If m is the wholesale margin, then $p_E = p_W (1 + m)$ and a wholesale tax rate
of t gives rise to a tax inclusive price given by $p_I = p_E + p_W t$, or:

$$p_I = p_W (1 + m + t) \qquad (7.26)$$

If the wholesale tax rate increases by the absolute amount Δt, the proportionate increase in p_I is given by:

$$\dot{p} = \frac{\Delta t}{1 + m + t} \qquad (7.27)$$

Hence if the initial tax rate is zero, the proportionate price increase resulting
from the imposition of a wholesale tax is just $t/(1 + m)$.

Values of retail margins are given in Broad and Bacica (1985, p.56),
but because the emphasis of their work is on calculating the tax revenue,
they defined the margins slightly differently. They give values of m^*, where
$p_W = p_E (1 - m^*)$, which means that $m = \{1/(1 - m^*)\} - 1$. The wholesale

Table 7.1: Wholesale Tax Rates

HES commodity group	Tax	m^*	m
Rate Property Maintenance Goods	0.10	0.20	0.25
Home Appliances	0.30	0.25	0.33
Household Equipment	0.10	0.25	0.33
Utensils, Furniture	0.10	0.20	0.25
Floor Coverings	0.10	0.20	0.25
Household Textiles	0.10	0.20	0.25
Household Supplies	0.10	0.20	0.25
Road Vehicles	0.30	0.10	0.11
Vehicle Ownership Expenses	0.20	0.20	0.25
Tobacco Products	0.40	0.20	0.25
Alcohol	0.25	0.20	0.25
Toiletries and Cosmetics	0.20	0.20	0.25
Personal Goods	0.30	0.20	0.25
Pets, Racehorses and Livestock	0.20	0.20	0.25
Publications, Stationery	0.25	0.20	0.25
Office Equip, Leisure and Rec. Goods	0.20	0.20	0.25
Recreational Vehicles	0.10	0.20	0.25
Goods N.E.C.	0.10	0.20	0.25

and other indirect tax rates used here were taken from the Statistics New Zealand computer files used in the Broad and Bacica (1985) study. These rates were used to construct appropriate rates for the appropriate Household Expenditure Survey commodity groups, as shown in Table 7.1. As mentioned above, the household survey uses 60 commodity groups, 10 of which relate to food. Wholesale tax rates for other commodity groups were of course set to zero.

A Consumption Tax

Consider next the case of a consumption tax, which is imposed on the tax exclusive price rather than the wholesale price. If t denotes the tax rate, then $p_I = p_E(1+t)$, and if this rate increases by the amount Δt, the proportionate increase in the price is now given by:

$$\dot{p} = \frac{\Delta t}{1+t} \tag{7.28}$$

Comparison of equations (7.27) and (7.28) shows, as expected, that a given tax rate change imposes a smaller price change for a wholesale tax compared with a sales tax, reflecting the different tax bases. The introduction of a sales tax from a base of a zero rate thus implies that the proportionate price change is simply equal to the tax rate, t.

A Change in the Tax Structure

Consider next the effect of a transition from a wholesale tax to a consumption tax, involving a change in both the tax rate and the tax base. Substituting for $p_E = (1+m)\, p_W$, the new price, following conversion from a wholesale tax to a GST and a change in the tax rate of Δt, is given by $p_W\,(1+m)\,(1+t+\Delta t)$. Hence, the proportionate price change, measured from the price given in equation (15.15) is given by:

$$\dot{p} = \frac{(1+m)\,(1+t+\Delta t)}{1+m+t} - 1 \qquad (7.29)$$

which can be simplified to give:

$$\dot{p} = \frac{tm + (1+m)\,\Delta t}{1+m+t} \qquad (7.30)$$

Hence the percentage price change resulting exclusively from a change in the tax base, where $\Delta t = 0$, is given by $tm/\,(1+m+t)$.

In several cases, such as alcohol, tobacco and motor vehicles, the pre-GST taxes were left in place and GST was added. If t represents the pre-GST rate expressed as a wholesale tax and if t^* now represents the tax-exclusive GST rate, the tax inclusive price is $p_W\,(1+m+t)\,(1+t^*)$. Hence the proportionate price increase, $(p_I - p_E)\,/p_E$, can be shown to be:

$$\dot{p} = t^* + \frac{t\,(1+t^*)}{1+m} \qquad (7.31)$$

This is the price change used for those particular groups when examining the post-GST structure. When examining the once-for-all change in these cases, it can be shown that the appropriate proportionate change for these groups is the same as in equation (7.28).

Table 7.2: Pre-GST Indirect Taxes

no.	y	CV	CV/y	EV	EV/y
1	284.40	15.34	0.0539	14.59	0.0513
2	332.20	17.95	0.0540	17.07	0.0514
3	387.80	21.02	0.0542	19.99	0.0515
4	505.60	27.39	0.0542	26.07	0.0516
5	566.20	30.57	0.0540	29.10	0.0514
6	624.90	33.71	0.0539	32.11	0.0514
7	766.60	40.93	0.0534	39.03	0.0509
8	876.80	46.55	0.0531	44.42	0.0507
9	1121.70	58.33	0.0520	55.77	0.0497

7.3.2   Empirical Estimates

The pre-GST indirect tax system can therefore be regarded as imposing a set of price increases, compared with a situation of no taxes, given by equation (7.27) with $t = 0$ and Δt equal to the rate as specified in Table 7.1, with all other values of $\dot{p}$ set equal to zero. The welfare changes, expressed in dollars per week, for each income group are given in Table 7.2. The values of y given in the first column correspond to the average weekly total expenditure of households in the specified income group. These total expenditures are assumed to remain fixed when the tax system is changed; only the allocation between commodity groups changes. The nine groups correspond to the groups in the 1993-4 Household Expenditure Survey. The compensating and equivalent variations are given, along with the values expressed as proportions of total expenditure.

It can be seen from Table 7.2 that, except for the slight reductions in the highest three groups, there is very little variation in these ratios. It could, therefore, be argued that the pre-GST system of indirect taxes did not impose a systematically higher burden on lower-income households.

Following the introduction of the GST in New Zealand, the rates imposed on road vehicles, vehicle ownership expenses, tobacco products and alcohol were held constant. However, a uniform tax-exclusive rate of 0.10 was imposed on all goods and services, with the exception of residential rents, which have a zero rate. Presumably this zero rating of rents was because the implicit rental from owner-occupied housing remains untaxed. The New Zealand GST therefore has a very broad tax base compared with those of many countries which have a range of exemptions and zero rating, or which use lower rates (for example, in the case of food and also domestic fuel and power).

Two approaches to the analysis of the GST were carried out. First, as in the pre-GST calculations, a comparison was made of no taxes compared with the GST; results are given in Table 7.3. Secondly, the effects of the once-and-for-all transition were examined by using equation (7.28), with the values of t set at their pre-GST levels and the values of Δt calculated accordingly. In this case, it is necessary to allow the different tax base used where wholesale taxes are relevant. The results are given in Table 7.4.

Finally, the welfare effects of a modified GST structure are reported in Table 7.5, where exemptions are given for food (except meals outside the home) and domestic fuel and power. These groups are exempt (or have lower rates than the standard rate) in many countries. These exemptions have been examined using the standard GST rate of 0.10, which means that total revenue is lower. A revenue neutral comparison would involve a slightly higher rate, and consequently very slightly more progression than is shown in Table 7.5. However, these results support the point, often made in this context, that exemptions are an expensive method of purchasing a small amount of progression.

It should be stressed that when the Goods and Services Tax was introduced in New Zealand, comprehensive adjustments to transfer payments were also made.

7.4 Conclusions

This chapter has examined compensating and equivalent variations for a range of income groups, resulting from several types of price change. The method involved the use of the linear expenditure system, estimated for each of a range of income (total expenditure) groups.

The results confirm those of previous studies which found that indirect

Table 7.3: Post-GST Indirect Taxes

no.	y	CV	CV/y	EV	EV/y
1	284.40	31.86	0.1120	28.65	0.1007
2	332.20	37.40	0.1126	33.58	0.1011
3	387.80	43.94	0.1133	39.45	0.1017
4	505.60	57.57	0.1139	51.77	0.1024
5	566.20	64.40	0.1137	57.94	0.1023
6	624.90	71.18	0.1139	64.06	0.1025
7	766.60	86.82	0.1133	78.29	0.1021
8	876.80	99.19	0.1131	89.48	0.1020
9	1121.70	125.41	0.1118	113.53	0.1012

Table 7.4: Once-and-for-all Changes From GST

no.	y	CV	CV/y	EV	EV/y
1	284.40	14.46	0.0508	13.75	0.0483
2	332.20	17.05	0.0513	16.20	0.0488
3	387.80	20.13	0.0519	19.11	0.0493
4	505.60	26.59	0.0526	25.25	0.0499
5	566.20	29.87	0.0527	28.36	0.0501
6	624.90	33.11	0.0530	31.44	0.0503
7	766.60	40.70	0.0531	38.65	0.0504
8	876.80	46.77	0.0533	44.39	0.0506
9	1121.70	59.96	0.0535	56.93	0.0507

Table 7.5: Modified GST

no.	y	CV	CV/y	EV	EV/y
1	284.40	25.17	0.0885	22.99	0.0808
2	332.20	29.98	0.0902	27.29	0.0822
3	387.80	35.75	0.0922	32.51	0.0838
4	505.60	47.95	0.0948	43.55	0.0861
5	566.20	54.19	0.0957	49.20	0.0869
6	624.90	60.41	0.0967	54.84	0.0878
7	766.60	74.96	0.0978	68.06	0.0888
8	876.80	86.45	0.0986	78.54	0.0896
9	1121.70	111.13	0.0991	101.03	0.0901

taxes in New Zealand did not have a substantially larger impact on low-income groups than on high-income groups. Furthermore, the introduction of the Goods and Services Tax does not appear to be regressive.

Chapter 8

The Distributional Effects of Inflation

Distributional implications of inflation exist because of the fact that prices do not all change by the same proportion over time. If there is a systematic tendency for the price of those goods which form a relatively higher proportion of the total expenditure of low income households to increase relatively more than other goods, inflation produces adverse effects on the distribution of real income. The effect of differential price changes on welfare also depends on the extent to which households substitute away from those goods whose prices increase relatively more. Studies of inflation in other countries, using a variety of approaches, have found a small effect of this type; see Muellbauer (1974) for the UK, and Blinder and Esaki (1978), Stoker (1986), Slottje (1987) and Slesnick (1990) for the US.

This chapter examines the redistributive effect of price changes in Australia over the sixteen year period from 1980 to 1995, and the effects of inflation in New Zealand over the period 1993-5. The distributional effects of inflation are examined in two ways. First, it examines the way in which equivalent variations vary with household income. Secondly, values of several alternative measures of inequality are reported, for a range of degrees of aversion towards inequality. The inequality measures are based on the distribution of 'equivalent income', following the concept explored in detail by King (1983). Results are obtained for 'all households' and for the two separate categories of 'married with dependants' and 'married without dependants'. It should be borne in mind that the analysis is based entirely on consumption and therefore ignores wealth accumulation and changes in asset prices.

The estimates of the distributional effects are based on the use of the Linear Expenditure System, which is applied to each income group separately. This follows the approach set out in chapter 7. Muellbauer (1974) measured welfare changes using estimates of the Linear Expenditure System (LES), using estimates based on aggregate data; but even if only a single set of parameters is used, the ratio of the compensating and equivalent variations to total household expenditure is higher in lower-income groups if the price of 'necessities' increases by relatively more than that of 'luxuries'.

The cost of the present approach is that it involves a large increase in the number of parameters to be estimated, so that very strong restrictions are imposed. Estimation of the LES for each income group is based on the expressions obtained by Frisch (1959) for the elasticities of demand for additive utility functions, of which the LES is a special case. The empirical results reported here use the 16 commodity groups for which data are given in the Australian Household Expenditure Survey. In the New Zealand Household Expenditure Survey, 60 commodity groups are used.

Section 8.1 presents the expressions for compensating and equivalent variations in the case of the Linear Expenditure System. These are given in more detail in chapter 7. The effects of inflation in Australia are then examined in section 8.2. The approach involves the application of proportionate annual price changes, for each year in turn, to the LES utility function parameters estimated using data for 1989. Section 8.2 therefore considers the following question: what would be the effect on the welfare of 1989 households of applying alternative sets of proportionate price changes? The effects of inflation in New Zealand are examined in section 8.3.

8.1 Welfare Effects of Price Changes

This section briefly derives the expressions used to calculate the welfare effects of price changes using the linear expenditure system.

8.1.1 The Linear Expenditure System

The direct utility function takes the form:

$$U = \prod_i (x_i - \gamma_i)^{\beta_i} \tag{8.1}$$

where $x_i \geq 0$ denotes the consumption of good i; $0 \leq \beta_i \leq 1$; γ_i is the committed consumption of good i; and $\sum \beta_i = 1$. Define the terms A and B respectively as $\sum_i p_i \gamma_i$ and $\prod (p_i/\beta_i)^{\beta_i}$. The expenditure or cost function, $E(p,U)$, is defined as the minimum expenditure required to achieve U at prices p, and is:

$$E(p,U) = A + BU \tag{8.2}$$

8.1.2 Compensating and Equivalent Variations

Suppose that the vector of prices changes from p_0 to p_1. The compensating variation, CV, is the difference between the minimum expenditure required to achieve the original utility level, U_0, at the new price, p_1, and the initial total expenditure, y_0, so that $CV = E(p_1,U_0) - E(p_0,U_0)$. Using equation (8.2) this becomes:

$$CV = A_1 + B_1 U_0 - y_0 \tag{8.3}$$

where subscripts refer to the set of prices used. After substituting for $U_0 = (y_0 - A_0)/B_0$, this can be rearranged to give, as in Allen (1975):

$$CV = A_0 \left[\frac{A_1}{A_0} + \frac{B_1}{B_0} \left(\frac{y_0}{A_0} - 1 \right) \right] - y_0 \tag{8.4}$$

The term A_1/A_0 is a Laspeyres type of price index, using the committed consumption of each good as the weight. The term B_1/B_0 simplifies to $\prod (p_{1i}/p_{0i})^{\beta_i}$, which is a weighted geometric mean of price relatives.

The equivalent variation, EV, is the difference between the post-change total expenditure and the minimum expenditure required to achieve post-change utility at the pre-change prices, so that $EV = E(p_1,U_1) - E(p_0,U_1)$. Substituting for E using (8.2) gives:

$$EV = y_1 - (A_0 + B_0 U_1) \tag{8.5}$$

Substituting for U_1, using equation (8.2), into (8.5) and rearranging gives:

$$EV = y_1 - A_0 \left[1 + \frac{B_0}{B_1} \left(\frac{y_1}{A_0} - \frac{A_1}{A_0} \right) \right] \tag{8.6}$$

It is possible to calculate the compensating and equivalent variations, given y_0, y_1, the set of proportionate price changes and the coefficients β_i, along with the initial cost of committed expenditure for each good, $p_i \gamma_i$. Separate values of γ_i and p_i are not required.

8.1.3 Equivalent Incomes

Equivalent income is defined as the value of income, y_e, which, at some reference set of prices, p_r, gives the same utility as the actual income level. The use of equivalent incomes was explored in detail by King (1983), and examples using this income concept, allowing for labour supply variation, include Apps and Savage (1989), who used the 'almost ideal' demand system, and Fortin *et al.* (1993), who used the linear expenditure system. An early brief discussion of equivalent incomes using the linear expenditure system was provided by Roberts (1980).

As is usual in this type of static framework, income and total expenditure are treated as synonymous. In terms of the indirect utility function, y_e is therefore defined $V(p_r, y_e) = V(p, y)$. Using the expenditure or cost function gives:

$$y_e = E(p_r, V(p, y)) \tag{8.7}$$

For the linear expenditure system, this is found to be:

$$y_e = \sum_i p_{ri} \gamma_i + \left\{ \prod_i \left(\frac{p_{ri}}{p_i} \right)^{\beta_i} \right\} \left\{ y - \sum_j p_j \gamma_j \right\} \tag{8.8}$$

The effect on welfare of a change in prices and income can then be measured in terms of a change in equivalent incomes, from y_{0e} to y_{1e}, where, as before, the indices 0 and 1 refer to pre- and post-change values respectively.

Furthermore, values of a social welfare function can be calculated using the distribution of values of y_{0e} and y_{1e} so that, according to the value judgements implicit in the welfare function, a change can be judged in terms of its overall effect.

An important feature of equivalent income is that it ensures that alternative situations are evaluated using a common set of reference prices. Consider the use of pre-change prices as reference prices, so that $p_{ri} = p_{0i}$ for all i. In this case it can be shown that the post-change equivalent income is the value of actual income after the change less the value of the equivalent variation; that is, $y_{1e} = y_1 - EV$. Hence the results of the previous subsection can be used. For an application to the analysis of carbon taxation, see Cornwell and Creedy (1997).

8.2 Australian Price Changes

The annual percentage price changes for each of the 16 Household Expenditure Survey (HES) commodity groups over the period 1980 to 1995 are shown in Tables 8.1 and 8.2. The price index data for each subgroup were obtained from March publications of the Consumer Price Index (Australian Bureau of Statistics cat. no. 6401.0). A problem arises because the commodity groups used by the HES do not correspond to those used in compiling the consumer price index (CPI) data. In some cases an approximation only could be used; for example, 'personal care products' was used for 'toiletries and cosmetics'. In obtaining the price changes for each group, the subgroups were combined using weights given by the 'contribution to total CPI' data. The HES commodity group 'household capital goods' has no adequate CPI equivalent, so price data for this group were obtained from March publications of the House Building Materials Price Index (Australian Bureau of Statistics cat. no. 6408.0).

The higher inflation during the early and late 1980s, along with the generally lower inflation during the 1990s, is clearly shown in the table. The price changes show a wide dispersion across commodity groups. The changes in the CPI for the corresponding years are given by: 10.5, 9.4, 10.5, 11.5, 5.9,

Table 8.1: Price Changes

Year	H'ng Costs	Power	Food	Alcohol	Tobacco	Clothing	Equip
1980	7.60	15.20	15.00	5.60	6.00	6.70	6.35
1981	10.10	14.30	9.70	8.00	4.60	7.60	10.02
1982	11.10	15.70	7.70	9.70	8.70	7.00	8.12
1983	10.60	21.10	9.00	12.30	18.50	6.10	8.69
1984	6.80	7.10	8.70	9.00	22.00	6.10	6.88
1985	7.20	6.50	4.40	7.10	7.70	6.20	3.25
1986	9.00	5.80	8.30	8.30	13.60	8.30	10.20
1987	7.20	4.40	7.90	10.20	11.40	10.10	7.31
1988	6.60	5.90	4.60	7.80	8.00	7.10	7.55
1989	11.60	4.50	9.40	3.20	10.30	7.30	5.87
1990	17.00	4.30	6.20	7.50	12.40	5.20	6.04
1991	1.60	5.60	5.20	7.10	12.40	4.90	4.45
1992	-4.80	4.30	1.30	3.20	8.90	1.30	1.02
1993	-3.80	5.40	2.70	2.70	23.60	1.10	0.03
1994	-0.70	1.10	0.70	3.10	12.70	-1.10	2.94
1995	9.70	0.80	3.10	3.60	7.10	-0.10	1.37

Table 8.2: Price Changes

Year	Service	Hlth Care	Trans	E'tain	Pers Care	Mort	Cap Gds
1980	8.39	27.80	11.60	10.18	8.80	0.00	15.30
1981	12.79	2.10	10.90	8.21	14.45	0.00	10.30
1982	11.22	46.10	9.80	11.28	9.23	0.00	10.00
1983	11.92	22.50	13.60	9.55	15.55	0.00	6.70
1984	5.81	-25.30	7.20	4.84	6.90	0.00	7.70
1985	4.99	-21.90	5.80	2.82	7.12	0.00	8.20
1986	9.05	7.90	10.90	9.80	8.94	0.00	6.30
1987	5.59	26.90	11.20	9.25	11.38	0.00	6.80
1988	5.89	14.90	6.70	7.62	6.53	3.70	8.40
1989	5.85	11.80	2.70	4.24	4.24	15.70	10.90
1990	2.09	6.50	9.90	6.27	5.95	29.70	6.70
1991	3.74	13.10	4.50	4.34	6.35	-2.90	4.10
1992	3.34	20.10	2.90	0.44	2.96	-14.20	-0.60
1993	1.53	-2.40	1.80	2.25	2.11	-11.20	2.90
1994	2.18	4.70	1.70	1.60	3.05	-6.60	4.60
1995	1.10	5.80	3.60	2.86	2.53	22.80	3.10

4.4, 9.2, 9.4, 6.9, 6.8, 8.6, 4.9, 1.7, 1.2, 1.4, and 3.9.

The LES parameters for each of a range of total expenditure or income groups were obtained using the Household Expenditure Survey for 1989. The approach involved the application of proportionate annual price changes, for each year in turn, to the LES utility function parameters estimated using data for 1989. The results therefore consider the following question: what would be the effect on the welfare of 1989 households of applying alternative sets of proportionate price changes?

Results were obtained for 'all households', and for two further categories of 'married with dependants' and 'married without dependants'. In each case the first stage involves producing a matrix of budget shares. The average budget shares were calculated for each commodity group within each of a range of total expenditure groups. For 'all households', 29 total expenditure groups were used (giving 29 separate sets of LES parameter estimates from 464 budget shares), while for the other categories, 9 groups were used (giving 144 budget shares to be calculated). The need to calculate many budget shares meant that there were insufficient observations in order to disaggregate the data by other household composition groups. For example, it would have been of interest to consider pensioner households, but there are too few in the HES sample once they are divided into income groups.

The precise method of computing the parameter values, and the resulting elasticities, is discussed in more detail in chapter 7. This requires a specified variation in the Frisch parameter. Based on these studies, and Frisch's own conjectures, the following flexible specification has been found to be useful for the variation in ξ with y:

$$\log\left(-\xi\right) = a - \alpha \log\left(y + \theta\right) \tag{8.9}$$

Suitable parameter values were obtained by experimenting with a range of alternatives. As a starting point, values of ξ corresponding to various values of y, conforming with *a priori* beliefs based on the studies mentioned above, were used to estimate the parameters of (12.27) using an iterative method based on maximum likelihood. For 'all households', 'married with dependants', and 'married without dependants' respectively, the following sets of parameters were used for a, α and θ: 15.2, 1.227, 8595.44; 16.3, 1.35, 1200; and 16.1, 1.35, 2000.

8.2.1 Equivalent Variations

Values of equivalent variations, expressed as ratios of total expenditure, are given in Tables 8.3 to 8.8 for each year and total expenditure group. The arithmetic mean weekly expenditure in each group, measured in cents, is given in the first column of each table. The equivalent variations were evaluated at the mean total expenditure levels by applying the LES parameters appropriate to each group. If the percentage price changes were the same for each commodity group, the equivalent variations (expressed as ratios of total expenditure) would be the same for each total expenditure group. An initial idea of the distributional effect of the price changes can therefore be seen by reading down the columns for each year's price changes.

In the early 1980s the price changes suggest a small systematic higher burden faced by lower income groups. But by the middle to late 1980s this effect becomes negligible, and in some cases the burden faced by the middle income groups is slightly higher than for the lower income groups. There is some suggestion that the periods during which the relative burden borne by the lower income groups is higher coincide with the periods of higher increases in the CPI.

8.2.2 Inequality Measures

Any assessment of the redistributive impact of a change cannot escape the use of value judgements. For this reason it is useful to make such judgements explicit by computing a range of inequality measures, reflecting different degrees of aversion towards inequality. Hence, a second analysis was carried out where each set of price changes was applied in turn to each household in the HES (for the three relevant household decompositions). The resulting distribution of equivalent incomes was then obtained and inequality measures were based on that distribution. In calculating the equivalent income for each household, each household was assigned the LES parameter values and

Table 8.3: Ratio of EV to Total Expenditure: All Households 1980-87

	1980	1981	1982	1983	1984	1985	1986	1987
8000.00	0.107	0.090	0.103	0.106	0.058	0.040	0.081	0.081
11581.18	0.106	0.090	0.103	0.105	0.058	0.040	0.081	0.081
14417.82	0.106	0.089	0.103	0.105	0.057	0.039	0.081	0.082
17132.45	0.106	0.089	0.103	0.104	0.057	0.039	0.081	0.083
19732.05	0.105	0.088	0.103	0.104	0.056	0.039	0.081	0.083
22178.05	0.105	0.088	0.103	0.104	0.055	0.038	0.082	0.084
24684.80	0.104	0.088	0.103	0.104	0.055	0.038	0.082	0.084
27227.80	0.104	0.087	0.103	0.103	0.055	0.038	0.082	0.084
29749.50	0.104	0.087	0.103	0.103	0.054	0.038	0.082	0.084
32461.45	0.103	0.087	0.103	0.103	0.054	0.038	0.082	0.085
35035.60	0.103	0.087	0.103	0.103	0.054	0.038	0.082	0.085
37624.65	0.103	0.086	0.102	0.102	0.054	0.038	0.082	0.085
40547.80	0.102	0.086	0.102	0.102	0.054	0.038	0.082	0.085
43534.55	0.102	0.086	0.102	0.102	0.054	0.038	0.082	0.085
46464.40	0.102	0.086	0.101	0.101	0.054	0.038	0.082	0.085
49313.00	0.101	0.086	0.101	0.101	0.054	0.038	0.082	0.085
52223.65	0.101	0.086	0.101	0.101	0.054	0.039	0.082	0.085
55318.80	0.101	0.086	0.101	0.101	0.054	0.039	0.082	0.085
58561.85	0.101	0.086	0.101	0.100	0.054	0.039	0.082	0.085
61798.95	0.100	0.086	0.100	0.100	0.054	0.039	0.082	0.085
65172.60	0.100	0.086	0.100	0.100	0.054	0.039	0.082	0.085
68908.10	0.098	0.086	0.100	0.100	0.054	0.040	0.082	0.085
73162.50	0.099	0.086	0.099	0.099	0.054	0.040	0.082	0.085
78105.30	0.099	0.086	0.099	0.099	0.054	0.040	0.082	0.084
83574.05	0.099	0.086	0.099	0.099	0.054	0.040	0.082	0.084
89947.85	0.099	0.086	0.098	0.098	0.055	0.041	0.082	0.084
97849.60	0.099	0.086	0.097	0.098	0.055	0.042	0.082	0.084
109671.60	0.099	0.086	0.097	0.097	0.056	0.043	0.082	0.084
128647.82	0.100	0.087	0.096	0.095	0.057	0.044	0.081	0.083

Table 8.4: Ratio of EV to Total Expenditure: All Households 1988-95

	1988	1989	1990	1991	1992	1993	1994	1995
8000.00	0.060	0.074	0.075	0.047	0.017	0.016	0.013	0.039
11581.18	0.061	0.073	0.076	0.047	0.017	0.016	0.014	0.039
14417.82	0.061	0.073	0.076	0.047	0.017	0.015	0.014	0.039
17132.45	0.061	0.072	0.077	0.047	0.017	0.015	0.014	0.040
19732.05	0.062	0.072	0.077	0.047	0.017	0.014	0.014	0.040
22178.05	0.062	0.072	0.077	0.046	0.017	0.014	0.014	0.040
24684.80	0.062	0.071	0.078	0.046	0.017	0.014	0.014	0.040
27227.80	0.062	0.071	0.078	0.046	0.016	0.013	0.014	0.040
29749.50	0.063	0.071	0.078	0.046	0.016	0.013	0.014	0.041
32461.45	0.063	0.071	0.079	0.046	0.016	0.013	0.014	0.041
35035.60	0.063	0.070	0.079	0.046	0.016	0.013	0.014	0.041
37624.65	0.063	0.070	0.079	0.046	0.016	0.012	0.014	0.041
40547.80	0.063	0.070	0.079	0.046	0.016	0.012	0.014	0.041
43534.55	0.063	0.070	0.079	0.046	0.015	0.012	0.014	0.044
46464.40	0.064	0.069	0.079	0.046	0.015	0.012	0.014	0.041
49313.00	0.064	0.069	0.080	0.046	0.015	0.012	0.014	0.041
52223.65	0.064	0.069	0.080	0.045	0.015	0.012	0.014	0.040
55318.80	0.064	0.069	0.080	0.045	0.015	0.011	0.014	0.040
58561.85	0.064	0.069	0.080	0.045	0.014	0.011	0.014	0.040
61798.95	0.064	0.068	0.080	0.045	0.014	0.011	0.014	0.040
65172.60	0.064	0.068	0.080	0.045	0.014	0.011	0.014	0.040
68908.10	0.064	0.068	0.080	0.045	0.014	0.011	0.014	0.040
73162.50	0.064	0.068	0.080	0.045	0.013	0.011	0.014	0.040
78105.30	0.064	0.067	0.080	0.045	0.013	0.011	0.014	0.040
83574.05	0.064	0.067	0.080	0.045	0.013	0.011	0.014	0.040
89947.85	0.065	0.067	0.079	0.044	0.013	0.011	0.015	0.039
97849.60	0.065	0.067	0.079	0.044	0.013	0.012	0.015	0.039
109671.60	0.065	0.067	0.078	0.044	0.012	0.012	0.016	0.038
128647.82	0.066	0.068	0.077	0.044	0.011	0.013	0.017	0.037

Table 8.5: Ratio of EV to Total Expenditure: With Dependants 1980-87

	1980	1981	1982	1983	1984	1985	1986	1987
25000.00	0.103	0.087	0.102	0.104	0.055	0.038	0.081	0.083
38839.30	0.103	0.086	0.102	0.102	0.054	0.037	0.081	0.084
46515.30	0.103	0.086	0.102	0.102	0.053	0.037	0.081	0.084
53756.60	0.102	0.086	0.101	0.101	0.053	0.037	0.081	0.084
60933.60	0.102	0.085	0.101	0.100	0.052	0.038	0.081	0.084
67988.20	0.101	0.085	0.100	0.099	0.052	0.038	0.081	0.084
76808.00	0.101	0.085	0.100	0.099	0.052	0.038	0.081	0.084
88159.40	0.100	0.085	0.099	0.098	0.053	0.039	0.081	0.084
105928.60	0.100	0.086	0.098	0.097	0.054	0.041	0.081	0.084

Table 8.6: Ratio of EV to Total Expenditure: With Dependants 1988-95

	1988	1989	1990	1991	1992	1993	1994	1995
25000.00	0.062	0.073	0.082	0.046	0.015	0.012	0.013	0.043
38839.30	0.062	0.072	0.081	0.046	0.015	0.012	0.013	0.043
46515.30	0.063	0.072	0.081	0.045	0.014	0.011	0.013	0.042
53756.60	0.063	0.071	0.081	0.045	0.014	0.011	0.013	0.042
60933.60	0.063	0.071	0.081	0.045	0.014	0.010	0.013	0.042
67988.20	0.064	0.070	0.080	0.045	0.014	0.010	0.013	0.041
76808.00	0.064	0.069	0.080	0.045	0.013	0.010	0.014	0.041
88159.40	0.064	0.068	0.080	0.044	0.013	0.011	0.014	0.040
105928.60	0.065	0.069	0.079	0.044	0.012	0.011	0.015	0.039

Table 8.7: Ratio of EV to Total Expenditure: Without Dependants 1980-87

	1980	1981	1982	1983	1984	1985	1986	1987
15000.00	0.111	0.088	0.107	0.106	0.053	0.034	0.081	0.086
22657.15	0.109	0.087	0.106	0.105	0.052	0.034	0.081	0.086
28307.95	0.108	0.087	0.106	0.105	0.051	0.034	0.082	0.087
35304.95	0.106	0.086	0.106	0.103	0.051	0.035	0.082	0.087
43683.20	0.104	0.086	0.104	0.102	0.051	0.036	0.082	0.087
52104.40	0.102	0.085	0.103	0.101	0.051	0.037	0.082	0.087
61054.25	0.101	0.085	0.102	0.100	0.052	0.038	0.082	0.086
72974.15	0.100	0.086	0.101	0.100	0.053	0.039	0.082	0.086
91060.00	0.100	0.086	0.099	0.099	0.055	0.041	0.083	0.085

Table 8.8: Ratio of EV to Total Expenditure: Without Dependants 1988-95

	1988	1989	1990	1991	1992	1993	1994	1995
15000.00	0.062	0.071	0.071	0.050	0.024	0.018	0.015	0.036
22657.15	0.063	0.070	0.072	0.049	0.023	0.017	0.015	0.036
28307.95	0.064	0.070	0.073	0.049	0.022	0.015	0.015	0.037
35304.95	0.064	0.069	0.075	0.048	0.020	0.014	0.015	0.038
43683.20	0.065	0.068	0.076	0.047	0.018	0.013	0.015	0.038
52104.40	0.065	0.067	0.077	0.047	0.017	0.012	0.015	0.039
61054.25	0.065	0.067	0.078	0.046	0.016	0.012	0.015	0.039
72974.15	0.065	0.066	0.079	0.045	0.015	0.012	0.016	0.039
91060.00	0.065	0.065	0.078	0.045	0.015	0.013	0.016	0.038

elasticities corresponding to the income group in which it fell.

For the three groups of all households and couples with and without dependants, the number of observations were respectively 7191, 2524 and 2176. The measures calculated include Atkinson's (1970) measure, $A(\varepsilon)$, for various values of the inequality aversion parameter, ε, and the extended Gini measure, $G(v)$, following Yitzhaki (1983), where the parameter v has a similar role to that of ε. When $v = 2$, the value of $G(v)$ corresponds to the standard Gini inequality measure; for further discussion of these measures see, for example, Lambert (1993a).

The inequality measures are shown in Tables 8.9 to 8.11. The measures for each year can be compared with the 'base' value, which is the inequality of equivalent income with zero proportional price changes in each commodity group. For all households combined and for married with dependants, the highest inequality measure, for all degrees of aversion, is for 1983 price changes. This is the year which experienced the largest increase in the CPI over the period investigated. The value for those married without dependants is highest for 1980, which is also a high inflation year. The next highest inequality value for all households combined and married with dependants is consistently for 1982, irrespective of the measure used; this is also one of the years for which inflation is highest. The results for those married without dependants are not so clear cut, and it should be remembered that there are fewer observations in this group.

Table 8.9: Inequality Measures of Equivalent Income: All Households

Year	A(0.2)	A(0.8)	A(1.4)	G	G(1.2)	G(1.6)	G(2.4)
1980	0.0399	0.1582	0.2760	0.3474	0.1124	0.2560	0.4121
1981	0.0397	0.1577	0.2752	0.3468	0.1122	0.2556	0.4114
1982	0.0400	0.1584	0.2761	0.3479	0.1127	0.2565	0.4124
1983	0.0401	0.1587	0.2766	0.3482	0.1129	0.2568	0.4127
1984	0.0396	0.1574	0.2749	0.3464	0.1120	0.2552	0.4109
1985	0.0394	0.1567	0.2738	0.3456	0.1117	0.2545	0.4100
1986	0.0397	0.1574	0.2744	0.3466	0.1123	0.2556	0.4111
1987	0.0397	0.1573	0.2742	0.3467	0.1123	0.2556	0.4110
1988	0.0395	0.1567	0.2735	0.3459	0.1119	0.2549	0.4103
1989	0.0398	0.1581	0.2758	0.3473	0.1124	0.2560	0.4119
1990	0.0397	0.1572	0.2741	0.3465	0.1123	0.2555	0.4109
1991	0.0398	0.1577	0.2751	0.3470	0.1124	0.2558	0.4115
1992	0.0399	0.1581	0.2756	0.3475	0.1126	0.2562	0.4120
1993	0.0397	0.1576	0.2752	0.3468	0.1122	0.2555	0.4113
1994	0.0395	0.1569	0.2739	0.3460	0.1119	0.2549	0.4105
1995	0.0398	0.1577	0.2748	0.3470	0.1125	0.2559	0.4114
Base	0.0397	0.1573	0.2745	0.3465	0.1122	0.2554	0.4110

Table 8.10: Inequality: Married with Dependants

Year	A(0.2)	A(0.8)	A(1.4)	G	G(1.2)	G(1.6)	G(2.4)
1980	0.0250	0.0956	0.1634	0.2721	0.0911	0.2026	0.3210
1981	0.0250	0.0953	0.1629	0.2716	0.0909	0.2022	0.3204
1982	0.0252	0.0960	0.1640	0.2727	0.0914	0.2032	0.3215
1983	0.0253	0.0963	0.1645	0.2731	0.0916	0.2035	0.3221
1984	0.0249	0.0951	0.1629	0.2713	0.0907	0.2019	0.3202
1985	0.0248	0.0946	0.1620	0.2706	0.0904	0.2014	0.3193
1986	0.0250	0.0953	0.1628	0.2717	0.0910	0.2023	0.3204
1987	0.0250	0.0953	0.1628	0.2717	0.0910	0.2024	0.3204
1988	0.0248	0.0948	0.1620	0.2709	0.0907	0.2017	0.3196
1989	0.0251	0.0958	0.1637	0.2725	0.0912	0.2029	0.3214
1990	0.0251	0.0958	0.1636	0.2724	0.0913	0.2030	0.3212
1991	0.0250	0.0955	0.1631	0.2719	0.0911	0.2025	0.3207
1992	0.0251	0.0957	0.1634	0.2722	0.0912	0.2028	0.3210
1993	0.0249	0.0952	0.1628	0.2715	0.0908	0.2021	0.3203
1994	0.0248	0.0948	0.1620	0.2709	0.0906	0.2016	0.3196
1995	0.0251	0.0959	0.1637	0.2725	0.0913	0.2031	0.3214
Base	0.0250	0.0952	0.1627	0.2716	0.0909	0.2022	0.3203

Table 8.11: Inequality: Married without Dependants

Year	A(0.2)	A(0.8)	A(1.4)	G	G(1.2)	G(1.6)	G(2.4)
1980	0.0349	0.1354	0.2315	0.3282	0.1071	0.2426	0.3880
1981	0.0345	0.1338	0.2288	0.3263	0.1064	0.2411	0.3858
1982	0.0349	0.1352	0.2308	0.3281	0.1072	0.2427	0.3877
1983	0.0348	0.1348	0.2304	0.3276	0.1069	0.2422	0.3872
1984	0.0343	0.1331	0.2281	0.3253	0.1060	0.2404	0.3848
1985	0.0342	0.1326	0.2268	0.3247	0.1058	0.2399	0.3840
1986	0.0344	0.1335	0.2279	0.3260	0.1063	0.2409	0.3854
1987	0.0346	0.1339	0.2285	0.3266	0.1066	0.2415	0.3860
1988	0.0344	0.1333	0.2274	0.3258	0.1063	0.2408	0.3851
1989	0.0348	0.1347	0.2300	0.3275	0.1070	0.2422	0.3871
1990	0.0343	0.1329	0.2267	0.3253	0.1063	0.2406	0.3845
1991	0.0347	0.1344	0.2295	0.3271	0.1067	0.2418	0.3866
1992	0.0348	0.1349	0.2306	0.3277	0.1069	0.2423	0.3874
1993	0.0346	0.1342	0.2295	0.3268	0.1066	0.2415	0.3864
1994	0.0344	0.1335	0.2280	0.3259	0.1063	0.2409	0.3854
1995	0.0345	0.1336	0.2280	0.3262	0.1066	0.2413	0.3855
Base	0.0345	0.1337	0.2283	0.3262	0.1065	0.2412	0.3857

For lower degrees of aversion towards inequality, there are several sets of annual price changes for which the inequality of equivalent incomes is less than or equal to that of the 'base' value. For all degrees of aversion, the price changes for 1985, 1988 and 1994, for all households, produce reductions relative to the base value. Hence the price changes in those years can be said to impose a higher burden on the higher income groups. The results for couples with and without dependants are very similar, but the former has an additional year, 1984, for which inequality is lower than the base value. The same is true of 1984, 1986 and 1990 for those without dependants.

8.3 Inflation in New Zealand

This section examines welfare measures in each income group resulting from imposing the percentage price changes for each commodity group experienced over the period 1993-4 and 1994-5. During these periods the consumer price index (CPI) increased by annual rates of 0.026 and 0.031 for the two periods respectively, but this involved a distribution of changes over commodity groups.

Information is available on price indices for 320 commodity groups, along with the weights used in the CPI, for December 1993, 1994 and 1995. These are available in unpublished data on the *INFOS Consumer Price Index – All Sections*, produced by Statistics New Zealand. The first task is to convert these 320 indices into price changes relating to the classifications used in the Household Expenditure Survey. Where there was no information corresponding to the Household Expenditure Survey category, the CPI change over the period was assigned to the Household Expenditure Survey group. The resulting proportionate changes are given in Table 8.12. This shows that even over a single year, there is a wide dispersion in the price increases over commodity groups.

The compensating variations resulting from these changes are given in Tables 8.13 and 8.14, for 1993-4 and 1994-5 respectively. The changes for the earlier period do not show any systematic variation with income, but for the later period it can be seen that there is an increase in the compensating and equivalent variations, expressed as ratios of total expenditure, as the latter increases. However, the differences are small.

8.4 Conclusions

This chapter has examined the distributional effects of the differential price changes associated with inflation in Australia over the period 1980-95, using equivalent variations and equivalent incomes, and in New Zealand over the period 1993-5. The Linear Expenditure System was applied to a range of income groups rather than using a single set of parameters. The analysis was applied to all households in the Household Expenditure Survey, and for households with and without dependants. The price changes were found to impose a relatively higher burden on lower-income groups in some years, although in other years the higher-income groups were affected relatively more. The years when the inequality of equivalent incomes was highest coincide with years of high overall inflation.

Table 8.12: New Zealand Price Changes

no.	1993-4	no.	1993-4	no.	1994-5	no.	1994-5
1	0.026	31	0.009	1	0.031	31	-0.028
2	0.025	32	0.022	2	0.047	32	-0.026
3	-0.049	33	0.007	3	-0.058	33	-0.027
4	-0.019	34	0.026	4	-0.010	34	0.031
5	-0.031	35	0.026	5	-0.018	35	0.031
6	-0.009	36	0.011	6	0.013	36	0.080
7	0.001	37	0.052	7	0.027	37	-0.024
8	0.134	38	0.017	8	-0.012	38	0.022
9	-0.018	39	-0.004	9	-0.019	39	-0.032
10	0.001	40	0.026	10	0.017	40	0.031
11	0.120	41	0.003	11	0.085	41	0.032
12	0.110	42	0.021	12	0.184	42	0.038
13	0.026	43	0.029	13	0.031	43	0.066
14	0.011	44	-0.010	14	0.021	44	0.018
15	0.011	45	0.004	15	0.021	45	0.013
16	0.006	46	0.026	16	0.012	46	0.031
17	0.046	47	0.015	17	0.054	47	0.065
18	-0.009	48	0.011	18	-0.037	48	0.014
19	-0.009	49	0.035	19	-0.037	49	0.028
20	0.030	50	0.026	20	0.023	50	0.031
21	0.026	51	0.026	21	0.031	51	0.031
22	0.057	52	0.026	22	0.006	52	0.031
23	0.005	53	0.088	23	-0.034	53	0.054
24	-0.024	54	0.026	24	-0.005	54	0.031
25	0.026	55	-0.011	25	0.031	55	0.073
26	-0.001	56	0.026	26	-0.015	56	0.031
27	-0.013	57	0.026	27	-0.008	57	0.031
28	-0.027	58	0.026	28	-0.014	58	0.031
29	-0.042	59	0.026	29	-0.043	59	0.031
30	-0.017	60	0.026	30	0.041	60	0.031

Table 8.13: New Zealand Price Changes 1993-4

no.	y	CV	CV/y	EV	EV/y
1	284.40	8.50	0.0299	8.28	0.0291
2	332.20	9.80	0.0295	9.56	0.0288
3	387.80	11.25	0.0290	10.97	0.0283
4	505.60	14.44	0.0286	14.06	0.0278
5	566.20	16.19	0.0286	15.76	0.0278
6	624.90	17.78	0.0284	17.30	0.0277
7	766.60	22.01	0.0287	21.40	0.0279
8	876.80	25.13	0.0287	24.42	0.0279
9	1121.70	32.84	0.0293	31.83	0.0284

Table 8.14: New Zealand Price Changes 1994-5

no.	y	CV	CV/y	EV	EV/y
1	284.40	8.65	0.0304	8.38	0.0295
2	332.20	10.27	0.0309	9.95	0.0299
3	387.80	12.17	0.0314	11.78	0.0304
4	505.60	16.33	0.0323	15.78	0.0312
5	566.20	18.58	0.0328	17.94	0.0317
6	624.90	20.72	0.0332	20.00	0.0320
7	766.60	26.17	0.0341	25.23	0.0329
8	876.80	30.41	0.0347	29.29	0.0334
9	1121.70	40.41	0.0360	38.79	0.0346

However, the measured effects on inequality are low: the highest increase in inequality over the 'base' value as a result of differential price changes is less than 1 per cent. Hence, over the period investigated, inflation does not appear to have had substantial redistributive effects, and in some cases a small 'progressive' effect was observed. In considering these results, it should be remembered that the analysis was restricted to household consumption, and did not consider the distributional implications of capital gains resulting from changes in asset prices, particularly housing prices, over the period.

Part III

Income Dynamics

Chapter 9

Dynamics of Income Distribution

Information about income in a single period such as a year is often inadequate for policy purposes. It is often required to have details of the distribution over a much longer period, or to know something about the process of relative income change and the factors associated with such dynamics. This chapter considers some of these longitudinal aspects. The basic sources of longitudinal data are discussed in section 9.1. Section 9.2 examines the possibility of obtaining some information about mobility indirectly from cross-sectional data. Section 9.3 considers sample attrition, which is an important form of non-response in panel surveys. Finally, section 9.4 discusses the question of the appropriate unit of analysis in panel surveys.

It should be recognised that many policy questions cannot be answered simply by collecting longitudinal data. Policy analysis often involves aspects which cannot be directly measured, even if there were no constraints on data collection. For example, it may be desired to know the likely effect on lifetime incomes of introducing a certain tax or transfer payment. Examples include introducing a government pension scheme, or changing the tax treatment of contributions towards, and revenue from, private superannuation schemes.

Furthermore, in considering labour market or tax policies it is desirable to specify a counterfactual so that some assessment can be made of the proposed policy in relation to an alternative, which may be 'no change'. A further desirable feature of policy analyses is that in many cases a constraint of revenue neutrality (suitably defined) should be imposed, or the implications of revenue changes examined explicitly.

Such policy analyses require the use of some kind of simulation model. It is therefore not surprising that much energy has been devoted to the production of simulation models, most of which generate results for a specified cohort of individuals. These range from the smaller models designed to examine the relationship between annual and lifetime income inequality, and the influence of a limited range of taxes and transfers, to the larger micro-simulation models which exploit the rich detail provided by household surveys. These models cannot be examined in the present chapter, but discussions of a variety of models and issues can be found in Gallagher (1990), Hellwig (1990), Hancock and Sutherland (1992) and Orcutt *et al.* (1986). For Australian simulation models, see also Atkinson *et al.* (1994), Cameron and Creedy (1994) and Harding (1994). An early study is Blinder (1974).

9.1   Longitudinal Data Sources

Longitudinal income data for selected cohorts can be obtained using three basic methods. First, official data which allow individuals to be identified but which have been collected for other purposes, may be used to produce earnings histories. This has been a popular approach, largely because it allows information to be compiled relatively cheaply and quickly. Secondly, in a panel survey consisting of multiple 'waves', a sample of households and individuals is surveyed repeatedly over a long period. This is obviously more time consuming but allows data on a wider range of characteristics to be collected. Sometimes the two methods have been combined, by going forwards and backwards, in order to lengthen the data series for some cohorts. These methods are discussed briefly below. A third method is to use retrospective surveys which ask individuals about various job characteristics and changes in earnings over their earlier working lives. However, the problems associated with the difficulty of recalling past details sufficiently accurately, combined with the *ex post* rationalisation of past events, have meant that this method has not been extensively used; see, however, Creedy and Whitfield (1988).

9.1.1 Types of Survey

Faced with the need to obtain some longitudinal data fairly quickly, it may, as suggested above, be possible to collect information from existing official data sources. For example, income tax records can be used to trace the incomes of selected individuals over several previous years. However, information is not available for those with taxable incomes below the tax-free threshold, and some individuals may move in and out of the sample. Nevertheless, the income data are generally more accurate than those obtained from household surveys. A further limitation of tax data is that they do not contain much information about the characteristics of individuals, such as occupation, education, household circumstances and hours worked. On balance, however, tax files can provide a quick method of collecting data which, in the absence of other sources, can provide valuable information on income mobility.

Limited longitudinal data may also be obtained from records which are held as part of the administration of social insurance schemes. Some government pension schemes, such as that in the UK, require information about the earnings and contributions history of individuals to be retained in order to calculate the pension on retirement. The administration of sickness and unemployment benefits may also involve the storage of longitudinal information about all individuals in the labour force, not only those who claim benefits. Such data, like tax records, can provide a useful source of information about mobility and can be produced quickly and relatively cheaply.

A possible problem in this context is that the earnings information may be truncated or censored; that is, if there are upper and lower earnings limits relevant to the administration of social insurance schemes, earnings outside the range may not be recorded. Similarly, information may be available in a particular year only if a minimum number or value of insurance contributions has been paid.

Longitudinal data may also be obtained from employment or labour market surveys. *The New Earnings Survey* in the UK obtains information about earnings in a wide range of occupations, and an advantage of such data is that information about skill levels, occupation and industry is usually available. This survey obtained information about the earnings of individuals in two consecutive years and the data, collected from employers, are relatively accurate. However, such data are generally restricted to one job for each individual and may be available only if a minimum number of weeks were worked. Such employment surveys often collect data about earnings in just one week in each year, rather than annual earnings, which can lead to biased estimates of the mobility process.

For more extensive information over a longer period, which provides details of changes in the household characteristics of individuals, there is really no alternative to a properly designed longitudinal or panel survey involving the repeated questioning of individuals. Although initial costs are higher, the subsequent waves of a panel survey are usually cheaper than a typical cross-sectional survey, since contact has already been established with the sample. For a summary of mobility data and results, see Atkinson *et al.* (1992) and Creedy (1994).

9.2   Synthetic Cohorts

Most countries have cross-sectional data which provide information about the distribution of income in various age groups at a single point in time. The question arises of whether it is possible to make inferences from such cross-sectional data about the dynamics of income over the life cycle. At first sight this may appear to be an impossible task as a cross-section contains no direct information about dynamics. However, it may be possible to make some inferences, based on a simple specification of the process of earnings change. Such estimates may be supplemented by short-term longitudinal data. In considering this problem it is useful to distinguish between general changes in earnings, governing the variation in average income with age for members of a cohort, and the process of relative earnings change which influences the pattern of individual movements within the distribution and hence its dispersion. These are considered in turn below.

9.2.1 The Age-earnings Profile

Systematic variations in earnings over the life cycle of a cohort of individuals can be decomposed into those arising from the process of ageing and those resulting from the passage of calendar time. Such age- and time-related factors can interact with cohort effects which arise from particular characteristics of each cohort, such as its size. These different influences are very hard to disentangle, and very strong restrictions have to be imposed on models in order to identify separate components, even when longitudinal data are available. If cohort-specific factors are negligible, and 'time effects' arise from constant rates of inflation and productivity growth which influence all cohorts equally, then the observed relationship between average income and age in cross-sectional data can be translated into a profile for a selected cohort.

In the general age-earnings model suggested by Aitchison and Brown (1957), and extended by Fase (1970) and Creedy (1985), individual i's earnings in year t, y_{it}, are given by:

$$y_{it} = y_{it-1} \exp \left[f\left(t\right) + u_{it} \right] \tag{9.1}$$

where $f(t)$ is a function of age; and u is a stochastic term governing relative changes. For the simple case where the u_{it}s are independent of previous values and current income, u is $N(0, \sigma_u^2)$. This kind of process is known as Gibrat's Law. If the variance of the distribution of proportional changes is constant over time, it can be shown that the variance of the logarithms of incomes grows linearly with age. Furthermore the slope of the relationship between inequality in each age group and age is equal to the variance of relative earnings changes. Many cross-sectional surveys do in fact reveal an approximately linear growth in relative earnings inequality with age.

This kind of approach has been used by Creedy (1982) to examine pensions in the UK; and direct and indirect taxes over the lifetime in Australia were examined by Cameron and Creedy (1994).

If a time series of cross-sectional data sets is available, then the various surveys can be combined to produce a set of pseudo cohort profiles. The experience of separate cohorts can be traced although the same individuals are not observed in each cross-sectional survey. This may be more difficult if only grouped data are available, depending on the time interval between surveys and the width of the age groups. This approach was used by Doll (1971) in an early study of the effects of smoking on lung cancer, and has been used to examine earnings profiles by Ruggles and Ruggles (1977), and age-wealth profiles by Shorrocks (1975a).

These approaches contrast with the production of synthetic cohorts in the larger scale microsimulation models, such as that of Harding (1994). In Harding's model, individuals in a single cohort consisting of 2000 males and 2000 females are 'aged' with attention paid to many demographic details such as marriage, divorce, births, children leaving home, schooling, and labour force entry and exit. The probabilities of the various demographic transitions are also based largely on available cross-sectional data and draw on a wide variety of sources. The final result of the simulations is a very large rectangular data set which can form the basis of a wide range of analyses.

9.3   Sample Attrition in Panel Surveys

It is widely known that non-response in a cross-sectional survey can lead to bias in the estimation of models. This arises if the selection of individuals (either in the initial design of the survey or in the non-response) is not random with respect to the heterogeneity characteristics of the population. Methods designed to deal with such sample selection bias were pioneered by Griliches *et al.* (1978) and Heckman (1979, 1990). The probability of an individual being included in the sample can be regarded as a function of a set of variables. These variables include all those which also influence the conditional mean of the dependent variable, along with additional variables which do not influence the dependent variable but only affect the selection process. This implies that the observed variables in the model to be estimated are correlated with the appropriate 'error' terms, resulting in the bias.

Sample attrition in panel surveys, where individuals leave the panel after several waves and do not return, is an additional type of non-response which can lead to bias. Other types of non-response may also be important, such as when information is missing on one or more variables for some individuals or when individuals are missing from one or more waves but return later. The US *Panel Study of Income Dynamics* had an initial non-response of 24 per cent in 1968, and after 17 years the cumulative non-response exceeded 50 per cent: for further discussion of attrition in the context of this survey, see Becketti *et al.* (1988).

The majority of statistical and econometric techniques require 'rectangular' data sets, so it is not surprising that most analyses have tended to ignore the problem. The methods designed to deal with selectivity bias, based on maximum likelihood or Heckman's two-stage procedure, are computationally much more difficult with panel data. In a pioneering study, Hausman and Wise (1979) estimated earnings functions using data from the Gary Income Maintenance experiment, which experienced an attrition rate of over one-third. Although they found a small correlation between earnings and the probability of attrition, the allowance for bias affected the estimates of some of the model's coefficients quite substantially. The Hausman and Wise method involved only two periods (given the short length of the income maintenance experiment), and has only recently been extended to longer periods; see Ridder (1990) and Verbeek and Nijman (1992). Selection problems have been treated in the analysis of labour demand and supply and in consumption and investment behaviour, but they have not so far been handled in studies of relative earnings mobility. This presents a very difficult challenge from both a theoretical and a computational point of view.

Another potential problem with longitudinal data concerns measurement errors. This has been extensively examined in the standard regression context, but is not so well understood in the context of panel surveys, although analyses include Griliches and Hausman (1986) and Lillard and Willis (1978). However, Duncan and Hill (1985a) compared individuals' reported earnings with those in employers' records, and found that the errors were correlated over two successive years and the variances were not constant. Both these findings violate the assumptions usually imposed in econometric modelling.

On the econometrics of panel data, see the various papers in Matyas and Sevestre (1992) and the two-volume collection in Maddala (1993). Useful full-length treatments include Chamberlain (1984) and Hsiao (1986). On measurement errors, see also Bound *et al.* (1990) and Rodgers *et al.* (1991). Further studies concerned with attrition include Abeles and Wise (1980), Olsen (1982), Stasny (1986), Robins and West (1986), and Christian and Frischmann (1989).

9.4   The Unit of Analysis in Panel Surveys

Changes in the structure of households take place over time for a variety of reasons, such as births, deaths, marriage, divorce, re-marriage, and children leaving or entering the household. For example, United States data have shown that approximately 20 per cent of households experience a change in composition during a period of one year, with the proportion increasing to over half during a five-year period; see Duncan and Hill (1985a).

A large proportion of changes in the economic status of individuals has been found to be associated with changes in household composition. Early panel studies attempted to allow for such changes by identifying so-called 'longitudinal households'. This essentially involves the classification of households according to whether they are in some sense the same over a period of time, and uses arbitrary rules based on the 'head' of the household, or the majority of members; see McMillen and Herriot (1984).

The problem with this kind of approach, in addition to the arbitrary nature of the definition, is that analyses thereby ignore the experience of many individuals who are deemed not to have been members of a longitudinal household. Furthermore, there is a great deal of heterogeneity within the group of households which are deemed to have remained the same.

A more satisfactory approach to dealing with compositional changes is to regard the individual rather than the household as the primary unit of analysis. This involves attributing to each individual the characteristics of the household in which each person lives. The case for this approach has been strongly made by Duncan and Hill (1985b), who show how the data storage problems can easily be overcome. Changes in household composition become attributes of individuals which can be treated in further analysis like other characteristics (such as age, education and occupation), rather than being treated as one of the criteria for sample selection.

This type of approach also has the advantage of allowing for greater flexibility. Thus, the household can, where required, easily be made the unit of measurement in studies of inequality or poverty. However, given that the focus of social policy is usually on individuals, it is more informative to consider, say, what proportion of individuals lived in poor households over a period, rather than the proportion of households that remained poor over the same period.

9.5 Conclusions

This chapter has discussed the sources of longitudinal data and problems associated with them. Although longitudinal data are clearly desirable, it is sometimes possible to use cross-sectional data on age and earnings to estimate simple models of age-earnings profiles. Indirect information concerning relative earnings mobility can often be obtained in the same way. Such models and estimates can be useful for the analysis of taxes and transfers over the life cycle, and particularly the analysis of alternative pension and superannuation schemes using simulation methods. Ideally, genuine longitudinal data are desirable, and a useful source consists of data collected as part of the administration of income taxation. Such data are in fact used to examine relative income mobility in New Zealand in chapter 11.

Chapter 10

Mobility and Inequality

Income distribution comparisons between countries are typically made using cross-sectional data. In most cases data limitations rule out comparisons on the basis of a longer-period measure of income, although limited information about relative income mobility is sometimes available. The question therefore arises of whether some general statements regarding alternative distributions can be made on the basis of cross-sectional data combined with summary measures of mobility. This requires an analysis of the relationships among alternative types of distribution. In particular, the aim of this chapter is to examine the general validity of the following two statements:

> *Statement 1.* If two countries have broadly similar degrees of income mobility, cross-sectional comparisons provide a good indication of differences in lifetime inequality.
>
> *Statement 2.* If an increase in cross-sectional inequality in a country is associated with an increase in income mobility, lifetime inequality increases by less than cross-sectional inequality.

Both of these statements may at first sight appear to be quite reasonable, and if true they would be very useful. The first extends the range of international comparisons that can be made with limited data, and the second statement suggests, for example, that greater labour market flexibility has a smaller impact on inequality when a longer-period measure is considered.

Both statements can be found in a lengthy report by the OECD (1996). Thus, 'Countries with higher cross-sectional earnings inequality do not appear to have correspondingly higher relative earnings mobility, so that international differences in earnings inequality at a single point in time probably provide a good approximation of the differences in life-time earnings inequality' (1996, p.60; see also pp.83, 94); and 'If the forces causing wider earnings dispersion within a single year also create a more fluid labour market, in which the relative position of workers within the earnings distribution varies more over time, then life-time inequality of earnings will increase by less than what is observed cross-sectionally' (1996, p.76). However, it was acknowledged that, 'the analysis [of mobility] undertaken in the chapter is exploratory. In particular, attempts to compare earnings mobility across different countries are hindered by fundamental conceptual and empirical difficulties' (1996, p.59).

This chapter shows that the two statements given above are not justified. It is shown that attention must be given to the specification of processes of relative earnings mobility. In particular, the distinction between cross-sectional distributions, which necessarily contain a large number of cohorts and are influenced by the age distribution of the population, and lifetime earnings distributions of particular cohorts need to be clarified. Furthermore, allowance must be made for the systematic variation in earnings over the life cycle of each cohort. Mobility estimates that are based on a sample containing many different cohorts can be highly misleading.

It is difficult to provide explicit formal results concerning the relationships among the various distributions, even with very simple specifications of the mobility process. For this reason, this chapter illustrates some of the problems of making comparisons of the type indicated above when using a simple model. The model is kept deliberately as simple as possible in order to highlight the essential elements of the comparisons. Section 10.1 provides a description of the model and gives some analytical results. Section 10.2 presents the results of simulations using the model.

10.1 A Simple Model

Consider a cohort of individuals, each of whom enters the labour market at the same age. Let y_{it} and m_t denote respectively the income of individual i ($i = 1, ..., N$), and the geometric mean income (defined by $\log m_t = \frac{1}{N}\sum_i \log y_{it}$) in age group t ($t = 1, ..., T$). If, furthermore, z_{it} is the logarithm of the ratio of person i's income to the geometric mean, so that $z_{it} = \log(y_{it}/m_{it})$, suppose that:

$$z_{it} = z_{i,t-1} + u_{it} \tag{10.1}$$

where u_{it} is a random variable that is assumed to be independently normally distributed as $N(0, \sigma_u^2)$. Hence the dynamic process of relative proportional income changes from year to year is a simple Markov process which, in the present context, is known as a Gibrat process. Taking variances of (10.1) gives:

$$\sigma_t^2 = \sigma_1^2 + (t - 1)\sigma_u^2 \tag{10.2}$$

and the variance of logarithms at age t, σ_t^2, is a linear function of age.

Suppose also that, in addition to the random proportionate change determined by u_{it}, all incomes are subject to growth at the constant rate α. This means that the arithmetic mean of logarithms of income at age t, μ_t, is given by:

$$\mu_t = \mu_1 + (t - 1)\alpha \tag{10.3}$$

10.1.1 Lifetime Income

The lifetime income of individual i, Y_i, is given (ignoring discounting) by:

$$Y_i = \sum_{t=1}^{T} \exp(z_{it} + \mu_t) \tag{10.4}$$

so that:

$$\log Y_i = (z_{i1} + \mu_1) + \log \left[1 + \sum_{t=2}^{T} \exp\left\{\sum_{s=2}^{t} u_{is} + \alpha\,(t-1)\right\}\right] \qquad (10.5)$$

and the variance of logarithms of lifetime income, $\sigma^2_{(T)}$, is equal to:

$$\sigma^2_{(T)} = \sigma^2_1 + V\,[X] \qquad (10.6)$$

where X is the second term on the right-hand side of (10.6) and depends in a rather awkward way on α, T and of course σ^2_u. Further progress can be made by using the linear approximation, $V\,[f\,(u)] = f'\,(E\,(u))^2\,V\,(u)$, and noting that all u_{it} are from the same distribution with mean 0, an approximation to (10.6) is given by:

$$\sigma^2_{(T)} = \sigma^2_1 + \sigma^2_u \left[\frac{\sum_{t=2}^{T} \exp\left\{\alpha\,(t-1)\right\}}{1 + \sum_{t=2}^{T} \exp\left\{\alpha\,(t-1)\right\}}\right]^2 \qquad (10.7)$$

This can be further rearranged to give:

$$\sigma^2_{(T)} = \sigma^2_1 + \sigma^2_u \left[1 + e^{\alpha}\left(\sum_{t=2}^{T} \exp\,(\alpha t)\right)^{-1}\right]^{-2} \qquad (10.8)$$

If there is no mobility, then of course the variance of logarithms of lifetime income is the same as that in the first year. Otherwise it may be written as $\sigma^2_{(T)} = \sigma^2_1 + (t^* - 1)\,\sigma^2_u$, where t^* can be regarded in terms of a number of 'equivalent years', by comparison with the expression for σ^2_t in equation (10.2). For treatment of the coefficient of variation of lifetime income, see Creedy (1985, p.101-118). It is therefore possible for the ranking of countries according to $\sigma^2_{(T)}$ to change as the length of time over which incomes are measured, T, is gradually increased.

10.1.2   The Cross-sectional Distribution

The cross-sectional distribution consists of individuals from each of the T cohorts. In order to avoid problems arising from growth and other factors leading to labour market differences between cohorts, which produce changes in the cross-sectional distribution over time as different cohorts become older, suppose that each cohort has a similar age-profile of geometric mean income; hence α is the same for all cohorts. The cross-sectional distribution is obtained by aggregating over many cohorts, which requires an age distribution to be specified. Suppose that h_t denotes the proportion of the population who are aged t in a given time period, so that $\sum_{t=1}^{T} h_t = 1$. The mean of logarithms in the cross section, μ, is therefore equal to $\sum_{t=1}^{T} \mu_t h_t$ and the variance of logarithms, σ^2, is given, following the standard decomposition into within- and between-age components, by:

$$\sigma^2 = \sum_{t=1}^{T} h_t \sigma_t^2 + \sum_{t=1}^{T} h_t \left(\mu_t - \mu\right)^2 \tag{10.9}$$

For $t \geq 2$, the terms in μ_t and σ_t^2 are given by simple expressions involving α and σ_u^2, so it is possible to expand equation (10.9). For example, expanding the first term, this becomes:

$$\sigma^2 = \sigma_1^2 + \sigma_u^2 \sum_{t=2}^{T} (t-1) h_t + \sum_{t=1}^{T} h_t \left(\mu_t - \mu\right)^2 \tag{10.10}$$

Hence, σ_1^2 provides a lower bound to the variance of logarithms in both cross-sectional and lifetime contexts, and σ_u^2 affects the variance of logarithms in the cross-sectional distribution only through the second term in (10.10). For an extensive treatment of the problem of aggregation over ages under alternative assumptions about the age-income profile and the age distribution, see Creedy (1985, pp.84-94).

10.1.3 Comparisons Between Distributions

A comparison of equations (10.7) and (10.9) shows immediately that in the extreme case where there is no relative income mobility within cohorts, then $\sigma_u^2 = 0$ and $\sigma_{(T)}^2 = \sigma_1^2$, while $\sigma^2 > \sigma_1^2$ because cross-sectional inequality depends on the steepness of the age-income profile and the age distribution. Two countries can therefore both have no mobility, but the cross-sectional distributions can give quite misleading indications of lifetime inequality, depending on the values of α and the distributions of h_t. Similarly, for common non-zero values of σ_u^2, the cross-section can be equally misleading. This argument therefore shows that *statement 1* above is incorrect. The idea that it would be useful to allow for differences in age distributions when comparing cross-sectional income distributions is of course not new, and a variety of earlier studies have proposed suitable adjustment methods. Nevertheless the OECD study cited above made no mention of age distributions or income profiles.

Consider next the argument of *statement 2*. By differentiating both (10.7) and (10.10) with respect to σ_u^2, it can be seen that $\partial\sigma^2/\partial\sigma_u^2$ depends only on the form of the age distribution, while the term $\partial\sigma_{(T)}^2/\partial\sigma_u^2$ depends only on the parameter α (and of course T). Hence there is no reason why an increase in mobility, reflected in an increase in σ_u^2, should be expected to increase lifetime inequality by less than cross-sectional inequality; they depend on quite different factors. The analysis has, for convenience, been in terms of the variance of logarithms and has required the use of a linear approximation, but the same basic properties may be expected to hold for other measures of inequality. This is to some extent demonstrated by the simulations reported below, which use a different measure, the popular Gini inequality measure.

10.1.4   Regression Towards the Mean

The above discussion has been confined to just one type of mobility, measured by the term σ_u^2. However, mobility can take other forms. For example, it is possible that there is a systematic tendency for relatively higher incomes to increase by an amount that is different from that of lower incomes. In the present context this phenomenon is referred to as regression towards or away from the (geometric) mean, following the famous use of the term by Galton when examining the heights of fathers and sons. In this type of process, equation (10.1) can be modified to give, for $t \geq 2$:

$$z_{it} = \beta z_{i,t-1} + u_{it} \tag{10.11}$$

where $\beta < 1$ indicates regression towards the mean, and $\beta > 1$ indicates regression away from the mean. This considerably complicates the type of analysis given above. The following section provides numerical examples of the role of regression, and reinforces the earlier results, using simulation methods.

10.2 Simulation Results

This section uses the above model in order to generate simulated cohort and cross-sectional earnings distributions. There are of course many inequality measures that could be used in comparing the alternative earnings distributions. In addition, a variety of lifetime income concepts is available, such as annuity measures, present values or annual averages. For simplicity, this section reports simulation results using only the Gini inequality measure and the present value of earnings, discounted back to the first period at the rate of 5 per cent.

10.2.1 Simulation Procedure

The model can be used to generate a simulated cohort of individuals, on the further assumption that incomes in the first period are lognormally distributed with mean and variance of logarithms of μ_1 and σ_1^2 respectively. Using a random $N(0,1)$ generator, if ν_{i1} is a random value selected from the standard normal distribution, then the income of the ith individual in period 1 is given by:

$$y_{i1} = \exp\left(\mu_1 + \nu_{i1}\sigma_1\right) \qquad (10.12)$$

and in subsequent periods is given using:

$$y_{it} = y_{i,t-1} \exp\left(\alpha + \nu_{it}\sigma_u\right) \qquad (10.13)$$

Equations (10.12) and (10.13) can be used to generate a set of income profiles for a specified cohort. When regression towards the mean exists, equation (10.13) becomes:

$$y_{it} = \left(\frac{y_{i,t-1}}{m_{t-1}}\right)^{\beta} \exp\left(\mu_t + \nu_{it}\sigma_u\right) \qquad (10.14)$$

Table 10.1: Parameter Values

Parameter	A	B
α	0.025	0.15
σ_1^2	0.400	0.05

where, as before, $m_t = \exp \mu_t$.

10.2.2   Hypothetical Values

Consider *statement 1*, regarding comparisons between cross-sectional and lifetime earnings distributions with similar degrees of mobility. Suppose that the value of σ_u^2 is the same in countries A and B, and takes the value of $\sigma_u^2 = 1$. Relative earnings mobility is described by this single parameter in the present model, which is very convenient. Suppose that the values of α and σ_1^2 in each country are as given in Table 10.1. This table shows that country A is assumed to have a relatively flat age-earnings profile, while it has a substantially higher degree of inequality in the first year of the life cycle, compared with country B. It may be added that no reference to age-earnings profiles was made by the OECD. There is much movement within the cross-sectional distribution that does not involve mobility within the distribution of members of the same cohort, simply because of the shape of the age-earnings profile. It was assumed that $\mu_1 = 9.5$ in each country.

In order to obtain the cross-sectional age distribution at any date, it is necessary to aggregate over five different cohorts. Information is required about the age distribution, that is, the number of people in each cohort existing at the specified date. The number of individuals in any cross-section is obviously very much larger than that in any single cohort; in the present context this can be up to five times as large. Unfortunately, no reference to age distributions was made by the OECD. For present purposes, suppose that A and B have age distributions as shown in Table 10.2. Hence, country A has a relatively young population while B's population is relatively old.

Table 10.2: Age Distributions

Age Group	A	B
1	1000	200
2	800	400
3	600	600
4	400	800
5	200	1000

10.2.3 Alternative Distributions

Table 10.3 presents the inequality measures for the two countries A and B. The first part of the table gives the Gini measures for each year of the five-period life cycle, based on a simulated cohort size of 1000 individuals. These cohort profiles are, by assumption, the same for every cohort. The increase in the Gini measure reflects the random proportional changes within the distribution of contemporaries that are influenced by the term σ_u^2. In order to examine *statement 1* regarding comparisons between lifetime and cross-sectional distributions, the value of σ_u^2 has been set at 1 for each country. Inequality in B begins at a much lower level than in A because of the assumption, given above, concerning the variance of logarithms of earnings in the first year of the life cycle, σ_1^2.

The second part of the table shows the present value of earnings for alternative time periods. The label 'PV 2' refers to the present value, at period 1, of earnings over the first two periods, while 'PV 3' refers to the present value of earnings over the first three periods. Lifetime inequality is therefore given in the row labelled 'PV 5'. It can be seen that lifetime inequality in A is higher than in B, partially reflecting the higher value of σ_1^2 in that country.

The Gini measure of inequality of the cross-sectional earnings distribution, based on the age distribution given in Table 10.2, is given in the last row of the table. Each cross-sectional distribution contains 3000 individuals. Country A, which has the flatter age-earnings profile and the younger population, has a lower degree of cross-sectional inequality than country B, which has the steeper age-earnings profile and the older population. (Even if

Table 10.3: Gini Inequality Measures: $\sigma_u^2 = 1$

Period	A	B
yr 1	0.343	0.123
yr 2	0.605	0.537
yr 3	0.717	0.682
yr 4	0.764	0.750
yr 5	0.836	0.822
PV 2	0.468	0.362
PV 3	0.557	0.509
PV 4	0.616	0.597
PV 5	0.688	0.685
X-S	0.693	0.780

the age distributions in each country were completely flat, the ranking would remain the same, with Gini measures for A and B respectively of 0.768 and 0.776.) The ranking of the countries by cross-sectional and lifetime earnings inequality, as shown by the last two rows of Table 10.3, are different. These results provide a clear example of a situation in which *statement 1*, that cross-sectional comparisons give an indication of lifetime inequality when relative earnings mobility is the same in each country, is incorrect.

10.2.4   Higher Mobility

Statement 2 concerns the effects of an increase in relative earnings mobility. It suggests that an increase in relative mobility increases cross-sectional inequality more than lifetime inequality. This can be examined by increasing the value of σ_u^2 used in the simulations. Results for the case where $\sigma_u^2 = 1.5$ are shown in Table 10.4. All other parameters are the same as in simulations underlying Table 10.3. The increase in the degree of relative earnings mobility means that in both countries inequality increases more rapidly over the life cycle, as shown in the first part of the table.

A comparison of Tables 10.3 and 10.4 shows that for country A, the Gini measure of lifetime earnings increases by 14.8 per cent whereas the Gini measure of earnings from the cross-sectional distribution increases by 15.3 per cent. This is indeed the kind of result suggested by *statement 2*.

Table 10.4: Gini Inequality Measures: $\sigma_u^2 = 1.5$

Period	A	B
yr 1	0.343	0.123
yr 2	0.676	0.624
yr 3	0.789	0.770
yr 4	0.839	0.834
yr 5	0.895	0.888
PV 2	0.530	0.449
PV 3	0.647	0.621
PV 4	0.714	0.712
PV 5	0.790	0.795
X-S	0.799	0.881

However, for country B, which has the steeper age-earnings profiles and the lower inequality in the first age group, the Gini measure of lifetime earnings increases by 16.02 per cent. This compares with an increase in the Gini measure for the cross-sectional distribution of 10.13 per cent. Hence lifetime inequality increases by more than in the cross-section. Country B gives the opposite result to that expected from *statement 2*. The important feature of these results is that the effects of an increase in relative mobility on cross-sectional and lifetime inequality depend on the age distribution as well as the precise nature of age-earnings profiles.

10.2.5 Regression Towards the Mean

The above discussion of the effects of an increase in relative mobility is simplified by the convenient assumption that mobility can be described in terms of a single parameter. An increase in the degree of random relative mobility, σ_u^2, inevitably involves an increase in the extent to which the inequality of earnings increases over the life cycle. Lifetime and cross-sectional inequality must also increase as a result of an increase in this type of mobility.

However, different types of relative mobility may take place simultaneously. Suppose that, in addition to the independent random variation governed by σ_u^2, there is some regression towards the mean, in the sense that those with relatively higher earnings (compared with other members of the

Table 10.5: Inequality Measures: $\sigma_u^2 = 1.5$ and $\beta = 0.85$

Period	A	B
yr 1	0.343	0.123
yr 2	0.661	0.622
yr 3	0.744	0.735
yr 4	0.777	0.776
yr 5	0.823	0.819
PV 2	0.511	0.446
PV 3	0.591	0.576
PV 4	0.628	0.633
PV 5	0.669	0.683
X-S	0.717	0.804

cohort) experience, on average, relatively lower percentage increases in earnings. This introduces a type of mobility that has an equalising tendency. It can be specified in terms of a single parameter, β, such that the absence of this type of equalising change arises when $\beta = 1$. The degree of regression towards the mean is reflected by the extent to which β is less than unity.

Instead of the previous case where only σ_u^2 is increased to 1.5, suppose that β is reduced from its implicit value of unity to 0.85. The inequality measures resulting from this process are given in Table 10.5. Comparisons can now be made between Tables 10.3 and 10.5. It can be seen that in both countries, A and B, the inequality of the cross-sectional distribution increases, whereas the inequality of the distribution of lifetime earnings falls. In contradiction of *statement 2*, additional mobility can produce changes that, from the cross-sectional perspective, appear to increase inequality while at the same time reducing lifetime inequality. The extra mobility has a sufficiently egalitarian element which can generate a reduction in lifetime earnings inequality. Hence, when discussing the effects of changes in mobility, it is very important to distinguish precisely which type of mobility is affected.

The first part of Table 10.5 shows that the Gini measure increases with age, despite the introduction of the egalitarian changes. However, the rate of increase is not so great, as comparison with Table 10.4 shows. The present value of earnings over four and five years is greater in country B than in A, which is the reverse of the ranking obtained when using the present value of earnings over the first two and three years. Furthermore, country B has lower inequality within each cohort in each year over the life cycle, but greater lifetime inequality.

10.3 Conclusions

This chapter has examined the relationship between cross-sectional and lifetime income distributions, using a simple model to provide simulation results. It was shown that simple inferences about lifetime income distribution comparisons cannot be made on the basis of cross-sectional distributions alone, as suggested in the study by the OECD.

Chapter 11

Income Dynamics over the Life Cycle

This chapter examines the pattern of income changes over the life cycle for males and females, using information from a special data set compiled by the New Zealand Inland Revenue Department. Information is available about the income and age of a large sample of individuals (the tax unit in New Zealand) over the three consecutive years 1991-2-3. For confidentiality reasons, only summary statistics for a range of cohorts have been available to the author; these statistics include appropriate sums and sums of squares of variables. Data relating to other variables such as occupation, education and location are not available, so that the only decomposition is between males and females. It is therefore not possible to examine the extent to which changes in incomes are associated with job changes or factors such as sickness and employment.

The analysis concentrates on tax payers whose income is obtained mainly from wages and salaries. The data give direct details about only three years, but information is available for many cohorts (defined by age in 1991). It is thus possible to combine the information relating to the experience of a range of cohorts. The approach is based on a decomposition of individuals' income changes from one year to the next into a systematic component depending on age and cohort and a component that reflects relative income mobility. The systematic component is the same for all members of a particular cohort as they age, while the mobility component governs the extent to which individuals move within the income distribution of their contemporaries. Despite the lack of exogenous variables which may help to explain why particular relative movements take place, it is possible to distinguish different statistical characteristics of the pattern of relative income movements. By pooling the information for a variety of cohorts in an appropriate way, it is possible to obtain a description of the pattern of income changes over the life cycle of males and females.

The specification of the pattern of relative income mobility is described in section 11.1, and empirical results are given in section 11.2. The cohort income profiles, governing the systematic component, are estimated in section 11.3 using a pooling of the longitudinal information for all cohorts. A lifetime income simulation model, based on the results of sections 11.2 and 11.3, is constructed in section 11.4, and preliminary simulations are reported.

11.1   Relative Income Mobility

11.1.1   The Framework of Analysis

The starting point of the analysis is a decomposition of proportionate earnings changes from one period to the next into a systematic component and one that reflects the movements of individuals' incomes relative to each other within the distribution of contemporaries. For any individual the proportionate change in income from one year to the next is regarded as being the same as that of the geometric mean income of the cohort, plus a term which governs the extent of relative movements within the distribution. This framework can be written, for a particular cohort, as:

$$
\begin{aligned}
\frac{1}{y_{it}} \frac{dy_{it}}{dt} &= \frac{1}{m_t} \frac{dm_t}{dt} + u_{it} \\
&= f(t) + u_{it}
\end{aligned}
\tag{11.1}
$$

where y_{it} is individual i's income at age t, m_t is the geometric mean income of the cohort in age group t and u_{it} governs the relative income changes. Thus, everyone's income is assumed to change by the same proportion, except for the term u_{it}, whose expected value must by definition be zero. For further discussion of the framework and associated estimation issues, see Creedy (1985).

In order to abstract, for the time being, from changes in the geometric mean income, it is convenient to consider proportionate changes in the ratio, y_{it}/m_t, of individual i's income to geometric mean income. Then equation (11.1) is rewritten as:

$$\frac{m_t}{y_{it}} \frac{d}{dt} \left(\frac{y_{it}}{m_t} \right) = u_{it} \tag{11.2}$$

and defining $x_{it} = \log y_{it}$, $\mu_t = \log m_t$ and $z_{it} = \log(y_{it}/m_t) = x_{it} - \mu_t$, equation (11.2) can be simplified further as:

$$dz_{it}/dt = u_{it} \tag{11.3}$$

The term μ_t is the arithmetic mean of the logarithms of incomes at age t (equivalent to the logarithm of geometric mean income), so that z_{it} is the difference between the logarithm of i's income and the mean of logarithms. This section concentrates on the characteristics of the u. First, it is convenient to rewrite (11.3) in discrete form, using these assumptions, to give:

$$z_{it} = z_{it-1} + u_{it} \tag{11.4}$$

This decomposition is quite general and it is necessary to add more empirical content by specifying the properties of the u in more detail.

11.1.2 Specification of Mobility

The characteristics of u determine the nature of changes in relative income status within the cohort, so it is necessary to add further structure to the specification by considering alternative patterns of relative mobility. The simplest model assumes that the u_{it} are distributed independently of previous changes, have constant variance, σ_u^2, and do not depend on the relative income position in the previous period. In statistical terms, this implies the direct use of the simple first-order auto-regressive form given in 11.4. In the present context this is known as the 'law of proportionate effect' or alternatively as a Gibrat process, following Gibrat (1931), though more generally it would be referred to as a Markov process.

It is also desirable to allow for a tendency for those in the higher deciles of the income distribution to obtain proportionately smaller increases than those in the lower deciles. This is specified by subtracting:

$$(1 - \beta) \log \left(x_{it-1}/m_{t-1} \right) = (1 - \beta) z_{it-1} \qquad (11.5)$$

from the right-hand side of (11.4). Thus when individual i's earnings at age $t - 1$ are below the geometric mean of the cohort (when $x_{it-1} < m_{t-1}$), the logarithm of relative earnings, z_{it-1}, is negative. This means that the average change is greater than that of the geometric mean, so long as $\beta < 1$. This gives:

$$z_{it} = \beta z_{it-1} + u_{it} \qquad (11.6)$$

Thus equation (11.4) is a special case of (11.6) where $\beta = 1$. If $\beta < 1$ there is a systematic egalitarian tendency for those in the higher income groups $(x_{it} < m_t)$ to receive, on average, lower proportionate increases than those in the lower groups. This type of phenomenon is known as 'regression towards the mean' (where the mean in this context refers to the geometric mean), following Galton's (1889) use of the term in the context of the heights of fathers and sons.

For example, for a value of β of 0.98, the average percentage increase for those with incomes of one-quarter of the geometric mean is 2.8 percentage points higher than for those with incomes at the geometric mean. This is reduced to 1.4 for those with incomes of one-half of the geometric mean. A small change in β to 0.95 increases the respective values to 7 and 3.5 percentage points. The first example is obtained using the fact that $-(1 - \beta) \log(0.25) = 0.028$. The percentage change is then obtained as $\exp(0.028) - 1$. For a decrease in income the percentage reduction is calculated as 1-$\exp(\log\text{-change})$. Thus log-changes are symmetric about the geometric mean, although this is not the case for percentage changes. This type of process

Table 11.1: Average Percentage Income Change

ϵ_{t-1}	x_t/m_t			
	0.25	0.50	2.0	4.0
-0.3	15.7	12.5	6.4	3.6
-0.2	12.2	9.2	3.3	0.5
0.2	-0.5	-3.1	-8.4	-10.9
0.3	-3.4	-6.0	-11.1	-13.5

has been used in the context of the growth of firms and of trade unions, in addition to incomes; see Hart and Prais (1956), and Hart (1981, 1982, 1983).

In addition, it is desirable to allow for the possibility that individuals move through the income distribution of their contemporaries in a systematic way. For example, there may be a tendency for significant improvements to depend to some extent on previous success. This can be modelled by assuming serial correlation in the form of a first-order auto-regressive process for the u_{it}, such that:

$$u_{it} = \gamma u_{i,t-1} + \epsilon_{it} \qquad (11.7)$$

where γ is assumed to be the same for all individuals, and ϵ_{it} is distributed independently of previous values with variance σ_ϵ^2. Combining this with (11.6), and eliminating the u's from each, gives:

$$z_{it} = (\gamma + \beta) z_{it-1} - \gamma\beta z_{it-2} + \epsilon_{it} \qquad (11.8)$$

Hence an individual's relative income depends on its value in the previous two years. Examination of this type of process therefore requires information about individuals' incomes in three successive years.

The total effect of regression towards the mean combined with dependence on the past is illustrated in Table 11.1 for hypothetical values of β and γ of 0.96 and -0.3 respectively. The table shows the average percentage change in income for various alternative 'previous changes', ϵ_{t-1}, and 'current relative positions', x_t/m_t. This change is in addition to the systematic change in m_t for the group as a whole, and is experienced by all members of the cohort.

The pattern of mobility thus depends on three factors. These are the degree of regression towards the mean, measured by β; the degree of serial correlation in successive relative changes, measured by γ; and finally the random variation influenced by the variance term σ_ϵ^2. It is obviously possible in principle to specify much more complex processes of relative income change. However, with the available data, containing only three years for each cohort and no exogenous variables, there would be little value in specifying a more complex type of process.

11.1.3 Estimation Procedure

It is required to estimate the parameters β, γ and σ_ϵ^2 of the mobility process for each cohort, using data for three consecutive years. First, rewrite equation (11.8) as:

$$z_{it} = az_{it} + bz_{it-1} + \epsilon_{it} \tag{11.9}$$

where $a = \gamma + \beta$ and $b = -\gamma\beta$. The parameters of equation (11.9) can be estimated using ordinary least squares, though in practice the x_{it}s can be used instead of z_{it}s, giving a constant term in the regression equation. The procedure is not straightforward, however, because of an identification problem. This arises from the lack of exogenous variables. From the two above equations relating γ and β to a and b, it is required to express β and γ as functions of the coefficients a and b. Using $\gamma = -b/\beta$ and substituting in $a = \gamma + \beta$ gives the following quadratic in β:

$$\beta^2 - a\beta - b = 0 \tag{11.10}$$

However, using the two equations to solve for γ gives a quadratic of precisely the same form. The approach used is to impose an *a priori* condition that β is close to unity, so the larger root of the quadratic (11.10) is taken as its estimate; the smaller root is taken as the estimate of γ. Hence the estimates are:

$$\beta = 0.5\left[a + \left(a^2 + 4b\right)^{0.5}\right] \tag{11.11}$$

$$\gamma = 0.5 \left[a - \left(a^2 + 4b \right)^{0.5} \right] \tag{11.12}$$

where a, b, β and γ are understood to be estimates, although for convenience 'hats' have been omitted. The estimated sampling variances are obtained using the following expressions:

$$V(\beta) = V(a) \left(\frac{\partial \beta}{\partial a} \right)^2 + V(b) \left(\frac{\partial \beta}{\partial b} \right)^2 + 2\text{Cov}(a, b) \frac{\partial \beta}{\partial a} \frac{\partial \beta}{\partial b} \tag{11.13}$$

$$V(\gamma) = V(a) \left(\frac{\partial \gamma}{\partial a} \right)^2 + V(b) \left(\frac{\partial \gamma}{\partial b} \right)^2 + 2\text{Cov}(a, b) \frac{\partial \gamma}{\partial a} \frac{\partial \gamma}{\partial b} \tag{11.14}$$

The variances and covariance terms involving a and b are obtained directly from the ordinary least squares regressions. From (12.19) and (12.20) it can be shown that:

$$\frac{\partial \beta}{\partial a} = 0.5 \left[1 + \frac{a}{\left(a^2 + 4b \right)^{0.5}} \right] \tag{11.15}$$

$$\frac{\partial \beta}{\partial b} = \frac{1}{\left(a^2 + 4b \right)^{0.5}} \tag{11.16}$$

$$\frac{\partial \gamma}{\partial a} = 0.5 \left[1 - \frac{a}{\left(a^2 + 4b \right)^{0.5}} \right] \tag{11.17}$$

$$\frac{\partial \gamma}{\partial b} = \frac{-1}{\left(a^2 + 4b \right)^{0.5}} \tag{11.18}$$

The estimated standard errors reported below, $\sqrt{V(\beta)}$ and $\sqrt{V(\gamma)}$, were obtained using the above procedure. An improved method is suggested by Hansen (1998), who nevertheless obtains similar results.

11.2 Empirical Estimates

11.2.1 The Inland Revenue Data

The data are from a random sample of income tax returns for the 1991 to 1993 March years. The 'master' sample comprises 2 per cent of IR3 and

IR5 returns. IR5 returns are filed by taxpayers whose income predominantly has tax withheld; that is income from wages and salaries, taxable welfare benefits, New Zealand superannuation, interest and dividends. Individuals who have income from other sources, or who have been paying provisional tax, must file an IR3.

A significant number of individuals are not required to file, provided their income is below $20,000 and has tax withheld at source, and they are not in receipt of income-related transfer payments or student loans. They may nevertheless choose to file, usually to receive a tax refund. However, people in the sample below $20,000 are not representative of the population with incomes below $20,000.

Taxable income

This is taxable income for IR5 taxpayers, incorporating wage/salary income, interest, dividends and 'other' income less tax agent fees. For IR3 the 'income after expenses' definition is used, incorporating current losses, but not losses brought forward from prior years. It includes income from wages and salaries, interest, dividends, overseas trusts, self-employment, partnerships, shareholder salaries, rents and 'other'. It also incorporates losses passed on from loss-attributing qualifying companies in 1993 (due to a legislative change). Private superannuation income is not taxable.

Wage/salary income

As well as wages and salaries, this summarises all income from which PAYE was withheld at source. This includes welfare benefits, superannuation, withholding payments, redundancy payments, lump-sum retirement allowances, and taxable ACC payments. Welfare beneficiaries and superannuitants cannot be separately identified, and their income is lumped together with any wage or salary income they may have received from other jobs during the year.

Age and sex

Age is calculated in years as at 31 March 1991. For example, someone born on 28 March 1971 will be 20, someone born on 4 April 1971 will be 19. Where date of birth information was corrupt or unavailable, the record was discarded.

Sex M/F was determined using a 'title' variable (Mr, Mrs, Brig., Rev. etc.). Where title was missing, sex was imputed assuming 50 per cent males. Where title was Dr, 79 per cent males were assumed. Where title was numeric, the assumption was 92 per cent males (this situation seems to be restricted to army serial numbers).

'Mainly' wage/salary income

A taxpayer was deemed to be a wage/salary earner if the following condition was true for all three years. If y and w denote taxable income and salary income respectively:

$$(2/3)w \le y \le (4/3)w \qquad (11.19)$$

The condition essentially ensures that the taxpayer is present in all three years, and has wages and salaries as a main source of income throughout. Benefits and superannuation can cause a distortion to the income distribution resulting in spikes at standard annual benefit levels, most of which are below $15,000 (there are a few exceptions where the beneficiary has children).

11.2.2 Regression Results

Using appropriate sums, sums of squares and cross-product terms, the estimates for males and females respectively are given in Tables 11.2 to 11.5. These results are given in each case for 26 cohorts, defined according to the age of individuals at March 1991. The income concept is that of taxable income. It is worth recognising here that taxable income in New Zealand does include some welfare benefits (and although the tax unit is the individual, the unit of assessment for transfer payments is the family and benefit

Table 11.2: Mobility Estimates: Males Aged 18-43

Age	c	z_{92}	z_{91}	R^2	β	γ	σ_ϵ^2
18-19	1.19	0.8227	0.0531	0.444	0.8830	-0.0600	0.3493
		(0.0027)	(0.0019)		(0.0019)	(0.0021)	
20-21	1.13	0.6687	0.2182	0.446	0.9090	-0.2400	0.3303
		(0.0029)	(0.0027)		(0.0018)	(0.0028)	
22-23	3.01	0.4444	0.2667	0.510	0.7840	-0.3400	0.1251
		(0.0017)	(0.0018)		(0.0013)	(0.0020)	
24-25	2.16	0.7255	0.0663	0.587	0.8080	-0.0820	0.1074
		(0.0017)	(0.0016)		(0.0014)	(0.0020)	
26-27	1.86	0.6208	0.1995	0.532	0.8540	-0.2330	0.1374
		(0.0017)	(0.0016)		(0.0010)	(0.0018)	
28-29	1.65	0.8900	-0.0492	0.653	0.8310	0.0590	0.0991
		(0.0014)	(0.0014)		(0.0011)	(0.0017)	
30-31	1.74	0.6442	0.1874	0.624	0.8620	-0.2180	0.1328
		(0.0012)	(0.0013)		(0.0009)	(0.0014)	
32-33	1.06	0.7835	0.1156	0.728	0.9100	-0.1270	0.0896
		(0.0011)	(0.0011)		(0.0006)	(0.0012)	
34-35	1.25	0.6059	0.2750	0.667	0.9090	-0.3030	0.1067
		(0.0012)	(0.0014)		(0.0006)	(0.0014)	
36-37	0.64	0.8210	0.1194	0.722	0.9470	-0.1260	0.1009
		(0.0013)	(0.0012)		(0.0007)	(0.0013)	
38-39	0.26	0.9882	-0.0136	0.787	0.9740	0.0140	0.0841
		(0.0011)	(0.0013)		(0.0007)	(0.0013)	
40-41	0.79	0.7818	0.1439	0.801	0.9360	-0.1540	0.0534
		(0.0011)	(0.0012)		(0.0005)	(0.0013)	
42-43	0.17	0.6954	0.2875	0.757	0.9870	-0.2910	0.0890
		(0.0013)	(0.0014)		(0.0007)	(0.0013)	

Table 11.3: Mobility Estimates: Males Aged 44-69

Age	c	z_{92}	z_{91}	R^2	β	γ	σ_ϵ^2
44-45	0.28	0.7293	0.2430	0.734	0.9780	-0.2480	0.1050
		(0.0014)	(0.0015)		(0.0005)	(0.0015)	
46-47	0.15	0.8966	0.0877	0.811	0.9860	-0.0890	0.0703
		(0.0014)	(0.0015)		(0.0006)	(0.0015)	
48-49	0.87	0.7262	0.1892	0.681	0.9300	-0.2040	0.1198
		(0.0019)	(0.0021)		(0.0010)	(0.0022)	
50-51	-0.50	0.7946	0.2503	0.835	1.0360	-0.2420	0.0951
		(0.0016)	(0.0017)		(0.0008)	(0.0016)	
52-53	0.41	0.8205	0.1400	0.771	0.9650	-0.1450	0.0949
		(0.0021)	(0.0022)		(0.0008)	(0.0023)	
54-55	-0.22	1.0121	0.0010	0.742	1.0130	-0.0010	0.1291
		(0.0025)	(0.0027)		(0.0010)	(0.0026)	
56-57	0.95	0.6258	0.2746	0.511	0.9230	-0.2970	0.2882
		(0.0042)	(0.0050)		(0.0023)	(0.0049)	
58-59	1.64	0.8171	0.0064	0.631	0.8250	-0.0080	0.2289
		(0.0033)	(0.0038)		(0.0024)	(0.0046)	
60-61	1.99	0.8113	-0.0286	0.695	0.7740	0.0370	0.1423
		(0.0025)	(0.0026)		(0.0019)	(0.0034)	
62-63	1.43	0.9455	-0.1021	0.831	0.8210	0.1240	0.0596
		(0.0021)	(0.0020)		(0.0014)	(0.0026)	
64-65	3.20	0.5989	0.0512	0.697	0.6750	-0.0760	0.0484
		(0.0024)	(0.0025)		(0.0021)	(0.0035)	
66-67	1.97	0.7148	0.0682	0.731	0.8000	-0.0850	0.0359
		(0.0031)	(0.0028)		(0.0015)	(0.0034)	
68-69	2.38	0.6022	0.1371	0.797	0.7780	-0.1760	0.0149
		(0.0026)	(0.0020)		(0.0015)	(0.0025)	

Table 11.4: Mobility Estimates: Females Aged 18-43

Age	c	z_{92}	z_{91}	R^2	β	γ	σ_ϵ^2
18-19	1.00	0.7854	0.1084	0.501	0.9050	-0.1200	0.2762
		(0.0024)	(0.0020)		(0.0019)	(0.0021)	
20-21	2.41	0.4962	0.2641	0.480	0.8190	-0.3230	0.2212
		(0.0019)	(0.0023)		(0.0017)	(0.0024)	
22-23	2.01	0.6747	0.1204	0.445	0.8210	-0.1470	0.2943
		(0.0021)	(0.0025)		(0.0022)	(0.0028)	
24-25	2.62	0.7280	0.0032	0.485	0.7320	-0.0040	0.2579
		(0.0020)	(0.0017)		(0.0018)	(0.0023)	
26-27	2.50	0.6703	0.0718	0.548	0.7640	-0.0940	0.3681
		(0.0015)	(0.0017)		(0.0014)	(0.0021)	
28-29	1.02	0.6499	0.2351	0.572	0.9090	-0.2590	0.4049
		(0.0018)	(0.0019)		(0.0013)	(0.0019)	
30-31	2.19	0.6456	0.1309	0.654	0.8080	-0.1620	0.2592
		(0.0015)	(0.0016)		(0.0011)	(0.0018)	
32-33	2.00	0.6609	0.1362	0.634	0.8260	-0.1650	0.2682
		(0.0017)	(0.0016)		(0.0011)	(0.0018)	
34-35	2.48	0.5723	0.1764	0.558	0.7940	-0.2220	0.2944
		(0.0017)	(0.0014)		(0.0010)	(0.0017)	
36-37	1.18	0.7607	0.1224	0.654	0.8970	-0.1360	0.2106
		(0.0019)	(0.0017)		(0.0012)	(0.0019)	
38-39	1.08	0.6631	0.2308	0.747	0.9150	-0.2520	0.1601
		(0.0015)	(0.0015)		(0.0007)	(0.0016)	
40-41	2.00	0.6367	0.1666	0.689	0.8360	-0.1990	0.1372
		(0.0013)	(0.0014)		(0.0007)	(0.0015)	
42-43	0.84	0.7003	0.2195	0.852	0.9350	-0.2350	0.0711
		(0.0011)	(0.0011)		(0.0005)	(0.0011)	

Table 11.5: Mobility Estimates: Females Aged 44-69

Age	c	z_{92}	z_{91}	R^2	β	γ	σ_ϵ^2
44-45	0.40	0.8633	0.0951	0.668	0.9620	-0.0990	0.1509
		(0.0021)	(0.0021)		(0.0011)	(0.0021)	
46-47	0.20	0.9501	0.0288	0.736	0.9800	-0.0290	0.1400
		(0.0021)	(0.0024)		(0.0013)	(0.0024)	
48-49	0.16	0.9391	0.0454	0.861	0.9850	-0.0460	0.0617
		(0.0016)	(0.0016)		(0.0009)	(0.0016)	
50-51	1.29	0.6498	0.2221	0.765	0.8970	-0.2470	0.0841
		(0.0020)	(0.0020)		(0.0008)	(0.0022)	
52-53	-0.07	0.8148	0.1847	0.743	1.0000	0.1850	0.1241
		(0.0034)	(0.0032)		(0.0013)	(0.0032)	
54-55	0.05	1.1384	-0.1495	0.850	0.9870	0.1520	0.0924
		(0.0025)	(0.0026)		(0.0013)	(0.0027)	
56-57	0.78	0.9386	-0.0205	0.878	0.9160	0.0220	0.0457
		(0.0026)	(0.0028)		(0.0013)	(0.0030)	
58-59	2.29	0.8715	-0.1146	0.712	0.7100	0.1610	0.0860
		(0.0031)	(0.0031)		(0.0025)	(0.0048)	
60-61	1.93	0.7956	-0.0061	0.732	0.7880	0.0080	0.0512
		(0.0026)	(0.0022)		(0.0017)	(0.0028)	
62-63	2.94	0.7139	-0.0332	0.707	0.6640	0.0500	0.0329
		(0.0021)	(0.0020)		(0.0016)	(0.0031)	
64-65	3.69	0.7784	-0.1782	0.504	0.0000	0.0000	0.0406
		(0.0035)	(0.0030)		0.0000	0.0000	
66-67	2.96	0.8598	-0.1810	0.713	0.4920	0.3680	0.0123
		(0.0025)	(0.0026)		(0.0122)	(0.0144)	
68-69	1.51	0.8219	0.0135	0.778	0.8380	-0.0160	0.0063
		(0.0027)	(0.0023)		(0.0016)	(0.0027)	

income is usually split between each member of a couple for payment and tax purposes).

These results show that in general there is some regression towards the mean, particularly in the younger age groups, and some negative serial correlation, except for older females. Hence those with relatively low incomes receive, on average, relatively larger proportionate increases, and there is no systematic tendency for success to breed success or for failure to lead to further failure. Some individuals may nevertheless experience several successive large increases (or decreases), and some rich individuals may experience proportionately large increases, because of the particular values of ϵ_{it} experienced. The latter is the 'chance' or random component of the income change. However, the average percentage change for those in a high-income decile is less than the average change experienced by low-income deciles.

These relative movements can thus be described as being to some extent egalitarian, such that incomes measured over a longer period are lower than if β were equal to unity. However, a value of β below unity does not necessarily imply that annual income inequality falls. The change in annual income inequality depends on the relative size of the regression effect and the correlation between incomes in the two periods. A corollary is that judgements about the mobility process cannot be made on the basis of comparisons between single-period measures of inequality; see Hart (1976b, pp.112-114). The values of σ_ϵ^2 for males and females are similar, though there appears to be slightly less regression towards the mean among females, and in the higher age groups the value of β becomes positive, though low. In comparing these results with other countries, the values for males are similar to those obtained for males in Sweden and the UK; see Creedy (1985, pp.45-46). Comparable data for females are not available.

11.2.3   Variations with Age

The above approach relies on an assumption that the values of β and γ remain constant over the three-year period, containing two observed consecutive proportionate income changes. Indeed, given that only three years are available and there are no exogenous variables, it would not be possible to identify any changes over such a short period. This assumption is therefore reasonable. However, it is of interest to examine whether there are systematic variations over a longer period during the life cycle. An advantage of the present data is that a wide range of cohorts defined by age in 1991 is available, so that comparisons can be made among cohorts.

The question immediately arises of whether comparisons among cohorts can be interpreted as reflecting changes in mobility characteristics that might be expected to occur as a particular cohort ages. If the characteristics are significantly influenced by the particular calendar dates at which the incomes have been observed and/or if they are cohort specific (perhaps depending in some way on the size of the cohort), then such comparisons could not be used to indicate life-cycle variations. This perennial problem should always be kept in mind, particularly as only one 'observation' for each of β, γ and σ_ϵ^2 is available for each cohort. Nevertheless, evidence presented below relating to the dispersion of incomes suggests that time effects are not significant.

In the case of males, there appears to be a tendency for β to rise with age and then to fall slightly in the older age groups, while the pure random component σ_ϵ^2 falls and then rises slightly. The degree of regression towards the mean and the extent of variability therefore falls with age, at least up to the late 50s. However, there appears to be no systematic variation in the value of γ with age. Further evidence on the variation in β and σ_ϵ^2 given by the regression results in Table 11.6. The values of β and σ_ϵ^2 are regressed on age and age-squared, where age is measured in integers from 1 (for age group 20-21), and estimated t-values are given in parentheses below the parameters.

For females, the variation is more complex, suggesting the use of a term in age-cubed. Corresponding results for females are shown in Table 11.7, where a significant variation in γ with age up to the late forties was found (unlike the case of males). In comparing various mobility studies, Atkinson *et al.* (1992, p.81) suggest that the regression coefficient, β, is generally 'hump-shaped' and, 'the variance of the pure random component ... declines with age'. These findings are consistent with the correlation coefficient between log-income in two successive years increasing with age. However, they did

Table 11.6: Mobility Characteristics and Age: Males

	β	σ_ϵ^2
C	0.7264	0.2684
	(18.4134)	(7.7381)
Age	0.0417	-0.0383
	(5.5092)	(-5.0314)
Age^2	(-0.00175)	0.0018
	(-5.72636)	(5.2051)
R^2	0.625	0.615

Table 11.7: Mobility Characteristics and Age: Females

	β	γ	σ_ϵ^2
C	0.9582	(0.3350)	0.257
	(0.3008)	(3.2391)	-5.084
Age	-0.0969	0.1096	0.0240
	(2.6641)	(-2.0223)	(-1.3439)
Age^2	0.0138	(0.0178)	-0.004
	(3.9731)	(2.2939)	-2.352
Age^3	-0.0005	0.0008	0.0001
	(-4.97184)	(2.5103)	(2.4380)
R^2	0.773	0.461	0.814

not allow for serial correlation in successive relative changes and were not able to make such systematic comparisons for so many cohorts.

11.3   Cohort Income Profiles

This section turns to an analysis of the systematic variation in geometric mean incomes over the life cycle of males and females, using a pooling of the information for different cohorts. The emphasis on geometric mean incomes arises naturally from the decomposition of relative income changes presented above, and hence the focus on logarithms of income (since the logarithm of the geometric mean is the arithmetic mean of logarithms). It then examines the variation in the relative dispersion of incomes over the life cycle, using a similar approach. The latter results are ultimately related to those of the

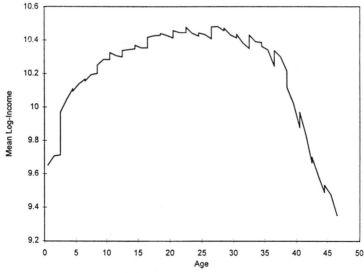

Figure 11.1: Income Profiles: Males

previous section. However, explicit analytical results relating the changing dispersion to changing mobility characteristics are not derived because of the considerable complexity involved. Nevertheless, they are later examined using simulation methods.

11.3.1 Age and Time Effects

In examining the systematic changes in income over the life cycle, the data provide information about the geometric mean income in each of three years, for a number of cohorts (defined by age at March 1991). If the three years of the mean of logarithms, μ_t, are plotted against t for each cohort and these are placed on a single graph, the result is the rather 'jagged' relationship shown in Figure 11.1. Each cohort is joined to its 'neighbours' by a vertical section, because of the overlap in t. It may be thought that a relationship between μ_t and t could be estimated using a dummy variable for each cohort, except the youngest, to deal with the different sections. An example of this type of approach is given in Creedy (1985, pp.70-75). In the present context, there are 23 cohorts shown, so the approach would involve a regression with 22 dummy variables, that is, one for each cohort, less one. Each dummy variable would take the value of zero for all ages except for the three age groups that are relevant for the particular cohort. Any allowance for differences between cohorts in the rate of growth of incomes with age would require a set of interaction terms, involving a further big increase in the number of dummy variables. Even if no multicollinearity problems were encountered (and such problems are very likely), few degrees of freedom would remain. Instead of using such an approach, the following specification is used.

Although only three years' data are available about the life cycle of each cohort, it is possible to pool the data in order to estimate cohort income profiles without using dummy variables. This requires strong assumptions about the nature of the 'age', 'time' and 'cohort' effects on incomes, though it should be remembered that strong assumptions would be required even with much more extensive longitudinal data. Suppose that there are no cohort effects, so that there are no distinctive features of particular cohorts that would affect the growth of incomes (cohort characteristics are not readily available anyway). Comparisons among cohorts generally show considerable stability in age-income profiles. However, for some evidence of cohort effects in the US, see studies by Weiss and Lillard (1978), Welch (1979), Connolly (1986) and Berger (1985). Suppose there are quadratic age and calendar time effects.

Let t denote age and s the calendar date. Then, following Creedy (1985, p.76; 1992, pp.81-90), the mean of the logarithms of income at age t and date s, $\mu_{t,s}$, can be specified as:

$$\mu_{t,s} = \alpha_0 + \alpha_1 t + \alpha_2 t^2 + \beta_1 s + \beta_2 s^2 \qquad (11.20)$$

The way in which the arithmetic mean log-income of a particular cohort varies with the age of the cohort can be seen by using the fact that $s - t$ gives the date of birth of a cohort, c, say (for example, people aged 20 in 1991 were born in 1971). Hence $s = t + c$. and substitution into (11.20) gives the variation in μ_t with age, t, for a particular cohort as:

$$\mu_{t|c} = \left(\alpha_0 + \beta_1 c + \beta_2 c^2\right) + \left(\alpha_1 + \beta_1 + 2\beta_2 c\right) t + \left(\alpha_2 + \beta_2\right) t^2 \qquad (11.21)$$

This result shows that both the intercept and the coefficient on age can differ between cohorts, depending on the time effects, even though no specific cohort effect operates. This also illustrates the problem of identifying any observed differences in age-income profiles as cohort effects. The relevant parameters are estimated directly by carrying out a regression using equation (11.20) above.

11.3.2 Empirical Results

Regressions of (11.20) were carried out for males and females separately, using the observed values of μ for cohorts aged from 20-21 up to 64-65 in 1991; that is, for 23 cohorts. The values of t were adjusted so that $t = 0$ for age 20; hence t was allowed to vary from 0.5 to 46.5. The values of s (calendar dates) were adjusted so that they took the values 1, 2 and 3 for 1991, 2 and 3 respectively. Hence for the first cohort (those aged 20-21 in 1991), three values of μ are available corresponding to (t, s) combinations of $(0.5, 1)$, $(1.5, 2)$ and $(2.5, 3)$ respectively. Similarly, for the second cohort (aged 22-23 in 1991), the three observed values of μ correspond to (t, s) combinations of $(2.5, 1)$, $(3.5, 2)$ and $(4.5, 3)$ respectively. Hence each cohort has one value of age, t, in common with its immediately younger cohort, but that value corresponds with a different value of calendar time, s, so there is no reason to expect the values of μ to be the same (unless the time effects are zero). This means that for each regression there are 69 observations (23 cohorts for three years). The values of μ used in the regressions were the observed values after adjusting for inflation; hence they are in constant 1991 prices. The 1992 values of μ were reduced by $\log (974/958)$ and the 1993 values were reduced by $\log(985/958)$.

It was found that, using taxable incomes, the coefficient on s^2 was negligible and insignificant. Hence regressions were re-run using only a linear time effect. The results for males are shown in Table 11.8. These parameter estimates can be substituted into (11.21) in order to obtain the age profile of any specified cohort. For example, those who 'enter' in year 1 (1991) at age 0.5 (in the cohort aged 20-21 in 1991) have a value of c of $1-0.5 = 0.5$. This gives

Table 11.8: Cohort Profiles: Males

Coefficient	Estimate	t-Value
C	9.7182	237.527
Age	0.0762	23.766
Age^2	-0.00173	-26.215
Date	-0.02046	-1.591
R^2	0.9188	
F (3, 65)	245.23	

Table 11.9: Cohort Profiles: Females

Coefficient	Estimate	t-Value
C	9.7883	191.621
Age	-0.02756	-3.284
Age^2	0.00228	5.522
Age^3	-0.000043	-7.412
Date	-0.02	0.292
R^2	0.769	
F (3, 65)	53.19	

an age-profile corresponding to (11) with a constant term and coefficients on t and t^2 of 9.70793, 0.05576 and -0.00173 respectively. Those who are aged 0.5 (that is, 20-21) five years earlier have a value of c of -5.5, so the constant term in their age-profile of μ becomes 9.83067. This is higher than the younger cohort previously considered because the time effect (the coefficient on s) is negative. More recent entrants to the labour force have slightly lower incomes, other things being equal. The advantage of the present approach is therefore that it can allow for the age-income profile of cohorts to differ slightly because they enter the labour market at different calendar dates, although of course it requires strong assumptions concerning the specification. Instead of using a large number of dummy variables, only the additional terms involving s and s^2 are needed. The finding that the coefficient on s^2 is insignificant is equivalent to the insignificance of interaction dummies.

The coefficient on age-squared in the regressions is highly significant and somewhat larger than has been found in, for example, the UK; see Creedy (1985). The cohort aged 20 years in 1991 would be expected to reach a

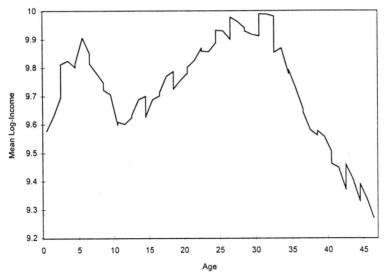

Figure 11.2: Income Profiles: NZ Females

maximum geometric mean income for $t = 16$, which corresponds to 36 years, on the assumption of no overall growth in incomes. If there is some growth, as a result of productivity and inflation, of say 5per cent, then 0.05 must be added to the coefficient on t, and maximum geometric mean income is reached at about 50 years.

The examination of the data for women, as shown in Figure 11.2, suggests that the quadratic specification of the age effects is not appropriate to capture the non-linearity. It was found that a cubic term is highly significant, as shown in Table 11.9. These results give a small positive (although not significant) linear time effect, showing that more recent entrants to the labour force have slightly higher initial incomes. Omitting this variable does not affect the other coefficients in the regression. However, the results for women should be treated with caution. Compared with other evidence for males, which shows a substantial degree of stability in their age-profiles, it is perhaps likely that there is a significant cohort effect for women, in view of the large changes in labour market participation over the last twenty years.

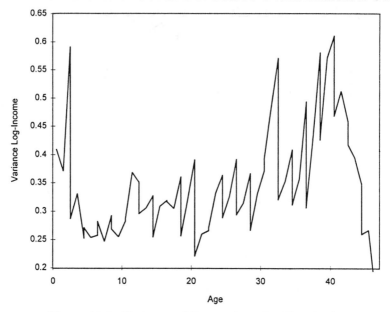

Figure 11.3: Variance of Logarithms Profiles: Males

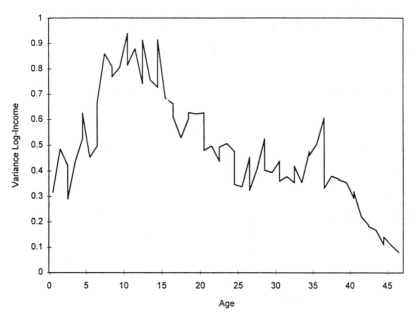

Figure 11.4: Variance of Logarithms Profiles: Females

Table 11.10: Cohort Variance Profiles: Males

Coefficient	Estimate	t-value
C	0.43920	10.848
Age	-0.03176	-4.314
Age^2	0.00171	4.731
Age^3	-0.00002	-4.603
R^2	0.360	
$F(3, 65)$	12.19	

11.3.3   Variance Profiles

A similar approach can be taken for the cohort profiles of the variance of logarithms. The variance of logarithms is plotted against age, for males and females respectively, in Figures 11.3 and 11.4. These figures suggest that a cubic profile for age is more appropriate than a quadratic. Regression results corresponding to (11.20), with the addition of a term in t^3 and replacing μ_t, $\sigma_{t,s}^2$, were carried out. The terms on the calendar date and its square were not significantly different from zero, and re-estimation without these terms gives the result in Table 11.10. A significant positive coefficient on the date variable would suggest that younger cohorts experience higher dispersion than otherwise. Corresponding results for females are given in Table 11.11. Again it can be seen that the goodness of fit is better for females than for males. While a cubic is appropriate for both males and females, the shape of the profiles is quite different, as a comparison of the coefficients (and particularly their signs) reveals. Furthermore, the cubic relationship for males does not capture the sharp increase in σ_t^2 in the first few years, shown in Figure 11.3. This should be kept in mind when considering the simulations reported in the next section, where this peak is in fact reproduced.

It is necessary to consider the possible connection between the relationship between σ_t^2 and t for a cohort and the process of relative income change considered earlier. If the various parameters describing the mobility process were constant over the life cycle, the existence of some regression towards the mean ($\beta < 1$) combined with $\gamma = 0$ would eventually lead to a stable value of σ_t^2, although it would initially increase depending on the extent of

Table 11.11: Cohort Variance Profiles: Females

Coefficient	Estimate	t-value
C	0.37568	5.998
Age	0.05496	4.824
Age^2	-0.00272	-4.846
Age	0.00003	4.005
R^2	0.680	
F(3, 65)	46.15	

the pure mobility term, s. The existence of some serial correlation leads to a rather intractable expression, but produces a rising profile for all ages; see Creedy (1985). The simplest case is that of a combination of $\beta = 1$ and $\gamma = 0$, which produces a linear and rising profile of σ_t^2 with age. The cubic nature of the profile shown by the results in Tables 11.8 and 11.9 arises from the variation in σ_ϵ^2 and β with age. Analytical expressions are unfortunately too intractable to be useful here, although further light on this aspect can be obtained by using the simulation approach of the following section.

11.4   A Simulation Model

This section combines the previous results in order to produce a simulation model of incomes over the life cycle. The model is then used to examine income inequality measured over a long time period rather than just one year. Furthermore, the implications for the age profile of the variance of log-income are compared with results obtained above. Any simulation model of this kind obviously involves a great deal of simplification, and of course the earlier estimates are based on strong assumptions regarding both systematic and random components of income change. However, such models, used with appropriate care and allowing for sensitivity analyses, can provide a very useful basis for policy simulations, particularly of tax policies. The fact that simulation can be produced using a small number of easily interpreted parameters means that the effects of specified types of change in the income mobility process can readily be investigated. It is seen that, despite the simple nature of the model used, the variation in inequality over the life cycle can be replicated surprisingly well. The precise results reported below must be regarded as illustrative only.

11.4.1 Specification of the Model

Sections 11.1 and 11.3 have examined the pattern of relative income mobility and the nature of cohort age-income profiles. It was found that there is some regression towards the mean and a small amount of negative serial correlation in proportionate changes from one year to the next, which may be regarded as 'equalising' changes when viewed in the context of incomes measured over a longer period. However, as stressed earlier, this does not necessarily mean that annual inequality falls with age; a crucial role is played by the degree of variability measured by the term σ_t^2. The parameters of the mobility process were also found to vary with age. The variation in geometric mean income with age for males can be described by a quadratic function, with the coefficients depending on the particular cohort of interest. For female taxable incomes, a cubic term was found to be important. These results suggest that the following model may be useful in simulating lifetime incomes for a selected cohort.

First, incomes in the first year, for which there is no 'history', need to be simulated, where μ_1 and σ_1^2 denote the mean and variance of logarithms of income in the first year. So far it has not been necessary to make an explicit assumption about the form of the distribution of income in each age group. For present purposes it is useful to make the assumption that incomes are lognormally distributed, so that y_t is distributed as $\Lambda(y_t|\mu_t, \sigma_t^2)$; for details of the properties of this distribution, see Aitchison and Brown (1957). It is known that no standard functional form can provide a complete description of all income distributions, but the lognormal form provides a reasonably good fit to the whole range of incomes and is extremely tractable. If incomes in the first year are assumed to be lognormally distributed, then the income, y_{i1}, of the ith person in year 1 can be obtained using:

$$y_{i1} = \exp\left(\mu_1 + u_{i1}\right) \tag{11.22}$$

where u_{i1} is a random variable distributed as $N(0, \sigma_1^2)$. Hence if v_i denotes the ith value of a random variable drawn from a standard normal distribution, $N(0, 1)$, then the corresponding value of u_{i1} is given by $\sigma_1 v_i$. The values of incomes for subsequent years, $t = 2, ..., T$, can be obtained using the expression:

$$y_{it} = \left(\frac{y_{i,t-1}}{m_{t-1}}\right)^{\beta_t} \exp\left(\mu_t + u_{it}\right) \tag{11.23}$$

where:

$$\mu_t = \mu_0 + \theta t - \delta t^2 \tag{11.24}$$

$$u_{it} = \gamma_t u_{i,t-1} + \epsilon_{it} \tag{11.25}$$

$$\epsilon_{it} = N\left(0, \sigma_{\epsilon,t}^2\right) \tag{11.26}$$

The parameters β, γ and σ_ϵ^2 are given t subscripts to allow for their variation over the life cycle. The above results suggest that for males, over a range of ages, quadratic functions are appropriate for β and σ_ϵ^2, although there is no systematic variation in γ. Hence:

$$\beta_t = b_0 + b_1 t + b_2 t^2 \tag{11.27}$$

$$\sigma_{\epsilon,t}^2 = d_0 + d_1 t + d_2 t^2 \tag{11.28}$$

In calibrating the model for males, the results in Table 11.8 can be used for the profile of μ_t. If nominal growth is assumed at the proportionate rate, g, then θ increases to $\theta + g$. For the β and σ_ϵ^2 profiles, the values in Table 11.6 need to be adjusted because they are obtained by carrying out regressions over 23 age groups. Denote the age group variable by r, where $r = 1, ..., 23$, so that $t = 2(r - 1) + 1$ with $t = 1, 3, 5, ..., 45$. Substituting for $r = (t + 1)/2$ means that if, say, the constant and coefficients on age (r) and age-squared (r^2) are denoted a, b and c respectively, then the adjusted values for use in

(11.27) and (11.28) are $(a + b/2 + c/4), (b + c)/2$ and $(c/4)$ respectively. This adjustment gives 0.74681, 0.01998 and -0.000438 for b_0, b_1 and b_2 in (11.27), and 0.24971, -0.01823 and 0.000457 for d_0, d_1 and d_2 in (11.28), where the latter applies only for $t \leq 40$, after which σ_ϵ^2 is assumed to be constant. Furthermore, the fit of the quadratic for σ_ϵ^2 in the very early years suggests that it may be appropriate to apply the formulae for $t \geq 3$, while holding σ_ϵ^2 fixed at 0.3 for the first two years.

11.4.2 Lifetime Incomes

The above model can be used to simulate the incomes of a specified cohort under a variety of assumptions. Given the complexities associated with simulating female incomes over the life cycle relating to variations in labour force participation, this section concentrates on males. Suppose that it is desired to simulate the incomes of the cohort aged 20 in 1991. The parameters for the profile of μ_t can be taken from the earlier results; thus μ_0, θ and δ are set respectively to 9.70793, 0.05576 and 0.00173. If nominal incomes increase at the rate of 0.05 over the lifetime, then the value of θ is adjusted accordingly. Suppose that the value of γ is constant at -0.120. Furthermore, the profiles for β and σ_ϵ^2 are based on the parameters given in the previous subsection.

Simulations of the incomes over 45 years (from age 20 to age 65) for 3000 individuals were produced using a random number generator, for random drawings from an $N(0,1)$ distribution. First, the resulting incomes were used to produce the simulated profile of σ_t^2 with age, for comparison with the estimated cohort profile using the above regression results. These two profiles are illustrated in Figure 11.5. It can be seen that the simulations are able to generate the general form of the variance profile, although there is room for improvement in the precise fit.

However, the simulated profile, showing a sharp increase in σ_t^2 in the early years, is in fact more realistic than the estimated cohort profile, as a comparison with Figure 11.3 shows. This is because, as mentioned earlier, the cubic cannot handle the initial sharp increase; the small number of years involved means that the addition of a term in t^4 is insignificant.

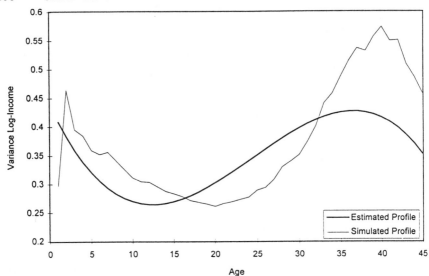

Figure 11.5: Estimated and Simulated Profiles

A further summary statistic worth considering is the variance of logarithms of the present value of income over the complete 45-year period, for
comparison with the annual values. Using a discount rate of 0.05, the present
value was found to be 0.1562 (the value for a zero discount rate was 0.1642).
This may be compared with the values over each of the 45 years, as shown
in Figure 11.5. The interesting result arises that the measure of inequality of
'lifetime income' is less than that obtained in any single year. Comparisons
with two and three years, using the actual data rather than simulations, are
made in an appendix. There is a substantial amount of relative income mobility that is uncorrelated with previous changes or income position. This,
as argued above, means that the variance of logarithms increases over a wide
range of the life cycle, despite the 'regression towards the mean' and the
negative serial correlation. Nevertheless, the systematic egalitarian changes
ensure that when incomes are measured over a long time period, inequality
is lower than in any single year.

An advantage of the simulation model is that it is able to capture the
main characteristics of income dynamics over the life cycle of a specified cohort using few parameters. Furthermore, these parameters are easily inter-

preted. Hence, it is possible to examine the implications of specified changes in the dynamic process. Such simulation results must nevertheless always be treated with caution. In the analysis of any particular policy issue, extensive sensitivity analyses should always be carried out.

11.5 Conclusions

This chapter has examined the dynamics of incomes over the life cycle of males and females in New Zealand, using special data compiled by the IRD. Attention has been given to the process of relative income movements within the income distribution and the systematic movements over age, for particular cohorts. A special pooling of information for a variety of cohorts observed over a three-year period was used.

Both males and females display some regression towards the mean, though the extent of this falls with age (until it is very low in the late forties and fifties) and then increases in the highest age groups.

For males there is some negative serial correlation in relative proportional income changes from year to year, which shows no systematic variation with age. Hence individuals do not move systematically up or down through the income distribution. For females there is some negative serial correlation in the early years, but this gradually falls and the higher ages show slight positive serial correlation.

There is a substantial amount of apparently 'random' relative movement from year to year within the income distribution. For males this is higher in the very young age groups, and falls with age until rising again in the older ages. For females, this rises with age and then gradually falls.

The relative movements generate a changing dispersion of annual income over the life cycle, as measured by the variance of logarithms. For men, the dispersion increases sharply in the first few years. It then follows a cubic variation with age; that is, it falls and then gradually rises to a maximum around age 60 after which it falls again.

Systematic variations in the mean of log-income for males can be described by quadratic age effects and a linear time effect, such that more recent entrants to the labour force have slightly lower incomes (on average) than their older cohorts at comparable ages. For females, a cubic age profile is produced, with recent entrants experiencing slightly higher average incomes than older cohorts at comparable ages. The results for females, in particular the finding that there are cubic age effects, should be treated with caution in view of the substantial changes that have taken place in labour force participation and the changes in participation over the life cycle.

The results described above can be used to specify a simulation model of lifetime incomes. A model was specified and applied to a cohort of males aged 20 years in 1991. It was found that the model was able to reproduce to a large degree the complicated profile of the variation in the variance of logarithms of incomes over the life cycle. An important result is the finding that the present value of income, over the 45-year period from age 20 to age 65, displays less inequality than in any single year. A significant advantage of the simulation model is that it is able to capture the earnings dynamics using few parameters, all of which have a straightforward interpretation. Hence, it is possible to use the model to consider the effects of specific changes in the mobility process and the systematic variations over the life cycle.

Chapter 12

Evaluating Income Tax Changes

Income tax is typically applied to each year's income, independently of other years. Some countries have averaging provisions for groups such as farmers, artists and performers, but the vast majority of individuals pay tax on an annual basis. This arrangement may be administratively convenient, but annual incomes may not be the most relevant from the point of view of distributional judgements. For some purposes it may be thought that the distribution of income measured over a longer period, perhaps including some concept of lifetime income, is more appropriate. In examining the effects of a given tax structure or comparing the effects of different tax structures, it may be more relevant to consider the effects on lifetime incomes or on incomes within separate cohorts of individuals (identified by age), rather than to use the cross-sectional income distribution which contains a mixture of many different cohorts.

This chapter provides an introduction to some of the issues raised by comparisons involving different time periods and population groups. It does not examine the effects of using alternative accounting periods for tax assessment purposes, but considers the possible effects on inequality and progressivity of evaluating income tax structures using different time periods. In particular, how do evaluations compare when using cross-sectional distributions compared with distributions of lifetime incomes? Furthermore, how do tax structures compare when, for a single cohort of individuals, the length of time is gradually increased from one year to the whole of the lifetime? Unfortunately, the answers to these questions are not clear except in some very simple situations. For this reason, numerical results are presented using simulated distributions based on a very simple model.

Before examining tax structures in detail, some preliminaries are required. Section 12.1 introduces some of the commonly used summary measures of the impact of taxation; this concentrates on just a few of the many available measures. Some numerical comparisons are presented in section 12.2. This section compares the use of alternative distributions and shows how comparisons between tax structures can be affected by the income distribution used. Welfare comparisons are then considered in section 12.3. The analysis assumes that incomes are exogenously given for each individual. This assumption means, for example, that it is not possible for individuals to shift some of their income from a period in which they face a relatively high marginal tax rate to a period (either later or earlier) in which they face a lower marginal rate. Such shifting undoubtedly takes place in practice, but it is not the focus of the present chapter.

Consider the extreme situation in which all members of a cohort have equal incomes in each year of their life cyle and no one in the cohort dies until the last year, but the common level of income increases steadily from one year to the next. There is therefore no inequality in lifetime incomes (as mentioned above, savings are ignored here). However, at any moment in time there are many cohorts alive simultaneously, and the number from any given cohort varies depending on cohort-specific birth rates. The form of the cross-sectional income distribution therefore depends on only two sets of factors. First, it is influenced by the shapes of the cohort income profiles; this is complicated by the fact that productivity and other changes which take place over time, along with cohort-specific differences such as the size of the cohort, may cause the profiles to differ between cohorts. Secondly, the cross-sectional distribution is influenced by the age distribution of individuals currently alive.

Suppose in addition that there is no inflation or productivity growth and no cohort-specific influences on incomes, so that the income profiles and lifetime incomes of each cohort are equal. This also implies that the cross-sectional age-income profile provides an accurate description of the profile of each cohort. In this case the cross-sectional income distribution depends only on the steepness of the common age-income profile and the age distribution. In view of the assumption (which is relaxed below) that all individuals of a given age have the same income, any attempt to redistribute income using a progressive tax and transfer system means that such redistribution is simply a matter of making transfers from old to young people at each point in time. No redistribution of lifetime income takes place since there are, by assumption, no non-income differences between individuals that are relevant for the tax system. The assumption that all cohorts are equal also rules out systematic transfers between cohorts. The use of a progressive tax and transfer scheme is therefore equivalent to a system of income smoothing over the life cycle, and any measure of redistribution or progressivity based on a cross-sectional income distribution is quite meaningless. In practice these extreme assumptions obviously do not hold. But the example serves to show that a spurious significance can be attached to cross-sectional comparisons which are substantially affected by demographic factors and the shapes of income profiles, factors which may not be regarded as relevant from the point of view of inequality comparisons.

12.1 Summary Measures

A progressive tax structure is one in which the average tax rate rises with income, but it is necessary to have a more precise measure of the degree of progression. For example, the two income tax structures shown in Table 12.1 are progressive, but it is not obvious which is the most progressive. Increasing marginal rates are not necessary for a tax structure to be progressive, although both systems shown in Table 12.1 have such rate structures. Tax structure 1 has more thresholds than structure 2, and the top marginal rate of structure 1 is substantially higher than in 2. However, the second structure, while 'flatter', has marginal rates that increase more rapidly at the lower end of the distribution.

The effect of these two structures on the distribution of tax payments and the distribution of net income cannot be assessed independently of the form of the distribution of pre-tax income, which determines the number of people who face the different rates. One approach to measuring the impact of a tax structure is to judge the system by its redistributive impact, that is the degree to which it alters a measure of inequality when moving from pre- to post-tax income. Alternatively, measures of the disproportionality of tax payments have been defined. These related measures are discussed below.

12.1.1   The Redistributive Effect

A basic concept in the analysis of redistribution and progressivity is that of the Lorenz curve. If individuals are ranked in ascending order according to their pre-tax incomes, denoted x_i, the Lorenz curve is defined as the relationship between the proportion of people and the associated proportion of total income obtained by those individuals. Both axes therefore vary from 0 to 1 and if all individuals have the same income, the Lorenz curve is a 45° line.

The Gini measure of inequality is a measure of the distance of the Lorenz curve from the line of equal distribution, defined as twice the area contained by the Lorenz curve and the 45° line. The area is doubled simply to ensure that the maximum value that the Gini measure can take is 1. In the case of the distribution of pre-tax income, x, where the incomes are arranged in ascending order, the Gini measure, G_x, can be calculated using:

$$G_x = 1 + \frac{1}{N} - \frac{2}{N^2} \sum_{i=1}^{N} (N + 1 - i) \left(\frac{x_i}{\bar{x}} \right) \tag{12.1}$$

Alternatively, it can be expressed in terms of the following covariance:

$$G_x = \left(\frac{2}{\bar{x}} \right) \text{Cov} \left(x, F(x) \right) \tag{12.2}$$

where $F(x)$ is the distribution function of income, so that $F(x)$ represents the proportion of individuals with incomes less than or equal to x, and $\bar{x}$ is the arithmetic mean pre-tax income; on such covariance expressions, see Jenkins (1988).

Table 12.1: Two Income Tax Structures

No.	Structure 1		Structure 2	
---	Threshold	MTR	Threshold	MTR
1	0	0.20	0	0.10
2	10	0.30	10	0.30
3	20	0.35	35	0.48
4	30	0.40	60	0.55
5	40	0.45		
6	50	0.58		
7	60	0.68		
8	80	0.80		

Suppose that the tax and transfer system is such that net or post-tax income, y, is given by:

$$y = x - t(x) \qquad (12.3)$$

It is possible to obtain a Lorenz curve and corresponding Gini measure of inequality of net income, G_y, by substituting y for x in equation (12.2). The redistributive effect of the tax system can be measured using the Reynolds-Smolensky (1977) measure, L, given by the difference between the two Gini measures, so that:

$$L = G_x - G_y \qquad (12.4)$$

12.1.2 Disproportionality of Tax Payments

The progressivity of a tax system can be defined to reflect the disproportionality of tax payments. It is useful to define a type of Lorenz curve in which the individuals are ordered according to their pre-tax incomes, and the proportion of people is related to the corresponding proportion of total post-tax income obtained by those individuals. This type of curve is called a concentration curve. This is not the same as the Lorenz curve of post-tax income because the tax system may lead to a re-ranking of individuals when moving from the pre-tax to the post-tax distribution.

The concentration curve gives rise to an area measure, the concentration index, that is similar to the Gini inequality measure. Hence, if the ranking of individuals by x is maintained, the concentration index of net income, C_y, is given by:

$$C_y = \left(\frac{2}{\bar{y}}\right) \text{Cov}\left(y, F(x)\right) \tag{12.5}$$

Similarly, it is possible to plot the proportion of people against the corresponding proportion of total tax paid by those individuals, when the individuals are also ranked in ascending order according to their pre-tax incomes. This gives rise to a tax concentration curve. The associated tax concentration index, C_t, may be obtained by substituting the arithmetic mean amount of tax paid, $\bar{t}$, for $\bar{y}$ and $t(x)$ for y in (12.5). Hence it is given by:

$$C_t = \left(\frac{2}{\bar{t}}\right) \text{Cov}\left(t(x), F(x)\right) \tag{12.6}$$

If the tax system is proportional, so that $t(x) = tx$ for all x, the concentration curve of taxation and the Lorenz curve of pre-tax income coincide. The curves differ if there is a degree of disproportionality in the tax system. If the tax system is progressive, the concentration curve of taxation shows more inequality than the Lorenz curve of pre-tax income. Kakwani's (1977, 1984, 1986) measure of disproportionality or progressivity, K, is the difference between the tax concentration index and the Gini measure of x. Hence:

$$K = C_t - G_x \tag{12.7}$$

12.1.3   The Effect of Re-ranking

The possibility of re-ranking of individuals when moving from the pre- to the post-tax income distribution was mentioned above. This type of re-ranking of individuals when moving from the distribution of x to that of y introduces an 'unequal treatment of unequals' which is contrary to the vertical redistribution intended by the form of the tax function. It can be distinguished from horizontal inequity, which may be said to refer to the 'unequal treatment of equals', and is discussed below. In a cross-sectional context, there is no reason why the ranking of individuals should be different when using pre-tax and post-tax incomes. However, re-ranking can occur in a life-cycle framework if marginal tax rates vary with income, because of the variability in incomes from year to year.

The Atkinson-Plotnick index, $P > 0$, measures re-ranking, or horizontal inequity, using:

$$P = \frac{G_y - C_y}{2G_y} \qquad (12.8)$$

The concentration measure, C_y, involves ranking by x and the Gini inequality measure, G_y, involves ranking by y, so an absence of re-ranking implies that $P = 0$; see Atkinson (1979), Plotnick (1981), and Jenkins (1988b).

12.1.4   A Decomposition

The various measures defined above can be related to each other using an explicit formula; this is not surprising given the reliance of the measures on areas in the basic Lorenz curve diagram. Define the effective total tax ratio, g, as the ratio of the total tax paid to the total pre-tax income (of all individuals combined). In the life-cycle framework, the value of g is the difference between the present values of gross and net income divided by the present value of gross income over all individuals. The relationship between the various measures is:

$$L = G_x - G_y = K \left\{ \frac{g}{1-g} \right\} - 2G_y P \qquad (12.9)$$

Thus the redistributive effect of the tax and transfer system, $G_x - G_y$, is proportional to the Kakwani progressivity measure, K, less a term that depends on the extent of re-ranking. An implication of this result is that a change in the tax system which increases tax disproportionality need not necessarily reduce the Gini inequality of net income.

Aronson *et al.* (1994) showed that a further decomposition of the redistributive effect is useful. Letting $R = 2G_y P$ denote the re-ranking effect, they showed that when the population is divided into groups with similar pre-tax incomes:

$$L = (G_x - G_0) - \sum \theta_x G_{F(x)} - R \qquad (12.10)$$

where G_0 is the 'between-groups' Gini measure of post-tax income obtained by replacing every post-tax income within each group by the arithmetic mean, θ_x is the product of the population share and the post-tax income share of those in the group with pre-tax income of x, and $G_{F(x)}$ is the Gini measure of inequality of post-tax incomes of those with pre-tax income of x. Computationally it is easier to calculate K and G_0 and then to obtain H using $H = (G_x - G_0) - gK/(1-g)$.

This shows that Kakwani's measure combines the effect of the first two terms on the right hand side of (12.10). These two terms measure 'vertical redistribution', V, and 'horizontal inequity', H, respectively. The horizontal inequity arises from the 'unequal treatment of equals'. A requirement of horizontal equity is that individuals with the same pre-tax income should have the same net income. If two individuals have the same present value of gross lifetime income, but one individual has a more variable income stream over time than another and therefore sometimes moves into higher-rate income groups, the person with the variable stream pays a higher present value of tax over the period.

In a cross-section where there are no tax-relevant non-income differences, the values of both H and R must be zero, and Kakwani's K is simply proportional to the redistributive effect, which is all of the 'vertical' kind. However, in a multi-period context, H can be non-zero in addition to R if the tax function is progressive. Both the horizontal inequity and the re-ranking effect reduce the redistributive effect of the tax structure. Unfortunately, it does not seem possible to provide an explicit treatment of the various measures in the context of a specified model of age-income profiles. Numerical simulations are presented in the following section.

12.2 Some Numerical Comparisons

Suppose that individuals work and live for five periods. For simplicity, the analysis abstracts from life-cycle saving behaviour and related issues concerning the taxation of interest-income. At any particular time, the cross-sectional distribution therefore contains five separate cohorts; the restriction to a small number of periods is made so that the presentation of results is easier. In order to avoid problems arising from growth and other factors leading to labour market differences between cohorts, suppose that each cohort has a similar age-profile of geometric mean earnings. This prevents changes in the cross-sectional distribution taking place over time as the 'cohort composition' of the cross-section changes. In particular, each individual's earnings are assumed to increase by a fixed percentage amount from one period to the next over the life-cycle; the profile of the geometric mean of earnings over the five year life-cycle is the same straight line for each cohort.

In addition to this systematic variation, suppose that there is some relative earnings mobility within each cohort, such that individuals move relative to others in the same cohort. Each individual is assumed to experience a random percentage change from one year to the next, in addition to the systematic variation described in the previous paragraph. This model is in fact the same as that used in chapter 10.

12.2.1 Income Profiles

Each member of a cohort enters the labour market at the same age. Let x_{it} and m_t denote respectively the earnings of individual i at age t (where t is measured from entry into the labour force, when $t = 1$) and the geometric mean earnings in age group t. If, furthermore, z_{it} is the ratio of person i's earnings to the geometric mean, so that $z_{it} = \log(x_{it}/m_{it})$, suppose that:

$$z_{it} = z_{i,t-1} + u_{it} \qquad (12.11)$$

where u_{it} is a random variable that is assumed to be independently normally distributed as $N(0, \sigma_u^2)$. In the present context, this is known as a Gibrat process. Taking variances of (12.11) gives:

$$\sigma_t^2 = \sigma_1^2 + (t-1)\,\sigma_u^2 \tag{12.12}$$

and the variance of logarithms at age t, σ_t^2, is a linear function of age, with σ_1^2 the variance of logarithms in the first year period.

Suppose also that, in addition to the random proportionate change, all earnings are subject to growth at the constant rate α. This means that the arithmetic mean of logarithms of earnings at age t, μ_t, is given by:

$$\mu_t = \mu_1 + (t-1)\,\alpha \tag{12.13}$$

This model can be used to generate a simulated cohort of individuals, on the further assumption that earnings in the first period are lognormally distributed with mean and variance of logarithms of μ_1 and σ_1^2 respectively. Suppose that $\sigma_u^2 = 1.0$, $\sigma_1^2 = 0.3$, $\mu_1 = 9.5$, $\alpha = 0.12$ and the nominal rate of interest is 0.05. As mentioned above, growth and inflation are assumed to be zero, so that comparisons between cohorts are reflected directly in differences between ages groups within a single cohort.

12.2.2   Annual Incomes Over the Life Cycle

The various summary measures using tax structure 1 from Table 12.1 in section 12.1 above, for a simulated cohort consisting of 1000 individuals, are shown in Table 12.2. Since inflation is assumed to be absent, the tax thresholds remain fixed. The first block of the table shows the measures for each year of the five-year lifetime of the cohort. The first two columns show the Gini inequality measures of pre- and post-tax income in each year; the increase with age reflects the assumptions of the simulation model described above. The difference between the two measures gives the Reynolds-Smolensky redistributive effect, L, which increases with age up to year 4, after which it decreases. The Kakwani tax disproportionality measure increases only up to year 2, after which it falls. There are therefore periods over the life-cycle when the redistributive effect increases while at the same time the progressivity falls. There are, by assumption, no non-income differences between individuals, so there is no horizontal inequity or re-ranking

Table 12.2: Tax Structure 1

Time	G_x	G_y	K	L	$100P$	g
Annual incomes over life-cycle						
1	0.299	0.272	0.081	0.027	–	0.249
2	0.587	0.482	0.147	0.105	–	0.417
3	0.703	0.564	0.112	0.139	–	0.553
4	0.759	0.611	0.088	0.148	–	0.628
5	0.832	0.713	0.048	0.120	–	0.712
Present value of income						
$\sum_{t=1}^{1}$	0.299	0.272	0.081	0.027	–	0.249
$\sum_{t=1}^{2}$	0.446	0.354	0.167	0.092	0.0366	0.357
$\sum_{t=1}^{3}$	0.551	0.415	0.162	0.136	0.1012	0.459
$\sum_{t=1}^{4}$	0.619	0.461	0.140	0.158	0.0934	0.533
$\sum_{t=1}^{5}$	0.698	0.529	0.107	0.170	0.0938	0.615
Cross-sectional distribution						
	0.788	0.633	0.090	0.155	–	0.632

reflected in the single-period measures; all the redistribution is 'vertical'.

The general upward movement in the incomes of the cohort over the five-year period means that (except for the random variability) the individuals are typically moving into higher tax brackets, and by the fifth year, the majority of the cohort is in the top tax bracket, so that the disproportionality of tax payments is low. This upward movement is also reflected in the increase in the aggregate tax rate, g.

12.2.3 The Present Value of Incomes

The second block of Table 12.2 gives summary measures for the distribution of the present value of income, discounted back to the first year using a fixed interest rate, r, of 0.05. The first row is simply a repetition of the first year, shown in the first block of the table, while the second row shows the present value of incomes over the first two years; finally, the fifth row is the present value of 'lifetime' income.

It can be seen that the inequality of lifetime income is approximately the same as the inequality of annual income during the third year of the life cycle. The longer-period inequality increases as extra years are added because the later years have higher annual inequality.

This second block reflects the effect of gradually increasing the length of time over which incomes are measured when calculating the various summary measures of progressivity and inequality; the accounting period for tax purposes is nevertheless the single year. The redistributive effect increases continually as the time period is increased, but the Kakwani disproportionality measure declines as the third and later years are added. The disproportional income tax does not automatically become more redistributive or disproportional when increasingly longer periods are used to evaluate its effect.

An important difference between the first and the second blocks of the table is that, when longer time periods are used to measure the effect of the tax structure, re-ranking can occur; this, measured by P, is shown to increase until the third year is added. As suggested above, horizontal inequity, as measured by H, can arise in this context. However, there is a practical problem of measuring H in this type of simulation, since it is extremely unlikely that any two individuals have identical pre-tax lifetime incomes. Some idea of the orders of magnitude involved may, however, be obtained by grouping individuals into narrow income ranges. For example, if the incomes of the 1000 individuals are divided into 800 income ranges of equal size, it is found that the value of $100H$ in the first year of the life cycle is 0.0005. This is negligible, thought it is of course known that in principle this should be zero for the single-year income measure. Nevertheless, when using the present value of lifetime income, the value of $100H$ increases to 0.0473. This means that the components, V, H and R form respectively 100.86, 0.28 and 0.58 per cent of the redistributive effect of the tax system on lifetime incomes.

12.2.4   The Cross-sectional Income Distribution

It is also of interest to compare the effects of using different time periods for a single cohort, with the measures obtained for a cross-section in any particular year. In practice, the relationship between cross-sectional and lifetime income distributions is very complex, but the simplifications used in this example make it possible to obtain the cross-section without much difficulty.

The 'steady state' assumption make it possible to obtain a representative cross-sectional distribution of individuals simply by suitable aggregation over different ages. All that is required is to specify an age distribution of the population and take an appropriate number of individuals at the required ages from the simulated cohort. For example, an individual age 5 is considered for this purpose to be a different person from when age 2. Suppose the vector of the number of individuals in each of the age groups, from 1 to 5 respectively, is [400, 600, 800, 1000, 800]. Hence the cross-section consists of 3,600 individuals.

The resulting summary measures are shown in the third section of Table 12.2. The first point to note is that the inequality of pre-tax incomes is greater for the cross-sectional distribution than for the distribution of lifetime incomes. This is influenced by the form of the age distribution, which reflects a relatively old population structure. Despite the fact that lifetime inequality is lower than in the cross-section, the Kakwani disproportionality measure and the redistributive effect are both higher using the lifetime distribution than for the cross-sectional distribution. Reliance on the cross-section may be said (in comparison with the lifetime distribution which is not affected by the population age distribution) to exaggerate inequality while understating the degree of progressivity and the redistributive effect of the tax structure.

Simulation studies of taxation in a life-cycle framework, such as Davies *et al.* (1984) and Fullerton and Rogers (1993), have suggested that income taxation is less progressive in terms of lifetime distributions compared with cross-sections. These results clearly contrast with those found in the present simulation model. Indeed, it is dangerous to make such generalisations in view of the fact that neither the pre-tax distribution nor the tax revenue are kept constant in comparing alternative time periods. The relative orders of magnitude will depend on the particular context under investigation.

12.2.5 Comparing Tax Structures

The corresponding results obtained using tax structure 2 from Table 12.1 are shown in Table 12.3. Consider first the results relating to annual incomes

Table 12.3: Tax Structure 2

Time	G_x	G_y	K	L	$100P$	g
Annual incomes over life-cycle						
1	0.299	0.261	0.170	0.038	–	0.183
2	0.587	0.509	0.161	0.078	–	0.328
3	0.713	0.627	0.106	0.076	–	0.417
4	0.759	0.693	0.078	0.066	–	0.460
5	0.832	0.790	0.041	0.042	–	0.505
Present value of income						
$\sum_{t=1}^{1}$	0.299	0.261	0.170	0.038	–	0.183
$\sum_{t=1}^{2}$	0.446	0.371	0.197	0.075	0.0192	0.276
$\sum_{t=1}^{3}$	0.551	0.463	0.165	0.089	0.0221	0.349
$\sum_{t=1}^{4}$	0.619	0.531	0.134	0.088	0.0164	0.398
$\sum_{t=1}^{5}$	0.698	0.619	0.098	0.079	0.0117	0.447
Cross-sectional distribution						
	0.788	0.716	0.084	0.071	–	0.459

over the life cycle. It can be seen that the redistributive effect of structure 2 is greater than that of structure 1 during the first year, while the Kakwani disproportionality measure of structure 2 is greater than that of 1 for the first two years. Despite the flatter rate structure of the second tax system, this effect arises because, in the early years of the life cycle, the majority of individuals are in the relatively lower tax brackets for which the marginal rate increases more rapidly than in the first structure.

When comparing the results for the present value of incomes, the second tax structure is found to have a higher Kakwani measure than the first struc-ture when using incomes up to the first three years, though the redistributive effect is lower after the second year is added. However, in terms of lifetime incomes (that is, five-year present values), the second tax structure is both less disproportional and less redistributive; the percentage reductions in the respective measures, K and L, are 8.41 and 53.53 per cent.

The question arises of how the tax structures would be judged if only the cross-sectional distribution were used. It can be seen that in this case the disproportionality and redistribution measures fall by 6.67 and 54.19 per cent respectively. Hence the cross-section is seen in this example to understate the effect of the tax structure change slightly when compared with the use of lifetime incomes. However, this is not a necessary result, and by a suitable choice of age structure and earnings profile it would be possible to obtain examples where the cross-section overstates the effect of the change. Although the cross-sectional comparison may be thought here to provide a reasonable approximation to the longer-term effect of a tax structure change, this is merely a coincidence that cannot be relied upon in practice. Robust generalisations are very difficult to make in this context.

A major difference between the two tax structures cannot even be observed when using cross-sectional income data. This is the extent to which the second structure reduces the degree of re-ranking of individuals. The flatter marginal rate structure of the second tax system implies an Atkinson-Plotnick measure for lifetime incomes that is 87.53 per cent lower than for the first tax structure. The flatter rate structure also implies less horizontal inequity in the second tax structure. When using 800 income groups, as before, the value of $100H$ is 0.0361, a reduction of 23.68 per cent. Nevertheless, in each case, the vertical redistribution is by far the most important contribution to the redistributive effect.

These results apply of course to comparative static changes where each tax structure is assumed to apply in each year of the life cycle. It would be possible to consider more complex cases in which the tax structure changes in a particular year; this would introduce differences between cohorts, so cross-sectional comparisons would be more awkward.

12.3   Welfare Comparisons

At the end of the previous section, it was shown that a flattening of the tax rate structure can have a substantial effect on horizontal inequity, which by its nature cannot be observed using cross-sectional income distributions. The question arises of how an overall evaluation of the tax structure change might take the change in horizontal inequity into account, along with the reduction in progressivity and the change in the aggregate tax revenue collected. This requires the use of an explicit statement of value judgements, summarised in the form of a social welfare, or evaluation, function that explicitly deals with this type of trade-off. The following treatment does not, however, consider how the tax revenue is spent; the revenue is treated as if it falls into a 'black hole'.

12.3.1   A Social Welfare Function

The use of the Gini inequality measure in the above comparisons suggests the use of a social welfare function involving the Gini measure. The abbreviated form of social welfare function that is known to be consistent with the use of the Gini measure is:

$$W = \overline{y}\left(1 - G_y\right) \tag{12.14}$$

where W represents social welfare per person; on abbreviated social welfare functions, see Lambert (1993b). This can be regarded as being written in terms of the distribution of net lifetime income for a particular cohort. The tax ratio, g, used above is thus expressed in terms of the present value of tax revenue, and $\overline{y} = \overline{x}\left(1 - g\right)$.

The information in Tables 12.2 and 12.3 can be used to show that social welfare per person, W, expressed as a ratio of $\overline{x}$, increases by an absolute amount of 0.029 as a result of the movement from the first tax structure to the second. If the cross-sectional distribution is used instead of that of lifetime income, this increase is lower, at 0.019. Hence, given this type of value judgement, the reduction in the redistributive effect of income taxation is willingly traded for the increase in average net income, $\overline{y}$, arising from the reduction in tax revenue.

The expression for social welfare in (12.14) can be decomposed by using (12.9), so that:

$$W = \overline{x}\left(1 - g\right)\left(1 - G_x + \frac{g}{1 - g}K - 2G_yP\right) \tag{12.15}$$

It is perhaps tempting to use this form of W to compare changes in P and K which have the same effect on social welfare. However, this would be somewhat artificial because it is very difficult indeed, with any given tax structure, to specify a change in tax parameters that leaves both g and G_y unchanged while changing K and P. Indeed, there may not be enough tax parameters to make such a change possible. For a discussion of variations in tax parameters and the above measures, using a very simple tax function, see below.

12.3.2 The Welfare Premium from Progression

A further concept that arises here is that of the welfare premium from progression, π, defined as the increase in W that arises from the actual tax structure compared with a proportional structure that raises the same total revenue. A proportional tax that raises the same revenue as the actual tax structure over the lifetime of the cohort, and which does not therefore involve any change in inequality, so that $G_y = G_x$, would produce a value of social welfare, W_P, say, given by:

$$W_P = \overline{x}\,(1-g)\,(1-G_x) \tag{12.16}$$

The welfare premium from progression is obtained by subtracting (12.16) from (12.14) to give:

$$\pi = \overline{x}\,(1-g)\,(G_x - G_y) \tag{12.17}$$

The second term in parentheses is simply the redistributive effect (measured by the Reynolds-Smolensky measure, L), so that using the decomposition in (??):

$$\frac{\pi}{\overline{x}} = gK - (1-g))\,R \tag{12.18}$$

Hence the welfare premium from progression, expressed as a ratio of average pre-tax income, is a weighted average of K and $R = 2G_yP$, with weights of g and $(1-g)$ respectively. Alternatively, using the Aronson *et al.* (1994) decomposition, $\pi/\overline{x} = (1-g)\,(V - H - R)$.

It is therefore possible for the welfare premium from progression to be increased by a change in the tax structure which reduces the value of K, provided that the degree of re-ranking is sufficiently reduced. However, as discussed in the previous subsection, it is important to recognise that the various terms in (12.18) cannot really be changed independently. A change in the tax structure is likely to change every term in the expression.

Using the numerical examples from the previous section, the change in the tax structure from 1 to 2 implies, in terms of lifetime incomes, a reduction in the welfare premium from progression of about one-third. This is despite the reduction in P and the increase in W itself, as noted above. Thus, the welfare premium from progression can fall while simultaneously the level of welfare itself rises. Much of the reduction in the premium actually arises from the reduction in g, since the reduction in K, as noted above, is relatively low. However, it is also the reduction in g which contributes towards raising the value of the social welfare function when moving from tax system 1 to 2.

12.3.3 Changes in Tax Parameters

In order to illustrate the link between specific tax parameters and the summary measures discussed above, consider the very simple case of a cross-sectional distribution (thereby ruling out re-ranking) with a tax function given by:

$$t\left(x\right) = t\left(x - a\right) \tag{12.19}$$

where is it assumed that all individuals are above the threshold, a, and therefore pay tax. This last assumption considerably simplifies the following expressions. Net income, y, is thus $at + x(1 - t)$, its mean is given by $\bar{y} = at + \bar{x}\left(1 - t\right)$, and the aggregate tax ratio, g, is given by:

$$g = t\left(1 - \frac{a}{\bar{x}}\right) \tag{12.20}$$

Hence, changes in the parameters, t and a, which leave g unchanged are given by:

$$\left.\frac{dt}{da}\right|_{g} = \frac{t}{\bar{x} - a} \tag{12.21}$$

and an increase in a must be matched by a suitable increase in t. This result can only be applied over the range of a for which it remains below the minimum income.

Consider the Gini inequality of net income, G_y. This requires the covariance term:

$$\text{Cov}(y, F(y)) = E(yF(y)) - E(y)E(F(y)) \qquad (12.22)$$

Since there is no reranking, $F(y) = F(x)$, and using $E(F(x)) = 0.5$, the second term in (12.22) is $\{at + (1-t)\bar{x}\}/2$. The first term in (12.22) is $E((at + x(1-t))F(x))$, so that:

$$E(yF(y)) = (1-t)E(xF(x)) + \frac{at}{2} \qquad (12.23)$$

and since $\text{Cov}(x, F(x)) = E(xF(x)) - \bar{x}/2$, this becomes:

$$E(yF(y)) = (1-t)\text{Cov}(x, F(x)) + \frac{at + (1-t)\bar{x}}{2} \qquad (12.24)$$

and $\text{Cov}(y, F(y)) = (1-t)\text{Cov}(x, F(x))$. Hence the Gini measure of net income is found, after substitution in the covariance form, to be:

$$G_y = \left\{1 + \frac{a}{\bar{x}}\left(\frac{t}{1-t}\right)\right\}^{-1} G_x \qquad (12.25)$$

so that the measure of redistribution, L, is:

$$L = \left[1 + \left\{\frac{a}{\bar{x}}\left(\frac{t}{1-t}\right)\right\}^{-1}\right]^{-1} G_x \qquad (12.26)$$

Using a similar type of approach, it can be found that the tax concentration measure is given by:

$$C_t = \left\{1 - \frac{a}{\bar{x}}\right\}^{-1} G_x \qquad (12.27)$$

which depends only on the threshold parameter, a.

The value of the social welfare function after taxation is given by:

$$W = \bar{x}(1-g)(1-G_y) \qquad (12.28)$$

which simplifies to:

$$W = at + (1 - t) W_x \qquad (12.29)$$

where $W_x = \bar{x} (1 - G_x)$. Hence, changes in a and t which leave social welfare unchanged are given by:

$$\left. \frac{dt}{da} \right|_W = \frac{t}{W_x - a} \qquad (12.30)$$

Notice that $\partial W_y / \partial t$ is negative. For a given small increase in a, it can be seen that, since $\bar{x} > W_x$:

$$\left. \frac{dt}{da} \right|_g < \left. \frac{dt}{da} \right|_W \qquad (12.31)$$

This means that an increase in a, accompanied by an increase in t in order to maintain revenue neutrality, involves an increase in W.

For more complicated tax structures and situations (such as the use of lifetime incomes) where re-ranking can occur, the explicit analysis of the relationship between the various summary measures and the tax parameters becomes very messy.

12.4   Conclusions

This chapter has discussed the evaluation of changes in the structure of the income tax system, focusing on the choice of time period and population group to use when calculating progressivity and inequality measures. It was argued that the use of cross-sectional income distributions may not be very meaningful because they are substantially influenced by factors such as the age distribution of the population and the shape of age-income profiles. Furthermore, cross-sections and distributions for a single year in the life cycle of a cohort are not able to capture the effect of a tax change on the degree of horizontal inequity and re-ranking that arises with progressive rate structures when individuals' incomes fluctuate from year to year. The use of alternative income concepts was examined for two tax structures using numerical examples based on simulated income profiles.

Cross-sectional distributions have invariably been used because of the difficulty (indeed the impossibility) of observing the appropriate lifetime incomes of various cohorts. Information about the impact of tax changes on a longer-period income concept must inevitably rely heavily on the use of simulation models. Such models can at best represent a considerable simplification of the vast complexity of actual lifetime income processes, but it is argued that, carefully constructed and used, relatively simple models can provide useful supplementary information about the potential effects of tax changes.

Chapter 13

Income Taxation and the Time Period

The previous chapter provided an introduction to the problems arising in comparing income tax structures using different accounting periods. The present chapter presents a more detailed analysis using the income simulation model developed in chapter 11. Measures of the degree of progressivity and the redistributive effects of taxation are usually based on cross-sectional data for a single year. However, the income distribution in any single year consists of individuals from a large number of separate cohorts, distinguished by date of birth. This would not matter if all individuals obtained the same income in each year of their life cycle, but it is well known that age profiles of mean earnings display a 'humped' shape and there is a considerable amount of mobility of individuals within the distribution of contemporaries. At any moment in time, the low-income groups may contain large numbers of both relatively young and old people, as well as many who, in terms of their lifetime incomes, may be in the higher deciles. Much redistribution in a tax and transfer system may be between stages of the life cycle rather than between the members of a cohort or between cohorts.

Cross-sectional studies of taxation are therefore potentially misleading as indicators of the progressivity in terms of lifetime incomes. In addition, the existence of income variability from year to year can produce a degree of horizontal inequity, when using a longer period framework. For example, of two individuals with the same present value of pre-tax income but different time profiles, the person with the greater variability pays more tax in a system having increasing marginal tax rates. This is the basis of arguments for averaging of income for tax purposes; see, for example, Creedy (1979) and Moffitt and Rothschild (1987).

The study of the lifetime effects of taxation is severely constrained by data limitations, so it is not surprising that there have been few studies. It has also been necessary to use simulation methods; examples include Davies *et al.* (1984), Poterba (1989), Fullerton and Rogers (1993), Casperson and Metcalf (1993), Harding (1994), Cameron and Creedy (1994) and Cornwell and Creedy (1996). When discussing some of the general problems of examining taxation in lifetime terms, Fullerton and Rogers (1991, p.21) make the point that, 'while practical considerations presently limit the widespread use of lifetime analysis as a routine procedure, academic studies of lifetime tax incidence can still provide policy economists with insights into the differences and similarities between the annual and lifetime perspectives. Any discussion about equity that is based on annual calculations could be supplemented, wherever possible, with potential lifetime effects'.

In this spirit, the present chapter examines some effects of taking a longer accounting period than the single year, using simulations for a single cohort. The chapter should be considered as exploring some of the relationships involved, by using a number of simplifying assumptions. In particular, it should not be treated as an attempt to assess the actual redistributive impact of any tax structure or change in structure.

This chapter therefore explores the use of alternative income accounting periods to examine the implications for tax progressivity and redistribution, using a simulation model to generate simulated profiles of pre-tax incomes for a cohort of males in New Zealand. The simulation model is based on estimates in chapter 10. Results are illustrated using the income tax schedules that operated over the second half of the 1980s. However, it is important to stress that the present study is concerned only with income taxation, and does not consider the wide range of government expenditure and its incidence, including transfer payments. This is particularly important in view of the finding of Lambert (1985a) that the effect of a single tax, within the context of a multiple tax and expenditure system, is far from obvious and, for example, regressive taxes can enhance the redistributive effects of government expenditure. The tax reforms that took place in New Zealand in the 1980s involved a considerable amount of base broadening, as well as a wide range of changes to direct and indirect taxation and expenditure. These changes are ignored in what follows.

The lifetime income simulation model is described in section 13.1. Before moving to the multiple period context, the variations in selected progressivity measures of annual incomes over the life cycle are examined in section 13.2. This is of interest in view of the dependence of such measures on the pre-tax income distribution, so that the measures vary over the life of the cohort even when the same tax structure is applied in each year. This is followed in section 13.3 by comparisons which involve the income period gradually being increased from one year to that of a working life of 45 years. Section 13.4 then provides comparisons with measures obtained using cross-sectional data.

The simulation model used to produce the earnings of a cohort of New Zealand males is quite complex, involving systematic changes over the life cycle in the degree of regression towards the mean and the extent of random variability within the income distribution. Section 13.5 therefore compares results with those obtained for a much simpler process of year-to-year relative income changes in which there is no regression and the degree of random variability remains constant.

In each tax structure comparison, the income tax schedule is held fixed over the whole of the period considered, except for the appropriate indexation of the thresholds. Section 13.6 turns to consider the implications of shifting to an entirely new tax structure at a given point in the life cycle. It examines the effects of varying the time periods over which two different tax structures apply within the life cycle of the cohort. Conclusions are in section 13.7.

13.1   The Simulation Model

The calculations reported below are based on the simulated incomes of a single cohort of males between the ages of 20 and 65. The members of the cohort are considered to be continuously employed over the period and no deaths take place. Alternative income tax structures are examined where (except for section 13.6) the same set of marginal tax rates and thresholds (suitably indexed) are used in each year. In order to simplify the analysis, interest-income taxation is ignored, which means that the time profile of saving by each individual can also be ignored.

13.1.1   Income Profiles

Incomes in each year are assumed to follow the lognormal distribution, so that x_t is distributed as $\Lambda\left(\mu_t, \sigma_t^2\right)$. For year 1, the income of the ith person, x_{i1}, is obtained using:

$$x_{i1} = \exp\left(\mu_t + v_i \sigma_1\right) \tag{13.1}$$

where v_i is a random variable drawn from a normal distribution, $N\left(0, 1\right)$, with zero mean and unit variance. Equation (13.1) is obtained from the basic relation $v_i = \left(\log x_{i1} - \mu_1\right)/\sigma_1$. The values of income in subsequent years are obtained using:

$$x_{it} = \left(\frac{x_{it-1}}{m_{t-1}}\right)^{\beta_t} \exp\left(\mu_t + u_{it}\right) \tag{13.2}$$

where:

$$\mu_t = \mu_0 + \phi t - \delta t^2 \tag{13.3}$$

and:

$$u_{it} = \gamma_t u_{it-1} + \epsilon_{it} \tag{13.4}$$

Furthermore, $m_t = \exp\left(\mu_t\right)$ and ϵ_{it} is a random variable drawn from a normal distribution with mean zero and variance $\sigma_{\epsilon t}^2$. The parameters β, γ

Table 13.1: Income Profiles: Males Aged 20 in 1991

no.	Parameter	Estimate
1	μ_0	9.707930
2	θ	0.055760
3	δ	0.001730
4	γ	-0.120000
5	b_0	0.746810
6	b_1	0.019980
7	b_2	-0.000438
8	d_0	0.200000
9	d_1	-0.018230
10	d_2	0.000457
11	σ_1^2	0.200000

and σ_ϵ^2 are given time subscripts in order to allow for their variation over the life cycle. The New Zealand data for males suggest that quadratic functions are appropriate, over a range of ages, for β and σ_ϵ^2 , although there is no significant variation in γ. Hence:

$$\beta_t = b_0 + b_1 t + b_2 t^2 \tag{13.5}$$

$$\sigma_{\epsilon t}^2 = d_0 + d_1 t + d_2 t^2 \tag{13.6}$$

The parameter values appropriate for a cohort aged 20 in 1991, when $t = 1$, are given in Table 13.1 and taken from chapter 7. However, equation (13.6) is applied only for $3 \leq t \leq 40$. After $t = 40$, σ_ϵ^2 is assumed to be constant at its value at $t = 40$, and before $t = 3$ it is fixed at 0.3 for the first two years. The value of u_{i1} is set equal to zero for all individuals.

Equations (13.1) to (13.6) can thus be used to generate the simulated income profiles for a cohort of males. The following analysis uses simulated incomes over the period $1 \leq t \leq 45$, corresponding to ages 20 to 45. No deaths or other exits from the labour force over that period are assumed to take place. Nominal income growth of 5 per cent per year is assumed to take place in each year over the life cycle, and the rate of inflation is assumed to be constant at 3 per cent. When discounting incomes and taxes, a nominal

Table 13.2: Income Tax Schedules 1985 to 1989

Threshold	Rate	Threshold	Rate	Threshold	Rate
1985	-	1986	-	1987	-
0	0.2	0	0.175	0	0.15
9693.84	0.33	8774.09	0.24	11676.58	0.30
40391.01	0.451	13892.31	0.315	36873.41	0.48
48469.21	0.561	36558.73	0.3755	-	-
61394.31	0.66	43870.48	0.5205	-	-
-	-	55569.27	0.57	-	-
1988	-	1989	-	-	-
0	0.15	0	0.15	-	-
10981.54	0.29	10518.24	0.28	-	-
34678.57	0.36	34184.29	0.33	-	-
35690.02	0.405	-	-	-	-

interest rate of 5 per cent is used.

13.1.2 Income Tax Structures

The incomes generated using the above model are then subject to a variety of income tax structures. The simulations apply to males, and the comparisons simply apply various New Zealand tax schedules directly to the simulated incomes. No consideration is given to transfer payments such as means-tested benefits which usually depend on household composition, and no allowance is made for other possible deductions from the tax base. The tax structures are first adjusted to 1991 using the consumer price index, and are given in Table 13.2. The price indices for 1985, 1986, 1987, 1988, 1989 and 1991 were respectively 601, 664, 790, 840, 877, 971.

The year 1985 refers to the 1985-6 tax year, and the marginal rates given are effective rates (including surtax where appropriate). In New Zealand there is no tax-free threshold, so the first dollar of income is taxable. The reduction in the top marginal rate of income tax over the period is evident. However, the precise impact of a given tax structure cannot be inferred from the schedule of marginal rates and thresholds alone; it depends on the nature of the pre-tax income distribution. This is one reason why differences may be expected as the time period changes.

The major tax changes of the 1980s were accompanied by a substantial amount of base broadening by eliminating many tax deductions. As explained above, these effects, along with any efficiency effects of the reforms, are not examined here. Hence the lifetime income profiles are assumed to be fixed independently of the income tax structure.

13.2 Annual Incomes Over the Life Cycle

This section examines the variation in progressivity and inequality over the life cycle of the simulated cohort, using a single year as the accounting period. This shows the complexity of the variations and the relationships among the various measures.

13.2.1 Taxation and Redistribution

The extent of redistribution of annual incomes produced by the income tax system can be measured by the difference between the inequality measures of the pre-tax and post-tax distributions. If, as above, x denotes pre-tax income, then post-tax income, y, is obtained using the transformation $y = x - t(x)$, where $t(x)$ is the tax function. If G denotes the Gini measure of inequality, the Reynolds-Smolensky (1977) measure, L, of the redistributive effect of the tax schedule is given, where the subscripts refer to the appropriate distribution, by:

$$L = G_x - G_y \qquad (13.7)$$

The variation in L with age can be seen in Figure 13.1 for the 1985, 1987 and 1989 income tax structures. The profiles of G_y for the 1986 and 1988 structures are not shown in the diagram to avoid cluttering it too much. The Gini measure of inequality of pre-tax income increases sharply in the early years, and then falls until it begins to increase from years 20 to about 40, corresponding to ages 40 to 60 years, until again falling. The profile of G_y follows quite closely that of G_x, although that for the 1985 structure is

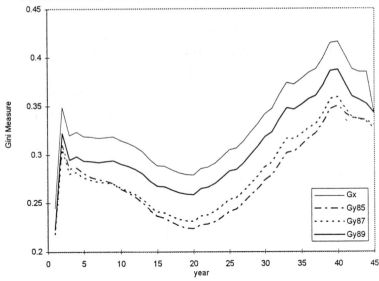

Figure 13.1: Inequality of Annual Income

consistently below that of the 1989 structure. The former therefore has a greater redistributive effect in every year of working life, though the profiles are closer together in the early and later years. However, the 1987 structure is more redistributive than the 1985 structure in the early and later years of the life cycle.

13.2.2   Tax Disproportionality

Redistribution, in terms of the difference between inequality measures, is often thought to translate directly into progressivity; hence a redistributive scheme is automatically said to be progressive, and vice versa. However, an alternative approach can be taken whereby progressivity is regarded as reflecting instead the extent of disproportionality of tax payments generated by the tax. This is the approach suggested by Kakwani (1977) and is based on measures that are closely related to Gini inequality measures.

The Gini inequality measure is related to the standard Lorenz curve, which plots the proportion of people against their corresponding proportion of total income, when individuals are arranged in ascending order of incomes. If the ordering of individuals by their pre-tax incomes is used, a similar type

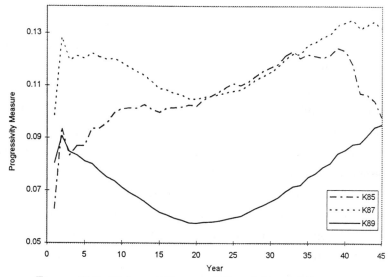

Figure 13.2: Kakwani Progressivity of Annual Income

of curve can be obtained using the tax paid by individuals; this gives a curve called the tax concentration curve. Hence the latter relates to the locus of points obtained by plotting the proportion of people against the corresponding proportion of total tax paid by those people. An analogous measure called the tax concentration measure, C_t, can be defined for this curve, corresponding to a Gini-type area measure. If the tax system is strictly proportional, then the tax concentration curve coincides with the Lorenz curve of the pre-tax incomes. But if the tax system is progressive, in the sense that the relatively richer pay proportionately more tax and the average tax rate increases with income, the tax concentration curve lies further from the diagonal line of equality than the Lorenz curve. This leads to the Kakwani measure, K, defined as:

$$K = C_t - G_x \tag{13.8}$$

The age profiles of K for each year under the 1985, 1987 and 1989 tax structures, suitably indexed, are shown in Figure 13.2. Despite the similarity in the profiles of G_y, shown in Figure 13.1, the variation in the progressivity with age is quite different. The application of the 1985 structure each year, with thresholds indexed according to inflation, produces a fairly steady increase until about age 60, after which K falls with age. By contrast, under the 1987 and 1989 tax structures, K falls until about age 40 and then rises steadily until age 65, although it is much higher for the 1987 schedule than for the 1989 schedule. Indeed, K is higher for the 1987 tax than for the 1985 tax schedule in most years. This arises because the marginal tax rates in the 1987 structure, despite its lower top marginal rate and smaller number of thresholds, increase more rapidly over the lower ranges of incomes than does the 1985 structure. Therefore it is more progressive over the years of the life cycle when incomes are on average lower. In considering this point it is worth keeping in mind that although the tax thresholds are adjusted each year to allow for inflation, the average incomes of the cohort grow faster than inflation until about the late forties. Average income reaches a peak and then declines, as shown by the quadratic profile of μ_t above.

The variation in μ_t with age also results in a systematic variation in the overall average tax rate with age. Let g denote the ratio of total tax revenue to total income. The age profiles of g for the three tax structures show a humped shape, with the 1985 structure having consistently higher values of g and a profile that is somewhat more 'peaked' than that of the 1989 structure. This characteristic reflects the greater extent to which marginal tax rates increase in the 1985 schedule.

13.3   Increasing the Accounting Period

This section examines the effect on the measures used in the previous section of gradually extending the time period over which incomes are measured. The longer period income measure used here is that of the present value at age 20 (when $t = 1$). Hence the present value of income measured over j years, $x_{(j)}$ is given by:

$$x_{(j)} = \sum_{t=1}^{j} x_t \left(1 + r\right)^{-(t-1)} \tag{13.9}$$

where r is the fixed rate of discount. Alternative income concepts could of course be used, such as annuity or annual average measures, but the present-value concept is the most frequently used. Furthermore, it has been shown that the various measures behave in very similar ways; see Creedy (1995).

13.3.1 Taxation and Redistribution

The Gini measures of pre-tax and post-tax incomes, for time periods of 1, 2, 3...., 45 years, are shown in Figure 13.3. The inequality of pre-tax income gradually falls, after its initial increase, as the time period is increased. However, it remains relatively stable for time periods of between 20 and 35 years. For very long accounting periods, the Gini measure is below all of the single-year measures. The profiles of G_y as the accounting period is increased show a similar pattern, although for the tax schedules of 1985, 1986 and 1987 the rankings change after about ten years.

Thus the structure of 1987 appears to be more redistributive when the accounting period is below ten years, but is less redistributive than the 1985 structure for longer accounting periods.

To the extent that the profiles spread out as the length of time over which incomes are measured increases, it can be said that the redistributive differences between the various tax structures increase with the accounting period. The redistributive effect, as measured by $G_x - G_y$, remains quite steady for the 1988 tax structure as the time period varies. It falls slightly for the 1989 structure, and for the 1985, 1986 and 1987 structures the redistributive effect increases initially as the time period increases, but then becomes stable.

13.3.2 Progressivity and the Time Period

The variation in the Kakwani progressivity (tax disproportionality) measure as the accounting period increases is shown, for each tax structure, in Figure 13.4. After an initial increase, the 1987, 1988 and 1989 tax structures display a reduction in the degree of progressivity, or disproportionality of taxes, as the period increases. For 1985 and 1986 structures, the progressivity increases with the length of time, until accounting periods of about 35 years are

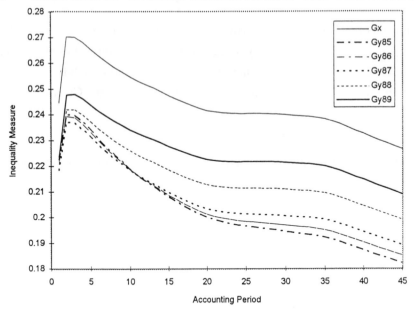

Figure 13.3: Inequality of Longer Accounting Periods

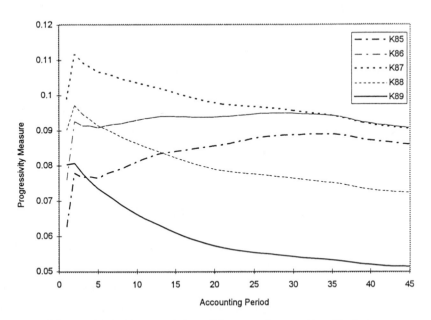

Figure 13.4: Progressivity of Longer Accounting Periods

exceeded. The rankings of the various structures can be seen to change as the accounting period increases, as shown by the intersections between schedules shown in Figure 13.4. Nevertheless, the 1986 and 1987 structures are always more progressive than the 1985 structure. This result contrasts with that found for the redistributive effects of those structures. These results therefore show how, when progressivity is associated with the disproportionality of tax payments, the degree of progressivity does not necessarily fall as the accounting period increases.

Measures of the redistributive effect and the degree of progressivity are linked, in part, by the effective overall tax rate, g, defined above. For each structure, g increases steadily as the accounting period increases, reflecting the systematic increase in average earnings of the cohort. The rankings of the various tax structures remain fixed, independent of the time period used.

13.3.3 Taxation and Re-ranking

It was mentioned above that the use of a multiperiod accounting framework can give rise, unlike the single-period case, to some re-ranking. This is because individuals with the same present value of gross income may pay different amounts of tax, depending on their time profile of income. This type of re-ranking of individuals can only occur for a tax schedule that has increasing marginal tax rates.

Reference was made in section 13.2 to the role played by the Lorenz curve in producing alternative measures. This device can also be used to produce a measure of re-ranking. If individuals are ranked in ascending order according to their pre-tax incomes, then it is possible to plot the locus of points which trace the increasing proportion of people in relation to the associated proportion of post-tax income. This curve (like the corresponding curve of tax paid) is called the concentration curve of post-tax income. It is possible to produce a Gini type of inequality measure, referred to as the concentration measure, C_y.

If the tax structure does not lead to any re-ranking of individuals, when moving from the pre-tax to the post-tax distribution of income, the concen-

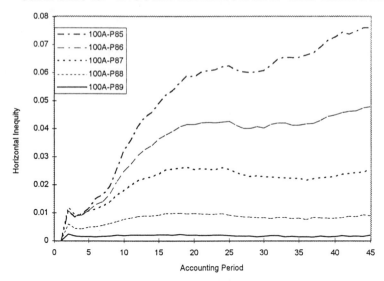

Figure 13.5: Re-ranking Inequity and the Accounting Period

tration curve of y corresponds exactly to the Lorenz curve of y. Hence the degree of re-ranking can be related to the difference between the two measures. The Atkinson-Plotnick measure, P, following Atkinson (1979) and Plotnick (1981), is given by:

$$P = \frac{G_y - C_y}{2G_y} \tag{13.10}$$

The variation in this measure, as the accounting period is extended, is illustrated in Figure 13.5. Each profile obviously begins with a value of zero when only the first year is used. The comparisons between the tax structures reveal the importance of the degree of marginal rate progression. The later structures, particularly the flatter 1989 structures, display very little re-ranking irrespective of the length of the accounting period used. The 1985 structure has substantially more re-ranking, which systematically increases as the accounting period is increased, because it has a more rapidly rising marginal rate structure.

Figures 13.3 to 13.5 each display different features of the tax structures. They reveal that unequivocal comparisons between them cannot be made. Furthermore, there are no simple statements about the role of the accounting period; although the results for g and P are relatively straight-forward, inequality and progressivity results are much more complex. The various measures can be related to each other, using a relationship given by Kakwani. This states that:

$$L = \left(\frac{g}{1-g}\right) K - 2G_y P \qquad (13.11)$$

This shows that higher values of g and K, together with lower values of P, contribute to produce higher values of L. But progressivity and redistribution need not move in the same direction, as revealed by the above numerical results. For example, a low degree of progressivity, when combined with a sufficiently high overall tax ratio, can give rise to a high degree of redistribution (despite also having a high degree of re-ranking). It is precisely this latter property that is demonstrated in some of the cases reported above. These considerations affect comparisons between tax structures and between different accounting periods using the same tax structure.

13.4   Cross-sectional Comparisons

This section examines the extent to which the summary measures of progressivity and redistribution of a tax structure are different when a life cycle framework is used, compared with results obtained when using cross-sectional income distributions. For this purpose the results based on the present value of income, measured over the 45-year period from age 20 to age 65, are compared with the single cross-section obtained from the relevant Household Expenditure Survey.

First, the lifetime measures are given in Table 13.3 for each of the five tax schedules used above (applied over each year of the life cycle and suitably indexed, as explained above). These results can be compared with Table 13.4, which shows the results of applying each tax structure to the male income distribution (wage and salary income) for that year. Hence the 1985 tax structure is applied to the 1985 male incomes, the 1986 tax structure is applied to the 1986 males incomes, and so on for later years. In Table 13.3,

Table 13.3: Present Value of Income over 45 Years

Tax Structure	Gini	K	L	g
1985	0.1822	0.0861	0.0445	0.3420
1986	0.1852	0.0909	0.0415	0.3144
1987	0.1892	0.0907	0.0374	0.2928
1988	0.1991	0.0724	0.0275	0.2758
1989	0.2091	0.0514	0.0176	0.2546

Table 13.4: Cross-sectional Distributions

TaxYear	Gini	K	L	g
1985	0.2719	0.0664	0.0295	0.3075
1986	0.2778	0.0878	0.0361	0.2914
1987	0.2883	0.0948	0.0339	0.2638
1988	0.3096	0.0829	0.0290	0.2595
1989	0.3250	0.0625	0.0205	0.2470

the simulated distribution of pre-tax income remains the same whichever indexed tax structure is applied over the 45-year period.

The first point to note is that the Gini inequality measure of post-tax income for each year, from the cross-sectional results of Table 13.4, is higher than the corresponding value for income measured over the 45-year period. Indeed, the Gini inequality of lifetime incomes is about 30 per cent lower than that observed in cross sections. This result reflects the substantial amount of relative income mobility from year to year, and in particular the regression towards the mean observed for males in New Zealand.

Earlier studies of taxation in cross-sectional and lifetime perspectives have found that the progressivity (or regressivity) of taxes is lower in the longer period context than in the single-year framework. However, Tables 13.3 and 13.4 show that for tax structures 1985 and 1986 the Kakwani measure of disproportionality of tax payments is higher in the 45-year case than in the corresponding cross section. Furthermore, the redistributive effect of the tax structure, as measured by the Reynolds-Smolensky index (the reduction in the Gini from pre- to post-tax incomes), is found to be higher in the longer-period context for the three tax structures 1985-6-7. The results obtained in previous studies cannot therefore be regarded as general; they apply only for the later tax structures used here.

Table 13.4 shows, more surprisingly, that the redistributive effect of income taxation appears to increase between 1985 and 1986. It should be remembered that in the cross-sectional results the pre-tax income distribution changes from year to year, so that the precise measures result from changes in both the tax structure and the income distribution. Further calculations showed that if the pre-tax distribution is held fixed, the redistributive effect falls as expected.

Consider the effect on the Gini measure of inequality of post-tax income of 'moving' from one tax structure to another. For example, from Table 13.3 the lifetime value of G_y increases by 1.65 per cent when moving from the 1985 to the 1986 structure in each year of working life, but the cross-sectional comparisons in Table 8.4 show a higher increase of 2.17 per cent. A change from the 1986 to the 1987 structure gives percentage increases in the Gini measure of respectively 2.16 and 3.78 for lifetime and cross-sectional distributions. A change from the 1987 to the 1988 structure gives respective percentage changes of 5.23 and 7.39. Hence in each case, the cross-sectional results overstate the increase in inequality resulting from the tax structure change. However, in moving from the 1988 to the 1989 tax structure, the Gini inequality measure of post-tax income increased by about 5 per cent irrespective of the framework used.

As suggested earlier, the results for cross-sectional distributions are affected substantially by the nature of age-income profiles and the age distribution of the population over the period, as well as the tax structure itself. The cross-sectional results also conceal the substantial reduction in re-ranking inequity associated with the flattening of the tax rate structure in moving from the 1985 to the 1989 structure, and discussed in the previous section. Indeed, when moving from the 1985 to the 1986 tax structure, the re-ranking measure falls by 37.14 per cent; the falls from 1986 to 1987, from 1987 to 1988 and from 1988 to 1989 are equal respectively to 46, 65 and 77 per cent. These changes must be set against any increase in the 'static' cross-sectional changes in inequality, but they are only revealed by a dynamic analysis.

13.5   A Simplified Income Mobility Process

The previous sections have used a simulation model in which the process of relative income mobility included several elements. It allowed for regression towards the mean, dependence on the past (serial correlation in year-to-year changes), and random movements, combined with systematic variations in the extent of random variability and regression to the mean over the life cycle. The dynamic simulation model was estimated using limited longitudinal data, and is able to capture the variation in inequality with age. As shown in Figure 13.1, inequality rises sharply in the early years, after which it follows an approximately cubic relationship, falling again in the later years. The resulting patterns of progressivity and redistribution, in both the single year and multi-year frameworks, are far from straightforward.

The present section provides a contrast with the previous results by examining the implications of a much simpler dynamic process of year-to-year changes. The extent to which the previous comparisons between tax structures are robust can therefore be judged. The income model used here continues to use equation (13.3) describe the variation in the mean log-income with age of the cohort. However, it is assumed that $\sigma^2_{\epsilon t} = 0$ and that $\beta_t = 1$ for all t, and that $\gamma_t = 0.005$ in all t. Hence equation (13.2) is replaced by:

$$y_{it} = y_{it-1} \exp\left\{(\mu_t - \mu_{t-1}) + u_{it}\right\} \tag{13.12}$$

where u_{it} is distributed as $N\left(0, \sigma^2_\epsilon\right)$. This simpler process of income dynamics corresponds to a Gibrat process, and implies a steady increase in the dispersion of log-income over age. Hence this process does not capture the peak in the profile revealed in the earlier ages, and the reduction in the later ages.

The Gini inequality measures for each year increase steadily, reflecting the simple Gibrat process discussed above. As with the more complex mobility case, the 1987 structure displays more redistribution than the 1985 structure in the younger and older stages of the life cycle. Variations in progressivity are also similar to the more complex case. The similarity occurs because the simpler model is able to generate the changing distribution of income with

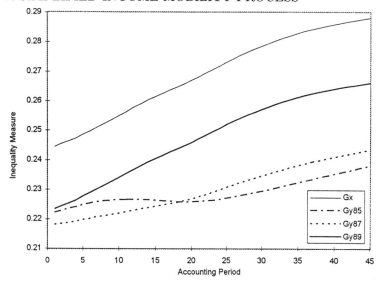

Figure 13.6: Inequality with Gibrat Process

age quite well. It simply approximates the relative inequality profile using a straight line rather than the more complex relationship shown above, yet it provides a good approximation for many of the years. The more interesting issue relates to the way in which the different dynamics affect the longer period measures.

13.5.1   Longer Time Periods

The Gini measures for time periods from 1 to 45 years are shown in Figure 13.6 for the 1985, 1987 and 1989 tax structures and the Gibrat mobility process. In this case a major difference from the earlier results is that the inequality of pre-tax income increases continually as the accounting period is lengthened. This contrasts with the previous situation, shown in Figure 13.3, where inequality falls as the period is increased. The reason for this difference is not simply that the inequality of annual incomes always increases in the Gibrat case. It arises largely because the Gibrat process does not contain the types of systematic egalitarian tendency of the more complex model. In the earlier case, there is systematic regression towards the mean and negative serial correlation in year-to-year relative movements. These

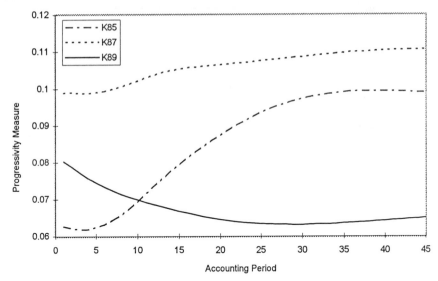

Figure 13.7: Progressivity with Gibrat Process

egalitarian tendencies operate to reduce inequality as the time period is increased, despite the fact that single-year inequality measures do increase over a substantial proportion of the life cycle. The substantial random variation operates against the other tendencies to generate the increase in the annual inequality measures over a wide range of years.

In comparing the redistributive effects of the tax schedules, however, it can be seen that the effect of the 1989 structure remains quite stable, irrespective of the accounting period. The same result was observed in Figure 13.3. The 1985 structure generates an increasing redistributive effect as the time period increases, although this becomes steady after an accounting period of about 25 years. Again, a similar result was observed for the more complex dynamic process.

The Kakwani progressivity measures for increasing time periods are shown in Figure 13.7. This again demonstrates that, even with a simpler dynamic process, no general statements are available about the behaviour of progressivity measures as the time period increases. Beyond the first few years of cumulation, the progressivity of the 1985 tax structure increases with the accounting period while that of the 1989 structure decreases for most of the range (until more than 30 years are involved). In addition, the 1989 structure, the less redistributive for all accounting periods, is the most progressive for periods up to ten years. The 1987 structure is more progressive than the other tax schedules for all accounting periods. In comparing the progressivity effects of these tax structures for varying accounting periods, the general picture is not substantially different for Figures 13.4 and 13.7, despite the difference in the income dynamics involved.

The results for the Atkinson-Plotnick measure show, as expected, that the reduced degree of income variability in the Gibrat process produces less re-ranking. As before, it is very low for the 1989 tax structure and varies very little as the accounting period is increased. The 1985 tax schedule produces substantially more re-ranking which, as in Figure 13.5, increases as the accounting period is increased. The main finding is therefore that, despite the different implications for the time profile of inequality over the life cycle and the effects on inequality of extending the accounting period, comparisons between tax structures in terms of their redistribution and progressivity are quite similar.

13.6 The Timing of Tax Structure Changes

The previous analyses have assumed that a given income tax structure applies during each year of the 45-year period (from age 20 to 65) for a single cohort. Only the tax thresholds were adjusted each year, and comparisons were made among several different structures. The major objective was to examine the way in which various measures of inequality and tax progressivity behave when the accounting period is increased. In practice, a policy change from one tax structure to another occurs at a particular point in the life cycle of each cohort; the same tax change occurs at different stages of the life cycle for different cohorts.

The purpose of this section is to consider the implications for lifetime inequality and progressivity of the date, or age, at which the income tax changes. For present purposes the simulation model is extended slightly. Instead of considering ages 20 to 65, each individual in the cohort is assumed to live in retirement for a further 14 years. The retirement is financed by accumulated savings, at a rate of 15 per cent of net, or disposable, income in each year. The resulting sum finances an annuity over the fixed period of retirement. Hence the model abstracts from the issue of differential mortality. The analysis assumes that there is an interest-income tax, unlike the previous simulations. In each case, the income concept used is the present value at age 20.

Simulations were carried out in which the 1985 tax structure (suitably indexed) applies. This was then changed to the 1989 structure at alternative points in the life cycle. Hence if the change occurs at year 10, the years 1 to 9 are taxed using the 1985 schedule and years 10 to 59 are taxed using the 1989 schedule. Comparisons are shown for the full simulation model and the simple Gibrat process.

13.6.1   Inequality and a Tax Switch

The Gini inequality measures of pre-tax and post-tax lifetime income are shown in Figure 13.8 for both income dynamic processes. The profiles for the Gibrat process are above the others, given the higher inequality of lifetime income observed above. The inequality of gross income is obviously constant, irrespective of the time at which the tax switch occurs. As the year at which the shift to the 1989 structure becomes later, the inequality of net income falls as the more redistributive 1985 schedule dominates. It can be seen that the profiles are in each case sigmoid, rather than linear, and are symmetric. The discounting does not negate the influence of the later years in taking present values. When changing in the first ten years there is little influence of the 1985 structure, and when changing in the last ten years there is little influence of the 1989 structure.

Figure 13.9 shows the Kakwani progressivity measures for alternative switching dates. The Gibrat process generates higher lifetime progressivity in all cases, but the two profiles are also sigmoid in shape. However, it is of interest that, for the Gibrat process, when the 1989 structure is introduced in the early years of the life cycle for this cohort, progressivity actually falls

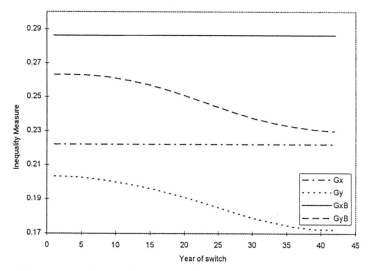

Figure 13.8: Inequality and a Switch in the Tax Structure

as the time for which the 1985 structure applies is increased. An increase in the amount of time that the 1985 structure applies would be expected to increase the progressivity. However, this is explained by Figure 13.7, which shows that, for the 1985 structure, progressivity falls as the accounting period is initially increased.

For the more complex process, it is found that progressivity falls slightly as the date of introduction of the 1989 structure is delayed, for the later dates. Again this is explained by the downturn in the profile in Figure 13.7 for the 1985 tax structure, for the very long time periods.

13.7 Conclusions

This chapter has used a cohort lifetime income simulation model in order to examine the effects on inequality and progressivity of extending the time period over which income and tax payments are measured. The income tax schedule typically displays increasing marginal rates, and there is a substantial amount of relative income mobility, along with a systematic variation in average incomes over the life cycle of the cohort. These factors mean that the accounting period may have an important impact on the summary measures

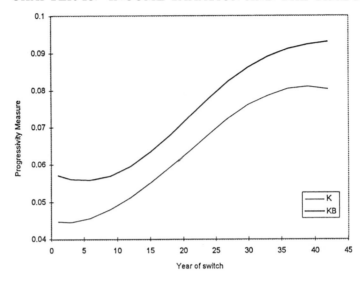

Figure 13.9: Progressivity and a Switch in the Tax Structure

used, but simulation methods are required in view of the intractability of an analytical approach.

The simulations showed that progressivity and inequality measures can often move in opposite directions, both over time for annual accounting periods and as the length of period is gradually increased. The relationship between summary measures is complicated by the role of the aggregate tax ratio, in addition to the horizontal inequity than can result in the longer-period framework.

Some tax structures operating in New Zealand during the second half of the 1980s were found to increase in progressivity as the time period increases, while others showed less progressivity as the time period increases. In view of the very different shapes of the profiles, the ranking of tax structures, according to the degree of redistribution and of progressivity produced, were found to change as the time period increases.

Re-ranking of individuals when moving from the pre-tax to the post-tax distribution, was found to increase as the accounting period increases. Not surprisingly, it is higher and increases more rapidly as the accounting period is increased for tax structures displaying more steeply rising rate structures.

The differences in progressivity and redistribution resulting from different income tax structures applied over the 45-year period from age 20 to
65 were compared with results obtained from cross-sectional data. It was
found that inequality is lower in the life cycle context than in cross-sections,
though both progressivity and redistributive effects can be either higher or
lower, depending on the particular structures and years being compared. The
changes in the inequality of post-tax income resulting from the use of different tax structures were found to be lower in the life cycle compared with the
cross-sectional results, except for the change from the 1988 to the 1989 tax
schedule. The cross-sectional comparisons combine the effects of the changing distribution of pre-tax income with those of the tax structure changes.
In addition, the cross-sectional framework ignores the re-ranking, revealed in
the longer-period comparisons for tax structures having increasing marginal
tax rates.

Comparisons were also made using a simple Gibrat process of relative
income mobility, implying a systematic increase in annual inequality with age.
While this process implies very different properties for the inequality of pre-
tax income as the accounting period increases, it was found that comparisons
between alternative tax structures gave similar results to those obtained for
the more complex process.

The analysis has displayed the extra valuable information which can be
revealed by analyses which allow for a longer accounting period, and the
potentially misleading nature of cross-sectional comparisons. The use of a
longer period framework also involves a considerable increase in complexity;
it is seen that the use of a longer period makes it necessary to consider explicitly a large range of relevant factors which are too easily ignored when using
the simpler cross-sectional approach to measuring tax progressivity. The
cost of the additional insights is of course the cost of obtaining appropriate
longitudinal data and of constructing appropriate tax models.

Chapter 14

Mobility and Social Welfare

If there is no income mobility from one year to the next, so that relative incomes remain unchanged over time, a relative measure of inequality has the same value irrespective of the accounting period used to measure income. It is sometimes suggested that the existence of income mobility, even if it causes the inequality of annual income to increase over time, leads to lower inequality of a longer-period measure. In discussing what he referred to as the denial of the growth in inequality in the US, Krugman (1994, pp.140-142) described the argument that annual inequality is highly misleading because of the existence of relative income mobility as 'the best' response. Krugman (1994, p.143) argued that the existence of a large amount of mobility is not the issue; what is important for the argument is that mobility must have *increased* significantly.

But the issue is more complex. Any statement about changes in mobility and the relationship between short- and longer-period inequality needs to be highly qualified, particularly as different types of income mobility may be distinguished, not all of which are egalitarian. Furthermore, so long as individuals have concave utility of income functions, income variability over time imposes a welfare loss, which may or may not be compensated by a higher annual average income. Consequently the implications of income mobility for individual and social welfare are not immediately clear.

This chapter examines the relationship between social welfare and different types of income mobility. The framework is one in which social welfare is

257

regarded as a function of individual utilities, with the latter depending on incomes in two periods. The social welfare function takes the much-used form introduced by Atkinson (1970) and reflects the judge's degree of aversion to inequality. Individuals are assumed to have an aversion to income variability over time. Hence for each individual, the utility-equivalent annuity, the constant income stream giving the same utility as the actual income stream, is less than the annual average income.

Two types of income mobility are distinguished. First, there is a general tendency for those with relatively higher incomes to receive, on average, relatively lower proportional income changes; thus there is 'regression towards the mean' in the Galtonian sense. Secondly, there is a purely stochastic component to income changes whereby each individual experiences a random proportional change which is independent of the current income and previous changes. Each type of mobility is described by a single parameter.

The central question examined in this chapter is the following. Given a fixed initial distribution of income in the first period, is it possible for a *change* in the mobility process (defined in terms of the two parameters describing the regression and stochastic components) to be associated simultaneously with an *increase* in inequality in the second period, a *decrease* in inequality when using a longer-period concept of income, and an *increase* in social welfare? It is found that strong conditions are required for all three results to hold simultaneously. It is worth stressing that the issue is framed in terms of changes in the mobility process, so comparative static results are relevant.

Section 14.1 describes the mobility process used, and examines the relationship between social welfare and the two types of mobility specified. It is found that, given the complexity of the relationship, comparative static exercises are much too cumbersome to be of any value. Hence numerical simulations are used in Section 14.2 to consider a wide range of alternative processes. It is found that three basic cases can be distinguished, and the type of mobility change required to achieve the three changes simultaneously is identified. Section 14.3 briefly reviews some limited evidence relating to income mobility.

14.1 Social Welfare and Mobility

14.1.1 A Dynamic Process

The mobility process contains a stochastic component and regression towards the mean. Let y_{it} denote individual i's income in period t, and let μ_t denote the mean of logarithms (log-geometric mean) in period t, with $m_t = \exp(\mu_t)$ as the geometric mean. The generating process can be written as:

$$y_{i2} = \left(\frac{y_{i1}}{m_1}\right)^{\beta} \exp(\mu_2 + u_i) \tag{14.1}$$

where u_1 is $N(0, \sigma_u^2)$. If $\beta = 1$ there is no regression towards the (geometric) mean and the mobility process is simply one in which proportionate changes in relative earnings are random. Equation (14.1) can be rewritten as:

$$(\log y_{i2} - \mu_2) = \beta(\log y_{i1} - \mu_1) + u_i \tag{14.2}$$

Hence the variance of logarithms of income in period 2, σ_2^2, is given by

$$\sigma_2^2 = \beta^2 \sigma_1^2 + \sigma_u^2 \tag{14.3}$$

The variance of logarithms is constant only in the special case where $\sigma_u^2 = \sigma_1^2(1 - \beta^2)$. In general, the variance of logarithms of income increases if the regression coefficient, β, exceeds the correlation between log-incomes in the two periods.

14.1.2 The Social Welfare Function

Write the utility of individual i, U_i, obtained from the income stream (y_{i1}, y_{i2}) as:

$$U_i = \sum_{t=1}^{2} \left(\frac{1}{1+r}\right)^{t-1} \frac{y_{it}^{1-\varepsilon_0}}{1 - \varepsilon_0} \tag{14.4}$$

where r is the rate of time preference and ε_0 measures the aversion to income variability. In the following analysis these are assumed to be the same for all individuals. The utility equivalent annuity, y_{ai}, is defined as the constant income stream giving the same utility as the actual stream, so that:

$$y_{ai} = \left\{ \left(\frac{1+r}{2+r} \right) \sum_{t=1}^{2} \left(\frac{1}{1+r} \right)^{t-1} y_{it}^{1-\varepsilon_0} \right\}^{1/(1-\varepsilon_0)} \tag{14.5}$$

Hence individuals are willing to trade income stability, measured by $y_{ai}/\overline{y_i}$, against the annual average $\overline{y_i} = \sum_{t=1}^{2} y_{it}/2$. Income variability, V_i, is measured by $1 - y_{ai}/\overline{y_i}$.

It is useful to rearrange the expression for utility in (14.4) as:

$$U_i = \left(\frac{y_{i1}^{1-\varepsilon_0}}{1-\varepsilon} \right) \left\{ 1 + \frac{1}{1+r} \left(\frac{y_{i2}}{y_{i1}} \right)^{1-\varepsilon_0} \right\} \tag{14.6}$$

Furthermore, equation (14.1) can be rearranged to give the ratio of incomes as:

$$\frac{y_{i2}}{y_{i1}} = \left(\frac{y_{i1}}{m_1} \right)^{\beta-1} \exp \left(\mu_2 - \mu_1 + u_i \right) \tag{14.7}$$

Hence if there is no regression towards the mean, so that $\beta = 1$, and no systematic growth, so that $\mu_2 = \mu_1$, the ratio of incomes is $\exp(u_i)$.

Social welfare, W, is defined in terms of the U_is as follows:

$$W = \frac{1}{1-\varepsilon} \sum_{i=1}^{N} U_i^{1-\varepsilon_1} \tag{14.8}$$

where there are N individuals and ε_1 represents the aversion to inequality of the judge. This chapter is concerned with the relationship between social welfare and the two measures of income mobility, β and σ_u^2. The substitution of (14.7) into (14.6), and the resulting expression for U_i into (14.8), gives social welfare as:

$$W = \frac{1}{1-\varepsilon_1} \sum_{i=1}^{N} \left(\frac{y_{i1}^{1-\varepsilon_0}}{1-\varepsilon_0} \right)^{1-\varepsilon_1} \times$$
$$\left[1 + \frac{1}{1+r} \left(\frac{m_1}{y_{i1}} \right)^{(1-\beta)(1-\varepsilon_0)} \exp \left\{ (\mu_2 - \mu_1 + u_i)(1-\varepsilon_0) \right\} \right]^{1-\varepsilon_1} \tag{14.9}$$

Hence, social welfare is a nonlinear function of the random variables y_{i1} and u_i, and depends on their corresponding density functions, the regression to the mean parameter β, the aggregate growth rate $\mu_2 - \mu_1 = g$, and the two aversion parameters. In order to focus on the relationship between social welfare and the parameters governing income mobility, consider a Taylor series expansion of (14.9) around the mean, $\bar{u}$, of the u_i distribution and any regression parameter β_0.

First note that (14.9) consists of two parts, a function of the β and u_i. For each individual define:

$$f_i(\beta, u_i) = \left[1 + \frac{1}{1+r} \left(\frac{m_1}{y_{i1}} \right)^{(1-\beta)(1-\varepsilon_0)} \exp\left\{ (g + u_i)(1 - \varepsilon_0) \right\} \right]^{1-\varepsilon_1} \quad (14.10)$$

Then social welfare can be viewed as a weighted average of these functions with weights defined by:

$$w_{i1} = \left(\frac{y_{i1}^{1-\varepsilon_0}}{1 - \varepsilon_0} \right)^{1-\varepsilon_1} \quad (14.11)$$

The weights are the judge's views of the distribution of period 1 utility, and do not depend upon β or the u_i. The functions f_i retain the i subscript to note their dependence on y_{i1}. For each individual i, the Taylor series expansion of f_i is a polynomial in $(\beta - \beta_0)$ and $u_i - \bar{u}$ with coefficients derived from f_i and its derivatives evaluated at β_0 and $\bar{u}$. Per capital social welfare can be expressed as the sum of these expansions:

$$\begin{aligned} W &= \frac{1}{N} \left(\frac{1}{1 - \varepsilon_i} \right) \sum_{i=1}^{N} w_{i1} \left\{ f_i^0 + f_{\beta,i}^0 (\beta - \beta_0) + f_{u,i}^0 (u_i - \bar{u}) \right\} \\ &\quad + \frac{1}{2!} \{ f_{\beta\beta,i}^0 (\beta - \beta_0)^2 + 2 f_{\beta u,i}^0 (\beta - \beta_0)(u_i - \bar{u}) \\ &\quad + f_{uu,i}^0 (u_i - \bar{u})^2 \} \end{aligned} \quad (14.12)$$

where the superscript 0 notes that the function is evaluated at β^0 and $\bar{u}$. The f_i^0 and its derivatives depend only on y_{i1} and not on u_i. Thus, the first term in the expansion of social welfare adds functions of y_{i1} and consequently depends only on the first period distribution of income. The second term depends on the first period distribution of income, multiplied by the regression parameter. The third term and other higher-order terms interacted with $(u_i - \bar{u})$ are covariances between (a nonlinear function of) the y_{i1} and $(u_i - \bar{u})$ and are zero because the two random variables are independent and $(u_i - \bar{u})$ vanish because u_i is assumed normal. Assuming that higher-order powers of $(\beta - \beta_0)$ are negligible, social welfare can therefore be expressed:

$$
\begin{aligned}
W \;=\; & \frac{1}{N}\left(\frac{1}{1-\varepsilon_1}\right)\Big\{\sum w_{i1} f_1^0 + (\beta - \beta_0)\sum w_{i1} f_{\beta,i}^0 + \frac{1}{2}\sigma_u^2 \sum w_{i1} f_{uu,i}^0 \\
& + \frac{1}{2}(\beta - \beta_0)\,\sigma_u^2 \sum w_{i1} f_{\beta uu,i}^0 + \frac{1}{4}3\sigma_u^4 \sum w_{i1} f_{uuuu,i}^0 \\
& + h\left(\beta, \sigma_u^2\right) + \text{higher order terms in } (\beta - \beta_0)\Big\}
\end{aligned}
\tag{14.13}
$$

where $h\left(\beta, \sigma_u^2\right)$ represents sixth- and higher-order even moments of the normal u_i all can be expressed as functions of σ_u^2 and fourth- and higher-order even moments interacted with $(\beta - \beta_0)$. Comparative statics when inequality aversion exists are too intractable to carry out analytically. Hence, numerical simulations are provided in the following section.

14.2   Some Numerical Simulations

14.2.1   The Simulation Strategy

In the model specified in section 14.1, changes in the pattern of relative income mobility arise from changes in the parameters β and σ_u^2. The question is whether a change in the mobility process can simultaneously produce an increase in inequality in period 2, a reduction in income inequality measured over the two periods, and an increase in social welfare. It would be possible simply to carry out simulations of incomes over two periods for a given population and to search for combinations of changes in β and σ_u^2 which produce the desired results. However, a more systematic analysis is required in order to provide further insight.

The strategy adopted was to consider, for given values of the aversion coefficients ε_0 and ε_1, along with the initial distribution determined by μ_1 and σ_1^2 , and the growth and discount rates, alternative values of β and σ_u^2. For each combination of these mobility parameters, the values of inequality in the second period, I_2, and of income measured over both periods, I_1, were calculated along with the value of social welfare, W. The inequality measures are Atkinson's measure for the appropriate degree of inequality aversion. In all cases μ_1 and σ_1^2 were set to 4 and 0.5, and values of σ_u^2 varied from 0 to 0.2 in steps of 0.02 while those of β varied from 0.5 to 1.2 in steps of 0.02. This gives 396 combinations. Having obtained these values, the following relationships were estimated:

$$W = c_1 + c_2\beta + c_3\beta^2 + c_4\sigma_u^2 \tag{14.14}$$

$$I_L = \delta_0 + \delta_1\beta + \delta_2\beta^2 + \delta_3\sigma_u^2 \tag{14.15}$$

$$I_2 = \gamma_0 + \gamma_1\beta^2 + \gamma_2\sigma_u^2 \tag{14.16}$$

These specifications were found to give very good fits to the simulated values. Using the estimated parameters in (14.14) to (14.16), it was then possible to generate combinations of β and σ_u^2 which gave constant values of W, I_2 and I_L; and iso-welfare and iso-inequality curves were plotted to pass through the same combination of β and σ_u^2. By examining in which direction a change in mobility gives rise to the required change in the inequality and welfare measures, it was thus possible to see whether the required combination is feasible.

14.2.2   Changes in Mobility and Welfare

The above procedure was applied to a very large range of assumptions regarding the aversion parameters, and three basic cases were identified, according to the configuration of the iso-welfare and iso-inequality curves. Case 1 is illustrated in Figure 14.1, where the arrows show the direction of change required (that is, in order to achieve a rise in W, a fall in I_L and a rise in I_2). The configuration in case 1 occurs when $\varepsilon_1 > \varepsilon_0$, that is when aversion to inequality exceeds the aversion of individuals to mobility. It is more likely to arise the higher is the general growth of incomes over the period. For high values of ε_1, the iso-welfare profile is initially rising, before falling as shown

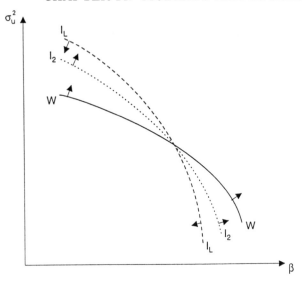

Figure 14.1: Mobility Case 1

in Figure 14.1, but this has no effect on the implications. The configuration shown for case 1 indicates that the combination of changes is feasible if β falls and σ_u^2 rises sufficiently. Hence the degree of regression towards the mean must increase and the extent of random variability governed by σ_u^2 must increase sufficiently in order for I_2 to increase. The increase must not, however, be too large, otherwise inequality of income measured over both periods would increase. While the combination of increasing W and I_2 with falling I_L can be achieved in this type of case, there is not a large range of movements in σ_u^2 and β for which it is possible.

The second type of situation, case 2, is illustrated in Figure 14.2. This case arises if $\varepsilon_0 > \varepsilon_1$, but the two aversion coefficients are relatively close. In case 2 it is also possible to achieve the required combination of changes, so long as β falls and σ_u^2 rises sufficiently. As ε_0 increases further, the situation turns into case 3, which is illustrated in Figure 14.3. This shows that it is not possible to achieve the required combination of changes in welfare and inequality. However, one interesting qualification does arise. If growth in incomes $(\mu_2 - \mu_1)$ is sufficiently large, the profile for W again cuts that for I_2 for a much lower value of β (and higher σ_u^2). This introduces a range of values

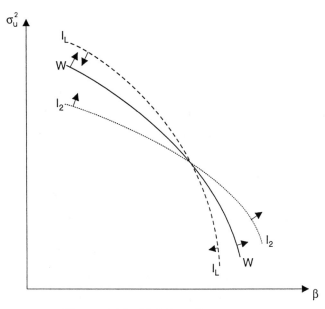

Figure 14.2: Mobility Case 2

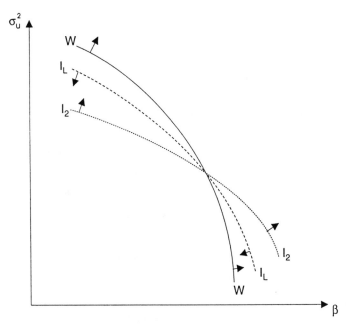

Figure 14.3: Mobility Case 3

over which the required changes in welfare and inequality can be achieved; however, starting from a given set of β and σ_u^2 it means that substantial changes are needed.

The simulations therefore show that the required changes in welfare and inequality can be achieved if there is an increase in regression towards the mean and simultaneously an increase in general variability, so long as the aversion to inequality is higher than the aversion of individuals to income variability. If ε_0 is only slightly higher than ε_1, it is still possible to achieve the desired combination. However, there is only a narrow range of changes which are capable of producing the desired result. If individuals' aversion to variability is relatively high compared with inequality aversion in the social welfare function, there is no combination of changes in β and σ_u^2 capable of producing an increase in W and I_2 along with a decrease in I_L. The empirical question thus arises of whether in practice any changes in mobility characteristics can be identified which may possible produce the required changes. Appropriate data are limited, but some evidence is considered in the following section.

14.3 Changes in Mobility

Evidence relating to *changes* in mobility and long-period inequality are required, given the comparative nature of the argument examined in this chapter. Hence, data relating to income mobility over a single specified period, showing that a certain degree of relative mobility exists, are not appropriate: an example is Hubbard *et al.* (1992). It is well known that inequality when measured over a longer period is less than in the years when it is highest (and may possibly be less than in all single years), and that a substantial number of inter-decile movements take place. The number of studies able to make appropriate comparisons is very limited.

Sawhill and Condon (1992) examined US data from the Michigan Panel Study of Income Dynamics (PSID) from 1967 to 1986, dividing the period into sub-periods of 1967 to 1976, and 1977 to 1986. They examined transition matrices and inequality measured over the ten-year periods. They found that long-period inequality was higher in the second period than in the first ten-year period. Furthermore, they were unable to find any 'discernible trend in mobility at all' (1992, p.3).

PSID data were also examined by Hungerford (1993), who used sub-periods of 1969 to 1976 and 1979 to 1986 and several statistical measures of association in order to measure mobility. He concluded that 'overall mobility within the income distribution appears to be the same in the 1970s and 1980s' (1993, p.407; see also p.409). A more detailed breakdown of movements showed that there were proportionately more upward movements from the lower deciles in the earlier period compared with the second period, while more people moved up from the higher deciles in the second period; this suggests the possibility of an increase in β.

A study of Current Population Survey (CPS) data in the US was carried out by Gittleman and Joyce (1994), covering the period 1967 to 1991. They were able to examine trends in year-to-year earnings mobility over the period (based on correlation coefficients between earnings in two successive years), finding no significant change. For men, there was, however, 'some evidence that short-term earnings mobility declined over the same period in which cross-section inequality increased' (1994, p.17). They also examined longer-period inequality measures, finding a slight increase in inequality in the 1980s relative to the 1970s for men. However, for women a slight increase in mobility was observed, along with a slight fall in longer-period inequality. Gittleman and Joyce conclude that 'mobility trends have not moved in such a way as to offset changes in annual inequality' (1994, p.26). Comparisons here are not straightforward, however, because their measure of mobility, the correlation coefficient, involves only one 'dimension' of the process of relative earnings change. They effectively used a model in which β was assumed to be unity.

14.4 Conclusions

This chapter has examined the relationship between relative income mobility, inequality and social welfare. While mobility is often regarded as reflecting opportunities for improvement and responses to incentives, income variability *per se* reduces individuals' utility where utility functions are concave (reflecting variability aversion). The question of whether social welfare, defined in terms of a social welfare function reflecting inequality aversion, and defined in terms of individuals' longer-period utility, can increase while mobility increases is far from straightforward. Furthermore, mobility is not a one-dimensional phenomenon, since one type of mobility (regression towards the mean) may be inequality reducing, while another type of mobility (relative movements uncorrelated with incomes) contributes to an increase in inequality. Whether a change in the pattern of income mobility can produce an increase in social welfare while at the same time reducing long-period inequality and increasing short-period inequality is also problematic.

Explicit analysis shows that comparative statics are too cumbersome, so simulations were carried out. It was found that if the aversion to variability of individuals is sufficiently larger than the aversion to inequality of the social welfare function, it is not possible to achieve all three changes simultaneously. If inequality aversion exceeds variability aversion, a small range of variations can produce the three changes; these involve an increase in the extent of regression towards the mean combined with a sufficient increase in the random variability of proportionate changes. The former change contributes to the reduction in longer-period inequality while the latter change is required for shorter-period inequality to increase. A brief review of evidence for the US suggests that, while annual inequality increased during the 1980s, the changes in mobility required to offset this increase did not appear to take place.

Chapter 15

Poverty Over Two Periods

The theory of poverty measurement is usually cast in a single-period framework within which the aggregate level of poverty is determined by incomes in that period. However, there is increasing concern with issues relating to the persistence of poverty; see Bane and Elwood (1986); Moffit (1992) Stevens (1994), Headey and Krause (1994) and Ravallion (1996). This concern is associated with the discussion of 'welfare-dependency' and of the growth of the 'underclass', which are based upon a distinction between the temporarily and the permanently poor.

It is not clear how the length of time that individuals spend below the poverty line should influence judgements about aggregate levels of poverty. The primary purpose of this chapter is to provide, within a two-period context, an analytical framework by means of which poverty-persistence might be incorporated into a index of aggregate poverty. In a two-period model, developed in section 15.1, aggregate poverty over both periods may be written as a weighted average of poverty in each of the periods. This allows a decomposition of aggregate multiperiod poverty in terms of the poverty of persons who are temporarily poor (poor in one period but not in the other) and the poverty of those who are permanently poor (poor in both periods). In calculating multiperiod poverty, a higher weight can be attached to the poverty of the latter group by means of a coefficient which represents the degree of aversion to 'poverty-persistence'.

A major analytical result, derived in section 15.1, is that transfers of persons from temporary to permanent poverty lead, even with positive aversion to poverty-persistence, to an unambiguous increase in aggregate multiperiod poverty only when poverty is measured by the headcount ratio. When more complex measures are deployed an increase in numbers in permanent poverty leads, within the context of a given number of total poor, to an unambiguous increase in aggregate poverty only under very restrictive assumptions. Consequently, simulation experiments were conducted in order to shed light on the relationship between mobility between temporary and permanent poverty and the level of aggregate poverty. These experiments are described in section 15.2.

15.1   A Poverty Decomposition

15.1.1   A Decomposition of Aggregate Poverty

Consider a framework in which there are two time periods $(t = 1, 2)$ and N persons in each time period, their incomes being arranged in ascending order as: $y_{1t}, y_{2t}...y_{Nt}$. If z_1 and z_2 are the poverty lines for periods 1 and 2, then $S_1 = \{j|y_{j1} \le z_1\}$ and $S_2 = \{j|y_{j2} \le z_2\}$ are the sets of poor persons in periods 1 and 2 respectively. The sets S_1 and S_2 may be written as:

$$S_1 = \left(S_1 \cap \bar{S}_2\right) \cup (S_1 \cap S_2) = A \cup C \tag{15.1}$$

$$S_2 = \left(\bar{S}_1 \cap S_2\right) \cup (S_1 \cap S_2) = B \cup C \tag{15.2}$$

where $\bar{S}_1$ and $\bar{S}_2$ are the converse sets of S_1 and S_2 respectively and A, B and C are disjoint sets.

Using the class of poverty measures defined by Foster *et al.* (1984), the measure of poverty in each period, P_t $(t = 1, 2)$ is given by:

$$P_t = \frac{1}{N} \sum_{j \in S_t} \left(\frac{z_t - y_{jt}}{z_t}\right)^\alpha \tag{15.3}$$

Let P_t^T and P_t^P denote respectively the poverty measures for period t including those who are poor only in period t and those who are poor in both periods. Then the above decompositions (15.1) and (15.3) can be used to show that:

$$P_t = P_t^T + P_t^P \tag{15.4}$$

An aggregate measure of poverty over the two periods, H, may be defined in terms of a weighted average of the P_ts with weights w_t so that $H = \sum_t w_t P_t$. Using (15.4), this becomes:

$$H = \sum_{t=1}^{2} w_t P_t^T + \sum_{t=1}^{2} w_t P_t^P \tag{15.5}$$

This illustrates that such an aggregate measure gives the same weight to permanent and temporary poverty in each period. A degree of 'persistence-aversion' may be introduced using the coefficient $\gamma \geq 1$, so that H is re-defined as:

$$H = \sum_{t=1}^{2} w_t P_t^T + \gamma \sum_{t=1}^{2} w_t P_t^P \tag{15.6}$$

Hence, when $\gamma > 1$ the aggregate poverty of the permanently poor is given a greater weight than that of the temporarily poor.

15.1.2 Effects of Mobility on Aggregate Poverty

In order to examine the effects of mobility on the aggregate poverty measure, consider first the headcount measure where $\alpha = 0$. Define M_t as the number of poor persons in period t. Denote by M_A, M_B and M_C respectively the number of persons who are poor in: period 1 but not in period 2; in period 2 but not in period 1; both periods. Then $M_1 = M_A + M_C$ and $M_2 = M_B + M_C$. Define $v_t = M_C/M_t$ as the proportion of the total poor, in period t, who are 'permanently' poor (poor in both periods) and let $m_t = M_t/N$ be the proportion in poverty in period t. Then:

$$H = \sum_{t=1}^{2} w_t (1 - v_t) m_t + \gamma \sum_{t=1}^{2} w_t v_t m_t \tag{15.7}$$

An increase in the number of people who are permanently poor, with the number of poor in each period, M_t, unchanged, produces a change in H given by:

$$\frac{\partial H}{\partial M_C} = (\gamma - 1) \sum_{t=1}^{2} w_t \left(\frac{m_t}{M_t} \right) \tag{15.8}$$

Thus $\partial H / \partial M_C = 0$ if $\gamma = 1$ and $\partial H / \partial M_C > 0$ if $\gamma > 1$.

In the case where $\alpha = 1$, the mean poverty gaps are relevant. Let g_t denote the mean poverty gap, expressed as proportions of the poverty line, of persons who are poor in only period t, and g_t^C the mean poverty gap of persons in set C (poor in both periods) calculated using period t's incomes. Then aggregate poverty is:

$$H = \sum_{t=1}^{2} w_t \left(1 - v_t \right) m_t g_t + \gamma \sum_{t=1}^{2} w_t v_t m_t g_t^C \tag{15.9}$$

In the case where, in each period, the incomes of all poor persons are equal, it can be shown that $\partial H / \partial M_C = 0$ if $\gamma = 1$ and $\partial H / \partial M_C > 0$ if $\gamma > 1$. However, in the general case, when poor incomes are unequal, it is not possible unambiguously to attach a sign to $\partial H / \partial M_C$ since the change in the mean poverty gaps consequent upon a change in the number of permanently poor persons, M_C, depends upon the incomes of poor persons transferring between permanent and temporary poverty, relative to the incomes of poor persons not making such a transfer; for details see Borooah and Creedy (1994).

For example, suppose the distribution of income is such that the permanently poor have the lowest incomes so that incomes arranged in ascending order are, for period t, given by $y_{1,t}, ..., y_{M_C,t}, y_{M_C+1,t}, ..., y_{M_t}$. Then $g_t^C > g_t$. Suppose the $(M_C + 1)$th person transfers in period 1 from temporary to permanent poverty; that is a person who was poor in period 1 only is now also poor in period 2. Then g_1^C / M_C and g_1 / M_C are both negative because the mean incomes, in period 1, of both the permanently and the temporarily poor both rise. On the other hand, with a fixed number, M_2, of poor persons in period 2, the increase in M_C in period 2 (which is the result of a person previously poor in period 1 entering poverty in period 2) is accommodated by a reduction in M_B, through a non-poor person in period 1 escaping poverty in period 2 as well. If this entry and escape in period 2 occurs at the highest end of the income distribution (in period 2) of, respectively, the permanently and the temporarily poor, then $g_2/M_C > 0$ and $g_2^C/M_C < 0$. Different scenarios for transfer between permanent and temporary poverty will yield different signs for the relevant partial derivatives.

Although it is not possible to predict the direction of change in H consequent upon a change in M_C, conditions under which change in the value of γ, the persistence aversion parameter, affect the magnitude of change, whatever the direction of change might be, can be derived. It can be shown that sufficient conditions for $\frac{\partial}{\partial \gamma} \left(\frac{\partial H}{\partial M_C} \right)$ to be positive are $\frac{\partial g_t}{\partial M_C} < \frac{y_t^C}{M_C}$ for $t = 1, 2$. In other words, provided that the change in the mean poverty gaps (expressed as a proportion of the poverty line) of the permanently poor, consequent upon a transfer between numbers of permanent and temporary poverty, is sufficiently small (informally, the percentage change in the mean poverty gap ratios of the permanently poor), an increase in the value of γ will attenuate the magnitude of the change in H consequent upon the above transfer.

When $\alpha = 2$, the poverty measures, P_t^T and P_t^P are:

$$P_t^T = (1 - v_t)\, m_t \left\{ g_t^2 + \left(1 - g_t^2 \right) \rho_t^2 \right\} \tag{15.10}$$

$$P_i^P = v_t m_t \left\{ (g_t^C)^2 + \left(1 - (g_t^C)^2 \right) \rho_{C,t}^2 \right\} \tag{15.11}$$

where ρ_t is the coefficient of variation of income of those poor in period t only, and $\rho_{C,t}$ is the coefficient of variation of period t's incomes of those poor in both periods. The aggregate poverty measure in this case can be obtained by substituting equations (15.10) and (15.11) into equation (15.6). As with the earlier case when $\alpha = 1$, it is not possible unambiguously to sign $\partial H/\partial M_C$. However, it is again possible to obtain conditions under which the size of the change is magnified through changes in the value of γ, the persistence-aversion coefficient. A sufficient condition for $\frac{\partial}{\partial \gamma} \left(\frac{\partial H}{\partial M_C} \right)$ to be positive can be obtained as in the case when $\alpha = 1$. Provided, as a consequence of a transfer of persons between the temporarily and permanently poor, the changes to the poverty gap ratios and the inequality coefficients of the two groups are sufficiently small, an increase in the persistence-aversion parameter γ magnifies the effects of this transfer on changes to aggregate poverty; for details see Borooah and Creedy (1994).

15.2   Income Mobility and Poverty

The previous section showed that the effects of income mobility on permanent and aggregate poverty are very complex, particularly for poverty measures which depend on the average poverty gap and the dispersion of income among the poor. The present section uses a model of income mobility in order to obtain some comparative static results using simulation methods. An advantage of the model is that it distinguishes between two basic types of relative mobility: income changes can have both a systematic inequality-increasing or -reducing component and a stochastic component.

Let y_{it} denote, as before, individual i's income in period t and let μ_t denote the arithmetic mean of logarithms of income in period t; then $m_t = \exp(\mu_t)$ is the geometric mean. The distribution of income in period 1 is given exogenously, and the mobility process generating period 2's incomes is written as:

$$y_{i2} = \left(\frac{y_{i1}}{m_1}\right)^{\beta} \exp(\mu_2 + u_i) \qquad (15.12)$$

where u_i is a random variable assumed to be distributed as $N(0, \sigma_u^2)$. This represents the stochastic component of income changes. The parameter β measures the degree of 'Galtonian' regression towards, or away from, the geometric mean. It influences the extent to which those with relatively higher incomes experience a relatively lower percentage change from year one to year two. If $\beta = 1$ there is no regression and mobility simply involves each individual receiving a random proportionate change. Equation (15.12) can be written as:

$$\log y_{i2} - \mu_2 = \beta (\log y_{i1} - \mu_1) + u_i \qquad (15.13)$$

so that taking variances gives the relationship between the variance of logarithms, σ_t^2, of income in each period as:

$$\sigma_2^2 = \beta^2 \sigma_1^2 + \sigma_u^2 \tag{15.14}$$

Hence income inequality, as measured by the variance of logarithms, is constant if $\sigma_u^2 = \sigma_1^2 (1 - \beta^2)$.

Using the assumption that income in the first period is lognormally distributed as $\Lambda(\mu_1, \sigma_1^2)$, a simulated set of y_{i1}s can be obtained with random
numbers, v_i, drawn from an $N(0,1)$ distribution, using $y_{i1} = \exp(\mu_1 + v_i\sigma_u)$.
Equation (15.12) can be applied for assumptions about β, σ_u^2, and μ_2 in order to obtain the corresponding y_{i2}s. The results reported below assume that
$\mu_1 = \mu_2 = 9.5$ and $\sigma_1^2 = 0.5$. Furthermore the poverty lines in each period
are set equal to 8000.

The income distribution in the first period is assumed to be fixed, so the
standard poverty measures applying to that period are constant whatever
the mobility process. However, the temporary and permanent components
P_1^T and P_1^P for that period vary as the mobility process varies. Changes in
the parameters β and σ_u^2 have different effects on the income distribution
of the second period. Increases in either β or σ_u^2 unequivocally increase the
dispersion of income in the second period. However, it is not immediately
obvious how such increases will affect the various components of poverty.
This is because of the way in which the two components of relative income
mobility interact. The links between the mobility processes, which have a
clear effect on income dispersion in the second period, and the various poverty
measures are complicated by the role of the covariance between incomes in
the two periods and the various integrals required.

The effects on the poverty measures of changing the mobility process can,
however, be examined numerically. Inspection of results for a variety of values
of β and σ_u^2 suggests that a specification with poverty expressed as a linear
function of β and σ_u^2, along with an interaction term, $\beta\sigma_u^2$, provides a good
approximation. Results are shown in Table 15.1 for each of the three poverty
measures, depending on the value of α. The table shows regression results for
two different dependent variables; these are the standard poverty measure for

the second period, P_2, and the permanent component of aggregate poverty, $\sum_t w_t P_t^P$. These results are based on simulated populations, with $N = 2000$, for variations in σ_u^2 from 0 to 0.6 in steps of 0.1 and variations in β from 0.4 to 1.6 in steps of 0.2. Hence the number of 'observations' used in the regressions is 49 in each case. These variations in the mobility parameters are very wide, as can be seen by considering the implied values of σ_2^2, the variance of log-income in period 2. The estimated t-values are given in parentheses.

Define the coefficients on β, σ_u^2 and the interaction term, $\beta\sigma_u^2$, for the regression involving P_2 as δ_1, δ_2 and δ_3 respectively, and the corresponding coefficients in the regression involving the permanent component of aggregate poverty as θ_1, θ_2 and θ_3. Then the changes in mobility parameters which leave P_2 unchanged are given, after total differentiation, by:

$$\frac{d\beta}{d\sigma_u^2}\Big|_{P_2} = -\left\{\frac{\delta_2 + \delta_3\beta}{\delta_1 + \delta_3\sigma_u^2}\right\} \tag{15.15}$$

Table 15.1 shows that for each poverty measure the value of δ_3 is negative, so the sign of the marginal rate of substitution in (15.15) is not unequivocal. However, substitution using the results from Table 15.1 shows that in the case where $\alpha = 0$ (the headcount poverty measure) and β is relatively large, $\frac{d\beta}{d\sigma_u^2}\Big|_{P_2}$ is positive; otherwise it is negative. Hence, if there is substantial regression away from the mean, a further increase in β must be matched by an increase in σ_u^2 in order to keep P_2 constant. But if there is regression towards the mean, an increase in β (implying a reduction in the degree of regression) must be matched by a decrease in σ_u^2, for the proportion in poverty in the second period to remain constant.

The change in mobility parameters which leaves aggregate poverty unchanged is seen to be:

$$\frac{d\beta}{d\sigma_u^2}\Big|_H = -\left\{\frac{w_2\delta_2 + (\gamma - 1)\theta_2 + \beta(w_2\delta_3 + (\gamma - 1)\theta_3)}{w_2\delta_1 + (\gamma - 1)\theta_1 + \gamma_2(w_2\delta_3 + (\gamma - 1)\theta_3)}\right\} \tag{15.16}$$

When $\gamma - 1$, corresponding to no aversion to permanent poverty, then it is clear that $\frac{d\beta}{d\sigma_u^2}\Big|_{P_2} = \frac{d\beta}{d\sigma_u^2}\Big|_H$. The difference between the two marginal rates of

Table 15.1: Regressions of Poverty on Mobility Components

Coefficient and α	Poverty in 2 P_2	Permanent Poverty $w_1 P_1^P + w_2 P_2^P$
$\alpha = 0$		
constant	0.0020	0.0335
	(0.204)	(2.869)
β	0.2148	0.1431
	(23.779)	(13.199)
σ_u^2	0.4717	0.0877
	(17.481)	(2.707)
$\beta\sigma_u^2$	-0.2963	-0.1303
	(-11.826)	(-4.333)
R^2	0.9600	0.8800
$\alpha = 1$		
constant	-0.0470	-0.0043
	(-30.254)	(-2.255)
β	0.1197	0.0688
	(83.061)	(38.787)
σ_u^2	0.1942	0.0430
	(45.105)	(8.121)
$\beta\sigma_u^2$	-0.0897	-0.0409
	(-22.430)	(-8.314)
R_2	0.9980	0.9870
$\alpha = 2$		
constant	-0.0381	-0.0082
	(-15.943)	(-22.812)
β	0.0742	0.0402
	(33.414)	(120.133)
σ_u^2	0.0944	0.0222
	(14.228)	(22.248)
$\beta\sigma_u^2$	-0.0255	-0.0121
	(-4.143)	(-12.995)
R_2	0.9880	0.9990

substitution increases as γ increases. Except for high values of β and the head count poverty measure, the substitution of values from Table 15.1 gives the result that $\frac{d\beta}{d\sigma_u^2}|_H$ is also negative. The absolute value of this marginal rate is less than that for which P_2 is constant.

Hence changes which involve a reduction in β, which compensate for an increase in σ_u^2 such that P_2 (and hence a conventional aggregate measure of poverty) is constant, result in a decrease in aggregate poverty when $\gamma > 1$. Alternatively, an increase in β, compensated by a fall in σ_u^2 to keep P_2 constant, results in an increase in aggregate poverty when $\gamma > 1$. These results are consistent with what would be intuitively expected of regression away from the mean. It is therefore possible for a change in mobility characteristics to have no effect on the time profile of a conventional single-period poverty measure, yet to increase permanent poverty. This makes it important for the design of poverty alleviation policies to establish the precise pattern of income mobility and changes in that pattern over time.

15.3   Conclusions

The aim of this chapter has been to incorporate poverty persistence in a measure of aggregate poverty over two periods. This was achieved by decomposing the Foster et al. (1984) class of poverty measures into two components, covering those temporarily in poverty and those in poverty in both periods. An additional weight was then added to the permanent component in forming an aggregate poverty measure over both periods; this weight reflects the degree of poverty-persistence aversion of the policy maker. It was found that the effect on the aggregate poverty measure of mobility between the categories of permanent and temporary poverty are not unambiguous (except in the special case of the headcount poverty measure). Simulations were then used, based on a process of income mobility, in order to investigate the relationship between poverty and mobility. The effects of two different types of mobility (random proportional income changes and a systematic regression towards or away from the median) were isolated.

Available evidence suggests that poverty persistence is an important phenomenon, so there is a clear need to allow for such persistence in measuring aggregate poverty. For example, given the observed correlation between unemployment and poverty, the increasing extent of long-term unemployment in many countries suggests that poverty persistence may also be increasing. The link with unemployment also suggests that there may well be a regional dimension to aggregate poverty, given an aversion to poverty persistence. The results demonstrate the need to have information about the process of income dynamics, in order to design appropriate policies to alleviate poverty.

Bibliography

[1] Abeles, R.P. and Wise, L.L. (1980) Coping with attrition in a longitudinal survey: the case of project talent. *Journal of Economics and Business*, 32, pp. 170-181.

[2] Aitchison, J. and Brown, J.A.C. (1957) *The Lognormal Distribution*. Cambridge: Cambridge University Press.

[3] Allen, R.G.D. (1975) *Index Numbers in Theory and Practice*. London: Macmillan.

[4] Apps, P. and Savage, E. (1989) Labour supply, welfare rankings and the measurement of inequality. *Journal of Public Economics*, 47, pp. 336-364.

[5] Aronson, J.R., Johnson, P. and Lambert, P.J. (1994) Redistributive effect and unequal income tax treatment. *Economic Journal*, 104, pp. 262-270.

[6] Atkinson, A.B. (1970) On the measurement of inequality. *Journal of Economic Theory*, 2, pp. 244-263.

[7] Atkinson, A.B. (1979) Horizontal equity and the distribution of the tax burden. In *The Economics of Taxation* (ed. by H.J. Aaron and M.J. Boskins). Washington DC: Brookings Institution.

[8] Atkinson, A.B. (1987) On the measurement of poverty. *Econometrica*, 55, pp. 749-764.

[9] Atkinson, A.B. (1991) Poverty, statistics and progress in Europe. *London School of Economics STICERD Discussion Paper* WSP/60.

[10] Atkinson, A.B. (1992) Measuring poverty and differences in family composition. *Economica*, 59, pp. 1-16.

[11] Atkinson, A.B. (1995) *Public Economics in Action*. Oxford: Clarendon Press.

[12] Atkinson, A.B. and Bourguignon, F. (1987) Income distribution and differences in needs. In *Arrow and the Foundations of the Theory of Economic Policy* (ed. by G.R. Feiwel). London: Macmillan.

[13] Atkinson, A.B., Bourguignon, F. and Morrison, C. (1992) *Empirical Studies of Earnings Mobility*. Philadelphia: Harwood.

[14] Atkinson, A.B., Gardiner, K., Lechene, V. and Sutherland, H. (1994) Comparing low incomes in France and the UK: evidence from household expenditure surveys. In *Social Policy Research Centre Reports and Proceedings*, No. 115 (ed. by B. Bradbury), pp. 61-101. Sydney: University of New South Wales.

[15] Australian Bureau of Statistics (1988) *Information Paper: Time Use Pilot Survey*. Cat. no. 4111.1. Sydney: AGPS.

[16] Bakker, A. and Creedy, J. (1997) Age and the distribution of earnings. In *Nonlinear Economic Models: Cross-sectional, Time Series and Neural Network Applications* (ed. by J. Creedy and V.L. Martin), pp.111-128. Aldershot, Hants: Edward Elgar.

[17] Bane, M.J. and D. Ellwood, (1986) Slipping into and out of poverty: the dynamics of spells. *Journal of Human Resources*, 21, pp. 1-23.

[18] Beckerman, W. (1979) The impact of income maintenance programmes on poverty in Britain. *Economic Journal*, 89, pp. 261-279.

[19] Becketti, S., Gould, W., Lillard, L. and Welch, F. (1988) The panel study of income dynamics after fourteen years: an evaluation. *Journal of Labour Economics*, 6, pp. 472-492.

[20] Berger, M. (1985) The effect of cohort size on earnings growth: a reconsideration of the evidence. *Journal of Political Economy*, 95, pp. 561-573.

[21] Besley, T. (1990) Means testing versus universal provision in poverty alleviation programmes. *Economica*, 57, pp. 119-29.

[22] Blinder, A. (1974) *Towards an Economic Theory of Income Distribution*. Cambridge, Mass: MIT Press.

[23] Blinder, A.S. and Esaki, H.Y. (1978) Macroeconomic activity and income distribution in the postwar United States. *Review of Economics and Statistics*, 60, pp. 604-608.

[24] Blundell, R. and Lwebel, A. (1990) The information content of equivalence scales. *Institute for Fiscal Studies WorkingPaper* W90/40.

[25] Borooah, V.K. and Creedy, J. (1994) The temporary versus the permanently poor: measuring poverty in a two period context. *University of Melbourne Department of Economics Research Paper* no. 433.

[26] Borooah, V.K and Creedy, J. (1998) Income mobility, temporary and permanent poverty. *Australian Economic Papers* (forthcoming).

[27] Borooah, V.K. and McKee, P.M. (1994) Intra-household income transfers and implications for poverty and inequality in the UK. In *Poverty, Taxation and Income Distribution* (ed. by J. Creedy). Aldershot, Hants: Edward Elgar.

[28] Borooah, V.K., McGregor, P.L. and McKee, P.M. (1991) *Regional Income Inequality and Poverty in the United Kingdom*. Aldershot, Hants: Dartmouth.

[29] Bound, J.C., Brown, C., Duncan, G.J. and Rodgers, W.L. (1990) Measurement errors in cross-sectional and longitudinal labour market surveys: validation study evidence. In *Panel Data and Labor Market Studies* (ed. by J. Hartog, G. Ridder and J. Theeuwes), pp. 1-19. Amsterdam: North-Holland.

[30] Bradbury, B. (1989) Family size equivalence scales and survey evaluations of income and well-being. *Journal of Social Policy*, 18, pp. 383-408.

[31] Bradbury, B. (1992) The welfare interpretation of family size equivalence scales. *University of New South Wales SPRC Discussion Paper*, no. 37.

[32] Bradbury, B. (1994) Poverty measurement with bounded equivalence scales: Australia in the 1980s. In *Social Policy Reseach Centre Reports and Proceedings,* no. 115 (ed. by B. Bradbury), pp. 27-52. Sydney: University of New South Wales.

[33] Bradshaw, J. (1991) How much is enough? *Basic Income Research Group Bulletin,* 12, pp. 13-14.

[34] Bradshaw, J., Mitchell, D. and Morgan, J. (1987) Evaluating adequacy: the potential of budget standards. *Journal of Social Policy,* 16, pp. 165-81.

[35] Brannen, J. and Wilson, G. (1987) *Give and Take in Families.* London: Allen and Unwin.

[36] Broad, A. and Bacica, L. (1985) *The Incidence of Indirect Taxes,* Vol. 2. Wellington: Institute of Policy Studies.

[37] Brown, J.A.C. (1976) The mathematical and statistical theory of income distribution. In *The Personal Distribution of Incomes* (ed. by A.B. Atkinson), pp. 72-97. London: Allen and Unwin.

[38] Buhmann, B., Rainwater, L., Schmauss, G. and Smeeding, T.M. (1988) Equivalence scales, well-being, inequality and poverty: sensitivity estimates across ten countries using the LIS data base. *Review of Income and Wealth,* 34, pp. 115-142.

[39] Cameron, L. and Creedy, J. (1994) Taxation and the distribution of lifetime income. In *Taxation, Poverty and Income Distribution* (ed. by J. Creedy), pp. 140-162. Aldershot, Hants: Edward Elgar.

[40] Casperson, E. and Metcalf, G. (1993) Is a value added tax progressive? Annual versus lifetime incidence measures. *National Bureau of Economic Research Working Paper* no. 4387.

[41] Central Statistical Office (1990) The effects of taxes and benefits on household income, 1987. *Economic Trends,* May, pp. 84-96.

[42] Chamberlain, G. (1984) Panel data. In *Handbook of Econometrics* (ed. by Z. Griliches and M. Intriligator), pp. 1247-1318. Amsterdam: North-Holland.

[43] Champernowne, D.G. (1953) A model of income distribution. *Economic Journal*, 63, pp. 316-351.

[44] Christian, C.W. and Frischmann, P.J. (1989) Attrition in the statistics of income panel of individual returns. *National Tax Journal*, 42, pp. 495-502.

[45] Cobb, L., Koppstein, P. and Chen, N.H. (1983) Estimation and moment recursion relations for multimodal distributions of the exponential family. *Journal of the American Statistical Association*, 78, pp. 124-130.

[46] Connolly, R. (1986) A framework for analysing the impact of cohort size on education and labour incomes. *Journal of Human Resources*, 21, pp. 543-562.

[47] Cornwell, A. and Creedy, J. (1996) The distributional impact of domestic fuel taxation. *Economic Analysis and Policy*, 26, pp. 129-143.

[48] Cornwell, A. and Creedy, J. (1997) *Environmental Taxes and Economic Welfare: Reducing Carbon Dioxide Emissions.* Aldershot, Hants: Edward Elgar.

[49] Coulter, F.A.E., Cowell, F.A. and Jenkins, S.P. (1991) Family fortunes in the 1970s and 1980s. *University College of Swansea Discussion Paper* no. 91-12.

[50] Coulter, F.A.E., Cowell, F.A. and Jenkins, S. (1992) Differences in needs and assessment of income distribution. *Bulletin of Economic Research*, 44, pp. 77-124.

[51] Coulter, F.A.E., Cowell, F.A. and Jenkins, S. (1994) Equivalence scale relativities and the extent of inequality and poverty. In *Poverty, Taxation and Income Distribution* (ed. by J. Creedy). Aldershot, Hants: Edward Elgar.

[52] Cowell, F.A. (1977) *Measuring Inequality.* Oxford: Philip Allen.

[53] Cowell, F.A. and Kuga, K. (1981) Inequality measurement: an axiomatic approach. *European Economic Review*, 15, pp. 287-305.

[54] Cox, D.R. and Miller, H.D. (1984) *The Theory of Stochastic Processes.* London: Chapman and Hall.

[55] Creedy, J. (1979) The inequality of earnings and the accounting period. *Scottish Journal of Political Economy*, 26, pp. 89-96.

[56] Creedy, J. (1982) The British state pension: contributions, benefits and indexation. *Oxford Bulletin of Economics and Statistics*, 44, pp. 97-112.

[57] Creedy, J. (1985) *Dynamics of Income Distribution*. Oxford: Blackwell.

[58] Creedy, J. (1991) Lifetime earnings and inequality. *Economic Record*, 67, pp. 46-58.

[59] Creedy, J. (1992) *Income, Inequality and the Life Cycle*. Aldershot, Hants: Edward Elgar.

[60] Creedy, J. (1994a) Taxes and transfers with endogenous earnings: some basic analytics. *Bulletin of Economic Research*, 46, pp. 97-130.

[61] Creedy, J. (1994b) Statics and dynamics of income distribution: an introductory survey. *Australian Economic Review*, 4, pp. 51-71.

[62] Creedy, J. (1995) Taxes and transfers: target efficiency and social welfare. *Economica*, 63, pp. S163-S174.

[63] Creedy, J. (1996a) *Fiscal Policy and Social Welfare: An Analysis of Alternative Tax and Transfer Systems*. Aldershot, Hants: Edward Elgar.

[64] Creedy, J. (1996b) Measuring income inequality. *Australian Economic Review*, 2, pp. 236-246.

[65] Creedy, J. (1996c) Earnings Dynamics of males and females: new evidence from New Zealand. *New Zealand Economic Papers*, 30, no.2, pp. 131-153.

[66] Creedy, J. (1997a) Evaluating alternative tax and transfer schemes with endogenous earnings. *Oxford Economic Papers*, 49, pp. 43-56.

[67] Creedy, J. (1997b) Labour supply and social welfare when utility depends on a threshold consumption level. *Economic Record*, 73, pp. 159-168.

[68] Creedy, J. (1997c) Inequality, mobility and income distribution comparisons. *Fiscal Studies,* 18, pp. 293-302.

[69] Creedy, J. (1997d) *The Statics and Dynamics of Income Distribution in New Zealand.* Wellington: Institute of Policy Studies.

[70] Creedy, J. (1998) Means-tested versus universal transfers: alternative models and value judgements. *Manchester School* (forthcoming).

[71] Creedy, J., Lye, J. and Martin, V.L. (1996) A labour market equilibrium model of the personal distribution of earnings. *Journal of Income Distribution,* 6, pp. 127-144.

[72] Creedy, J. and Martin, V.L. (1993) Multiple equilibria and hysteresis in simple exchange models. *Economic Modelling,* 10, pp. 339-347.

[73] Creedy, J. and Martin, V.L. (1994) A model of the distribution of prices. *Oxford Bulletin of Economics and Statistics,* 56, pp. 67-76.

[74] Creedy, J. and Martin, V.L. (eds) (1997) *Nonlinear Economic Models: Time Series, Cross-sectional and Neural Network Applications.* Aldershot, Hants: Edward Elgar.

[75] Creedy, J. and van de Ven, J. (1997) The distributional effects of inflation in Australia 1980-1995. *Australian Economic Review,* 30, pp. 125-143.

[76] Creedy, J. and Whitfield, K. (1988) Job mobility and earnings: an internal labour market approach. *Journal of Industrial Relations,* 30, pp. 100-117.

[77] Creedy, J. and Wilhelm, M. (1995) Income mobility, inequality and social welfare. *The University of Melbourne Department of Economics Research Paper,* no. 479.

[78] Davies, J., St-Hilaire, F. and Whalley, J. (1984) Some calculations of lifetime tax incidence. *American Economic Review,* 74, pp. 633-49.

[79] Deaton, A.S. (1974) A reconsideration of the empirical implications of additive preferences. *Economic Journal,* 84, pp. 338-348.

[80] Deaton, A.S. and Muellbauer, J. (1980) *Economics and Consumer Behaviour.* Cambridge: Cambridge University Press.

[81] Deaton, A.S. and Muellbauer, J. (1986) On measuring child costs: with applications to poor countries. *Journal of Political Economy,* 94, pp. 720-744.

[82] Doll, R. (1971) The age distribution of cancer. *Journal of the Royal Statistical Society,* A, 134, pp. 133-166.

[83] Duncan, G.J and Hill, D.H. (1985a) An investigation of the extent and consequences of measurement error in labour-economic survey data. *Journal of Labour Economics,* 3, pp. 508-532.

[84] Duncan, G.J. and Hill, M.S. (1985b) Concepts of longitudinal households: fertile or futile? *Journal of Economic and Social Measurement,* 13, pp. 361-375.

[85] Ebert, U. (1995) Consumer's surplus: simple solutions to an old problem. *Bulletin of Economic Research,* 47, pp. 285-294.

[86] Edwards, M. (1981) *Financial Arrangements Within Families.* Canberra: National Womens' Advisory Council.

[87] Fase, M.M.G. (1970) *An Econometric Model of Age-Income Profiles.* Rotterdam: Rotterdam University Press.

[88] Fortin, B., Truchon, M. and Beauséjour, L. (1993) On reforming the welfare system: workfare meets the negative income tax. *Journal of Public Economics,* 51, pp. 119-151.

[89] Foster, J.E. (1984) On economic poverty: a survey of aggregate measures. *Advances in Econometrics,* 3, pp. 215-251.

[90] Foster, J., Greer, J. and Thorbecke, E. (1984) A class of decomposable poverty measures. *Econometrica,* 52, pp. 761-2.

[91] Frisch, R. (1959) A complete scheme for computing all direct and cross demand elasticities in a model with many sectors. *Econometrica,* 27, pp. 177-196.

[92] Fuchs, V.R. (1986) His and hers: gender differences in work and income 1959-79. *Journal of Labor Economics*, 4, pp. 245-271.

[93] Fullerton, D. and Rogers, D.L. (1991) Lifetime vs annual perspectives on tax incidence. *National Bureau of Economic Research Working Paper* no. 3750.

[94] Fullerton, D. and Rogers, D.L. (1993) *Who Bears the Lifetime Tax Burden?* Washington, DC: Brookings Institution.

[95] Gallagher, P. (1990) Australian tax benefit and micro simulation models. In *Tax-Benefit Models and Micro Simulation Methods* (ed. by B. Bradbury), pp. 29-79. Sydney: University of New South Wales.

[96] Galton, F. (1889) *Natural Inheritance*. London: Macmillan.

[97] Gershuny, J., Jones, S. and Godwin, M. (1988) Collection and preliminary analysis of SCEl time budget data. University of Bath.

[98] Gibrat, R. (1931) *Les Inegalities Economiques*. Paris: Sirey.

[99] Gittleman, M. and Joyce, M. (1994) Earnings mobility and long-run inequality: an analysis using matched CPS data. *Bureau of Labor Statistics*.

[100] Glendinning, G. and Millar, J. (eds) (1987) *Women and Poverty in Britain*. Brighton, E. Sussex: Wheatsheaf.

[101] Griliches, Z. and Hausman, J. (1986) Errors in variables in panel data. *Journal of Econometrics*, 31, pp. 93-118.

[102] Griliches, Z., Hall, B.H. and Hausman, J. (1978) Missing data and self-selection in large panels. *Annales de d'INSEE*, pp. 30-31.

[103] Gronau, R. (1988) Consumption technology and the intrahousehold distribution of resources: adult equivalence scales re-examined. *Journal of Political Economy*, 96, pp. 1183-1205.

[104] Gronau, R. (1991) The intra family allocation of goods: how to separate the adult from the child. *Journal of Labour Economics*, 9, pp. 207-235.

[105] Haddan, L. and Kanbur, R. (1990) How serious is the neglect of intra-household inequality? *Economic Journal,* 100, pp. 866-881.

[106] Hancock, R. and Sutherland, H. (eds) (1992) Micro simulation models for public policy analysis: new frontiers. *London School of Economics STICERD Occasional Paper,* no. 17.

[107] Hansen, P. (1998) Inference on 'Earnings dynamics over the life cycle: new evidence for New Zealand'. *New Zealand Economic Papers,* 31 (forthcoming).

[108] Harding, A. (1994) Lifetime vs annual income distribution in Australia. In *Taxation, Poverty and Income Distribution* (ed. by J. Creedy), pp. 104-139. Aldershot, Hants: Edward Elgar.

[109] Hart, P.E. (1973) Random processes and economic size distributions. University of Reading.

[110] Hart, P.E. (1976) The comparative statics and dynamics of income distributions. *Journal of the Royal Statistical Society,* 139, pp. 108-125.

[111] Hart, P.E. (1981) The statics and dynamics of income distributions: a survey. In *The Statics and Dynamics of Income* (ed. by N.A. Klevmarken and J.A. Lybeck), pp. 1-22. Clevedon, Somerset: Tieto.

[112] Hart, P.E. (1982) The sizes and growths of trade unions. *University of Reading Discussion Paper in Economics,* Series A, no. 128.

[113] Hart, P.E. (1983) The size mobility of earnings. *Oxford Bulletin of Economics and Statistics,* 45, pp. 181-193.

[114] Hart, P.E. and Prais, S.J. (1956) The analysis of business concentration: a statistical approach. *Journal of the Royal Statistical Society,* Series A, 119, pp. 150-81.

[115] Hartog, J. (1988) Poverty and the measurement of individual welfare. *Journal of Human Resources,* 23, pp. 243-266.

[116] Hausman, J. and Wise, D.A. (1979) Attrition bias in experimental and panel data: the Gary income maintenance experiment. *Econometrica,* 47, pp. 455-473.

[117] Headey, B. and Krause, P. (1994) Inequalities of income, health and happiness: the stratification paradigm and alternatives. In *Social Policy Research Centre Report and Proceedings* (ed. by B. Bradbury), pp. 133-172. Sydney: University of New South Wales.

[118] Heckman, J.J. (1979) Sample bias as a specification error. *Econometrica*, 47, pp. 153-161.

[119] Heckman, J.J. (1990) Varieties of selection bias. *American Economic Review*, 80, pp. 313-318.

[120] Hellwig, O. (1990) Overseas experience with micro simulation models. In *Tax-benefit Models and Microsimulation Methods* (ed. by B. Bradbury), pp. 5-29. Sydney: University of New South Wales.

[121] Hsiao, C. (1986) *Analysis of Panel Data*. Cambridge: Cambridge University Press.

[122] Hubbard, R.G., Nunns, J.R. and Randolph, W.C. (1992) Household income mobility during the 1980s: a statistical assessment based on tax return data. Office of Tax Analysis, US Department of the Treasury.

[123] Hungerford, T.L. (1993) US income mobility in the seventies and eighties. *Review of Income and Wealth*, 39, pp. 403-417.

[124] Jenkins, S.P. (1988) Empirical measurement of horizontal inequity. *Journal of Public Economics*, 37, pp. 305-329.

[125] Jenkins, S.P. (1991a) The measurement of income inequality. In *Economic Inequality and Poverty: International Perspectives*, pp. 3-38. London: M.E. Sharpe.

[126] Jenkins, S.P. (1991b) Poverty measurement and the within-household distribution: agenda for action. *Journal of Social Policy*, 20, pp. 457-483.

[127] Jenkins, S.P. (1992) Accounting for inequality trends: decomposition analysis for the UK 1976-1986. *University of New South Wales Centre for Applied Economic Research Working Paper*, no. 8.

[128] Jenkins, S.P. and Lambert, P.J. (1993) Ranking income distributions when needs differ. *Review of Income and Wealth*, 39, pp. 337-356.

[129] Jenkins, S.P. and Lambert, P.J. (1997) Three 'I's of poverty curves, with an analysis of UK poverty trends. *Oxford Economic Papers*, 49, pp. 317-327.

[130] Johnson, N.L. and Kotz S. (1970) *Continuous Univariate Distributions.* New York: John Wiley.

[131] Johnson, P. and Webb, S. (1989) Counting people with low incomes: the impact of recent changes in official statistics. *Fiscal Studies*, 10, pp. 66-82.

[132] Juster, F.T. and Stafford, F.P. (1991) The allocation of time: empirical findings, behavioural models and problems of measurement. *Journal of Economic Literature*, 29, pp. 471-522.

[133] Kakwani, N.C. (1977) Measurement of tax progressivity: an international comparison. *Economic Journal*, 87, pp. 71-80.

[134] Kakwani, N.C. (1984) Welfare rankings of income distributions. *Advances in Econometrics*, 3, pp. 191-213.

[135] Kakwani, N.C. (1986) *Analysing Redistribution Policies: A Study Using Australian Data.* Cambridge: Cambridge University Press.

[136] Kanbur, R. and Keen, M. (1989) Poverty, incentives and linear income taxation. In *The Economics of Social Security* (ed. by A. Dilnot and I. Walker), pp. 99-115. Oxford: Oxford University Press.

[137] Kanbur, R., Keen, M. and Tuomala, M. (1994) Optimal non-linear income taxation for the alleviation of poverty. *European Economic Review*, 38, pp. 1613-1632.

[138] Kapteyn, A. and van Praag, B. (1976) A new approach to the construction of family equivalence scales. *European Economic Review*, 7, pp. 313-335.

[139] Kay, J.A. (1980) The deadweight loss from a tax system. *Journal of Public Economics*, 13, pp. 111-119.

[140] Kesselman, J.R. and Garfinkel, I. (1978) Professor Friedman, meet Lady Rhys-Williams: NIT vs CIT. *Journal of Public Economics*, 10, pp. 179-216.

[141] King, M.A. (1983) Welfare analysis of tax reforms using household data. *Journal of Public Economics*, 21, pp. 183-214.

[142] Klein, L.R. (1962) *An Introduction to Econometrics.* Englewood Cliffs, NJ: Prentice-Hall.

[143] Krugman, P. (1994) *Peddling Prosperity.* New York: W.W. Norton.

[144] Lambert, P.J. (1985a) On the redistributive effect of taxes and benefits. *Scottish Journal of Political Economy,* 32, pp. 39-54.

[145] Lambert, P.J. (1985b) Endogenising the income distribution: the redistributive effect, and Laffer effects, of a progressive tax-benefit system. *European Journal of Political Economy,* 1, pp. 3-20.

[146] Lambert, P.J. (1988) The equity-efficiency trade-off: Breit reconsidered. *Oxford Economics Papers,* 42, pp. 91-104.

[147] Lambert, P.J. (1993a) *The Distribution and Redistribution of Income: A Mathematical Analysis.* Manchester: Manchester University Press.

[148] Lambert, P.J. (1993b) Evaluating impact effects of tax reforms. *Journal of Economic Surveys,* 7, pp. 205-242.

[149] Lambert, P.J. (1994a) Redistribution through the income tax. In *Taxation, Poverty and Income Distribution* (ed. by J. Creedy), Aldershot, Hants: Edward Elgar.

[150] Lambert, P.J. (1994b) Measuring progressivity with differences in tax treatment. *In Taxation, Poverty and Income Distribution* (ed. by J. Creedy). Aldershot, Hants: Edward Elgar.

[151] Lazear, E.P. and Michael, R.T. (1986) Estimating the personal distribution of income with adjustment for within-family variation. *Journal of Labour Economics,* 4, pp. 216-244.

[152] Lazear, E. P. and Michael, R.T. (1988) *Allocation of Income Within the Household.* Chicago: University of Chicago Press.

[153] Lewis, G.W. and Ulph, D.T. (1988) Poverty, inequality and welfare. *Economic Journal,* 98, pp. 117-131.

[154] Lillard, L.A. and Willis, R.J. (1978) Dynamic aspects of earnings mobility. *Econometrica*, 46, pp. 985-1012.

[155] Lydall, H.F. (1976) Theories of the distribution of earnings. In *The Personal Distribution of Income* (ed. by A.B. Atkinson), pp. 15-46. London: George Allen and Unwin.

[156] Lydall, H.F. (1979) *A Theory of Income Distribution.* Oxford: Clarendon Press.

[157] Lye, J.N. and Martin, V.L. (1993) Robust estimation, non-normalities and generalized exponential distributions. *Journal of the American Statistical Association*, 88, pp. 253-259.

[158] Maddala, G.S. (1993) *The Econometrics of Panel Data*, 2 vols. Aldershot, Hants: Edward Elgar.

[159] Mandelbrot, V. (1960) The Pareto-Levy law and the distribution of income. *International Economic Review*, 1, pp. 79-106.

[160] Marron, J.S. and Schmitz, H.P. (1992) Simultaneous estimation of several income distributions. *Econometric Theory*, 8, pp.476-488.

[161] Matyas, L. and Sevestre, P. (eds) (1992) *The Econometrics of Panel Data.* Boston, Mass: Kluwer.

[162] McClements, L. (1978) *The Economics of Social Security.* London: Heinemann.

[163] McMillen, D.B. and Herriot, R.A. (1984) Towards a longitudinal definition of households. *Bureau of the Census Survey of Income and Program Participation WorkingPaper*, no. 8402.

[164] Mincer, J. (1970) Distribution and labour incomes: a survey. *Journal of Economic Literature*, 8, pp. 1-26.

[165] Mitchell, D. (1991) *Income Transfers in Ten Welfare States.* Aldershot, Hants: Avebury.

[166] Mitchell, D., Harding, A. and Gruen, F. (1994) Targeting Welfare: a survey. *Economic Record*, 70, pp. 315-340.

[167] Moffitt, R. (1992) Incentive effects of the US welfare system: a review. *Journal of Economic Literature*, 30, pp. 1-61.

[168] Moffitt, R. and Rothschild, M. (1987) Variable earnings and nonlinear taxation. *Journal of Human Resources*, 22, pp. 405-421.

[169] Muellbauer, J. (1974) Prices and inequality: the United Kingdom experience. *Economic Journal*, 84, pp .32-55.

[170] Nolan, B. (1985). Direct taxation, transfers and reranking: some empirical results for the UK. *London School of Economics STICERD/TIDI Discussion Paper*, no. 87.

[171] OECD (1996) *Employment Outlook.* Paris: OECD.

[172] Olsen, R.J. (1982) Independence from irrelevant alternatives and attrition bias: their relation to one another in the evaluation of experimental programs. *Southern Economic Journal*, 49, pp. 521-535.

[173] Orcutt, G., Merz, J. and Quinke, J. (1986) *Micro Analytic Simulation Models to Support Social and Financial Policy.* New York: North-Holland.

[174] Pahl, J. (1983) The allocation of money and the structuring of inequality within marriage. *Sociological Review*, 31, pp. 237-62.

[175] Pahl, J. (1989) *Money and Marriage.* London: Macmillan.

[176] Parker, S. (1994) An enquiry into the structure of the earnings distribution: how are individuals and households related? *University of Durham Department of Economics Discussion Paper.*

[177] Pauwels, W. (1986) Correct and incorrect measures of deadweight loss of taxation. *Public Finance*, 41, pp. 267-276.

[178] Pazner, E.A. and Sadka, E. (1980) Excess burden and economic surplus as consistent welfare indicators. *Public Finance*, 35, pp. 439-449.

[179] Phelps Brown, E.H. (1977) *The Inequality of Pay.* Oxford: Oxford University Press.

[180] Piachaud, D. (1982) Patterns of income and expenditure within families. *Journal of Social Policy*, 11, pp. 469-482.

[181] Plotnick, R. (1981) A measure of horizontal inequity. *Review of Economics and Statistics*, 63, pp. 283-287.

[182] Pollack, R. and Wales, T. (1979) Welfare comparisons and equivalence scales. *American Economic Review*, 69, pp. 216-221.

[183] Poterba, J.M. (1989) Lifetime incidence and the distributional burden of excise taxes. *American Economic Review*, 79, pp. 325-330.

[184] Ravallion, M. (1996) Issues in measuring and modelling poverty. *Economic Journal*, 106, pp. 1328-1343.

[185] Reynolds, M. and Smolensky, E. (1977) *Public Expenditures, Taxes and the Distribution of Income: The United States 1950, 1961, 1970.* New York: Academic Press.

[186] Ridder, G. (1990) Attrition in multi-wave panel data. In *Panel Data and Labour Market Studies* (ed. by J. Hartog, G. Ridder and J. Theeuwes). Amsterdam: North-Holland.

[187] Robbins, L. (1930) On the elasticity of demand for income in terms of effort. *Economica*, 10, pp. 123-129.

[188] Roberts, K. (1980) Price-independent welfare prescriptions. *Journal of Public Economics*, 18, pp. 277-297.

[189] Robins, P.K. and West, R.W. (1986) Sample attrition and labor supply response in experimental panel data. *Journal of Business Economics and Statistics*, 4, pp. 329-338.

[190] Rodgers, W.L., Duncan, G.J. and Brown, C. (1991) Errors in Survey reports of earnings, hours worked and hourly wages. *University of Michigan Survey Research Centre Working Paper.*

[191] Ruggles, N. and Ruggles, R. (1977) The anatomy of earnings behaviour. In *The Distribution of Economic Wellbeing* (ed. by F. Juster). New York: NBER.

[192] Sadka, E., Garfinkel, I. and Moreland, K. (1982) Income testing and so-
      cial welfare: an optimal tax-transfer model. In *Income Tested Transfer
      Programs: The Case For and Against* (ed. by I.Garfinkel), pp. 291-313.
      New York: Academic Press.

[193] Salem, A.Z.B. and Mount, T.D. (1974), A convenient descriptive model
      of income distribution: the gamma density. *Econometrica*, 42, pp. 1115-
      1127.

[194] Saunders, P. (1994) Married women's earnings and family income in-
      equality in the eighties. *Australian Bulletin of Labour,* 19, pp. 199-217.

[195] Sawhill, I.V. and Condon, M. (1992). Is US income inequality really
      growing? Sorting out the fairness question. *Policy Bites, no. 13.* Wash-
      ington: Urban Institute.

[196] Scott, C., Goss, P. and Davis, H. (1985) *The Incidence of Indirect
      Taxes,* Vol. 1. Wellington: Institute of Policy Studies.

[197] Sen, A.K. (1973) *On Economic Inequality.* Oxford: Clarendon.

[198] Sen, A.K. (1982) *Choice, Welfare and Measurement.* Oxford: Basil
      Blackwell.

[199] Sen, A.K. (1984) *Resources, Values and Development.* Oxford: Basil
      Blackwell.

[200] Shorrocks, A.F. (1975a) The wealth-age relationship: a cross-section
      and cohort analysis. *Review of Economics and Statistics,* 57, pp. 155-
      163.

[201] Shorrocks, A.F. (1975b) On stochastic models of size distribution. *Re-
      view of Economic Studies,* 42, pp. 631-641.

[202] Shorrocks, A.F. (1976) Income mobility and the Markov assumption.
      Economic Journal, 86, pp. 556-578.

[203] Shorrocks, A.F. (1983) Ranking income distributions. *Economica,* 50,
      pp. 1-17.

[204] Shorrocks, A.F. (1984) Inequality decomposition by population sub-
      groups. *Econometrica,* 52, pp. 1369-1386.

[205] Slesnick, D.T. (1990) Inflation, relative price variation, and inequality. *Journal of Econometrics,* 43, pp. 135-151.

[206] Slottje, D.J. (1987) Relative price changes and inequality in the size distribution of income. *Journal of Business and Economic Statistics,* 5, pp. 19-26.

[207] Smeeding, T.M., O'Higgins, M. and Rainwater, L. (eds) (1990) *Poverty, Inequality and Income Distribution in Comparative Perspective.* London: Harvester Wheatsheaf.

[208] Soong, T.T (1973) *Random Differential Equations in Science and Engineering.* New York: Academic Press.

[209] Stasny, E.A. (1986) Estimating gross flows using panel data with non-response: an example from the Canadian Labor Force Survey. *Journal of the American Statistical Association,* 81, pp. 42-47.

[210] Stern, N.H. (1976) On the specification of models of optimum income taxation. *Journal of Public Economics,* 6, pp. 123-162.

[211] Stevens, A.H. (1994) The dynamics of poverty: updating Bane and Ellwood. *American Economic Review,* 84, pp. 34-37.

[212] Stoker, T.M. (1986) The distributional welfare effects of rising prices in the United states. *American Economic Review,* 76, pp. 335-349.

[213] Townsend, P. (1979) *Poverty in the United Kingdom.* Harmondsworth, Middx: Penguin.

[214] Travers, P. and Richardson, S. (1993) *Living Decently: Material Well-being in Australia.* Melbourne: Oxford University Press.

[215] Verbeek, M. and Nijman, T. (1992) Incomplete panels and selection bias. In *The Econometrics of Panel Data* (ed. by L. Matyas and P. Sevestre), pp. 262-299. Boston, Mass: Kluwer.

[216] Weiss, Y. and Lillard, L.A. (1978) Experience, vintage and time effects in the growth of earnings. *Journal of Political Economy,* 87, pp. 427-447.

[217] Welch, F. (1979) Effects of cohort size on earnings: the baby boom babies' financial bust. *Journal of Political Economy*, 88, pp. 565-597.

[218] Whiteford, S.P. (1991) Inequality and average living standards: changes in the 1970s and 1980s. *Fiscal Studies*, 12, pp. 1-28.

[219] Wilson, G. (1987) *Money in the Family: Financial Organisation and Women's Responsibility.* Aldershot, Hants: Avebury.

[220] Yitzhaki, S. (1983) On an extension of the Gini index. *International Economic Review*, 24, pp. 617-628.

[221] Young, M. (1952) Distribution of income within the household. *British Journal of Sociology*, 3, pp. 305-321.

Index